RELIGIOUS PERFORMANCE
IN CONTEMPORARY ISLAM

Child preparing to march in Muharram procession.

RELIGIOUS PERFORMANCE
IN CONTEMPORARY ISLAM

Shi'i Devotional Rituals
in South Asia

by Vernon James Schubel

UNIVERSITY OF SOUTH CAROLINA PRESS

STUDIES IN COMPARATIVE RELIGION

Frederick M. Denny, Editor

The Holy Book in
Comparative Perspective

Dr. Strangegod:
On the Symbolic Meaning
of Nuclear Weapons

Native American Religious Action:
A Performance Approach to Religion

The Confucian Way of Contemplation:
Okada Takehiko and the Tradition
of Quiet-Sitting

Human Rights and the Conflict of Cultures:
Western and Islamic Perspectives
on Religious Liberty

The Munshidin of Egypt:
Their World and Their Song

The Buddhist Revival in Sri Lanka:
Religious Tradition, Reinterpretation
and Response

A History of the Jews of Arabia:
From Ancient Times to Their
Eclipse Under Islam

Arjuna in the Mahabharata:
Where Krishna Is, There Is Victory

Ethics, Wealth, and Salvation:
A Study in Buddhist Social Ethics

Ritual Criticism:
Case Studies in Its Practice, Essays on Its Theory

The Dragons of Tiananmen:
Beijing as a Sacred City

The Other Sides of Paradise:
Explorations into the Religious Meanings
of Domestic Space in Islam

Ritual Masks:
Deceptions and Revelations

Religion and Personal Autonomy:
The Third Disestablishment in America

Religion in Relation:
Method, Application and Moral Location

Islam and the Heroic Image:
Themes in Literature and the Visual Arts

Minoan Religion:
Ritual, Image, and Symbol

Religious Performance
 in Contemporary Islam:
Shi'iDevotional Rituals in South Asia

Copyright © 1993 University of South Carolina

Published in Columbia, South Carolina, by the University of South Carolina Press

Manufactured in the United States of America

Library of Congress Cataloging-in-Publication Data

Schubel, Vernon James, 1953–
    Religious performance in contemporary Islam : Shi'i devotional rituals in South Asia / by Vernon James Schubel.
        p. cm. — (Studies in comparative religion)
    Includes bibliographical references and index.
    ISBN 0–87249–859–X (alk. paper)
    1. Shi'ah—Pakistan—Karachi.   2. Tenth of Muḥarram.   3. Karachi (Pakistan)—Religious life and customs.   I. Title.   II. Series: Studies in comparative religion (Columbia, S.C.)
BP194.5.T4S38   1993
297'.302'09549183—dc20   92–40889
                                                                                          CIP

For Donna Heizer

CONTENTS

ILLUSTRATIONS

Frontispiece. Child preparing to march in Muharram procession.

SERIES EDITOR'S PREFACE

Islamic studies in the West and in the greater part of the Islamic world itself have long shared a bias that Sunni Islam is the normative tradition, whereas Shi'ism is at best heterodoxy and at worst heresy. In fact Shi'ism is earlier than Sunnism in its main and enduring emphases, which center in allegiance to 'Ali and through him the Prophet Muhammad and Allah. Sunni Islam developed over a long period, drawing from politically dominant, centrist tendencies and movements within the Umayyad and Abbasid caliphates. But the winners get to write the history books. So, the eventual Sunni hegemony over much of the Dar al-Islam by the second and third centuries after the Hijra read its own prefoundations as having been normative all along. This myth of the silent center has given Sunnis a sense of being heirs to a providential dispensation in ruling most Muslim domains, even where, as in Iraq and Lebanon, Shi'ites comprise a major part of the population.

Vernon Schubel's *Religious Performance in Contemporary Islam* provides a much needed corrective to Sunni-oriented, often invidious views of Shi'ism by viewing the followers of 'Ali as a distinctive religious movement focused on loyalties to and identification with spiritually authoritative human beings. According to Schubel, Sunnis see in the Qur'an God's authentic voice because of the miraculous qualities of the book itself. Shi'ites, however, accept the Qur'an as God's Word because their beloved Prophet said it was. The charisma of the Book, thus, is grounded in the charisma of Muhammad, and in the infallible spiritual guides, the Imams, who descended from him: 'Ali, Husayn, and others.

Schubel provides a rare view of Shi'ism in its ages-old ritual performances observed in the hidden, private world of domestic life and women's religious action, and in the public world of male ritual performance during Muharram observances and at other times. A special dimension of the Shi'ite worldview is the redemptive power of suffering. The primordial, foundational sufferings of the *ahl al-bayt*, "People of the House" (the Prophet's family), are rendered present through self-flagellation, the "wounds of devotion." Schubel draws upon contemporary ritual theory as he lays out his richly abundant textual and field data to show how urban Pakistani Muslims—both Shi'ite and Sunni—actually view their lives and their destinies in today's world.

Frederick Mathewson Denny

PREFACE

In 1983 I spent a year in Pakistan under the auspices of a grant from the American Institute of Pakistan Studies for the purpose of gathering materials for this book. The following is a study of Islam as a living religion in a particular cultural context. For far too long the academic study of Islamic civilization has been divided between textualists whose primary expertise has been theological and philological and anthropologists whose training has not always granted them an in-depth understanding of Islam as a religious system which both transcends and penetrates many different cultures. This examination of Shi'i rituals in the city of Karachi attempts to combine the theoretical approaches of the disciplines of history of religions and cultural anthropology with an understanding of Islam as a religion, both in its classical textual formulation and popular contexts.

This book differs from most scholarship on Shi'i Islam on three counts. First, it uses categories which define Shi'i Islam according to its intrinsic characteristics rather than by comparison to the majority Sunni school. Second, it focuses on the ritual and popular elements of the faith. Even though ritual performances such as the ones described in this book are crucial to the religious life of Shi'i Muslims, there has been surprisingly little research on Shi'i mourning rituals in the West. Shi'i studies as a whole suffer from a general bias in the field of Islamic studies, which tends to view Shi'i Islam as an heretical offshoot of Sunni Islam. Even among scholars of Shi'i Islam, however, popular piety and its ritual manifestations have been neglected in favor of "the high tradition" of Shi'ism as it is manifested in law, theology, and philosophy. What attention has been given to popular piety has often come from anthropologists with a minimal understanding of Islam as a religion. This study examines Shi'i practice and belief from the bottom up. It focuses on the practices of ordinary people while exploring the relationship between popular piety and the high tradition of the classical sources.

Finally, this study differs from the bulk of scholarship on Shi-
'ism because it focuses on the practice of Shi'ism outside of Iran.
While Iran is certainly the major center for the study of Islamic
law and scholarship, the fact that it is a country with a Shi'i majority makes it something of an anomaly in the Islamic world.
The geographical focus of this study is Karachi, Pakistan, where
Shi'i Muslims constitute an important minority surrounded by
an at times hostile majority—a situation more nearly approxi-
mating the historical experience of the majority of the Shi'a.

For the purposes of this book I have made use of a number of
different materials. As this project focuses on ritual performances I observed ritual activities in different areas of the city
and conducted interviews with participants in those rituals from
varied economic and ethnic backgrounds. I combined this data
with relevant textual sources. These included texts and pamphlets recommended to me by members of the local community
as popular and authoritative, as well as more classical materials.
In this way I have attempted to paint a picture of the religious
self-understanding of the Shi'i community of Karachi. This was
not always easy as that community like any other is heterogeneous in many of its practices and attitudes. The question of
what is authoritative and who is to be trusted in matters of religion is one which had to remain always in my mind. Certain
subjective factors constantly came into play.

The theoretical models which I chose to use were primarily
those of the late Victor Turner and Clifford Geertz as they allowed for the possibility of multivocality in the interpretation of
symbols and thus helped to provide a partial explanation for the
multiplicity of experiences and viewpoints surrounding Shi'i rituals. I strove to speak to a wide variety of informants and to
make use of those texts and documents which were almost universally recommended to me by them. Still, there are valid questions which can be raised by my choice of theoretical models or
sources of information. I do not claim this work to be definitive
but rather to be one particular approach to a complex problem,
an approach that has yielded some useful insights into the culture of South Asian Islam.

I would like to thank the many people who helped to make
the completion of this work a reality. In particular, I would first
like to thank the American Institute of Pakistan Studies for fund-
ing this project. My deepest appreciation goes out to Professor
Karrar Hussain, whose insights guided me through a vast ocean
of material, and to everyone at the Khurasan Islamic Research
Center for their assistance, especially S. M. Hasan Rizvi. I would

like to thank the persons at Mehfil-i Murtaza for allowing me to attend their services and take photographs and for their willingness to explain many aspects of their activities to me; the Bilal Muslim Trust for their assistance; William Jones and Lee Irwin for their support; Professor T. H. Naqvi for his help and instruction in Urdu translation; Zamir Akhtar for access to his library; Shafqat Shah for his hospitality; Maktab at-ul Ulum for allowing me to use their resources; and Abbas Hussain of the University of Karachi and Mrs. Zubayda Curmally for their friendship. I would also like to show my appreciation to Professor Habib Zuberi for help in translation; Donna Heizer for her patience and support; Walter Hauser for his assistance in drafting my research proposal; Professor Roger Hatch for his assistance in editing the manuscript; and Teri Severns for clerical help above and beyond the call of duty. I am especially indebted to the late Victor Turner in whose seminar the ideas for this project took shape. My thanks also to Professor Ravindra Khare for his enthusiasm; Benjamin Ray for his comments and support; and most importantly my adviser and friend Abdulaziz Sachedina for his vast knowledge and patient guidance. To all those in Pakistan and North America who added to this work, whom I did not mention, I also extend my thanks.

TRANSLITERATION

For Urdu, Persian, and Arabic words I have used a simplified
version of the Library of Congress system for Urdu transliteration.
Initial *hamzas* are deleted but I have retained ʿ*ayns* even
though they are not pronounced in Urdu and Farsi. Long vowels
are marked only in the glossary and in the first use of the
word in the text. The same is true for diacritical markings distinguishing
between the various h, s, t, and z sounds in Arabic and
retroflex consonants in Urdu. I have followed the convention of
using Shiʿa for both the singular and collective noun. I have
used Shiʿi for the adjectival form throughout the text.

RELIGIOUS PERFORMANCE
IN CONTEMPORARY ISLAM

INTRODUCTION

The following work is an exploration of the role of ritual and performance in South Asian Shi'i Islam. It focuses explicitly on Muharram rituals commemorating the martyrdom of the Prophet's grandson Imam Husayn at the battle of Karbala. These rituals are among the most striking and provocative public performances in the Muslim world. During the first ten days of Muharram, Shi'i Muslims congregate in lamentation assemblies to listen to retellings of the story of Husayn's martyrdom. At these assemblies men and women weep vociferously as they emotionally relive the events of the battle of Karbala. In large cities elaborate processions are staged which publicly affirm the Shi'i identity of the participants. Some of the community may even engage in acts of corporate self-flagellation in order to demonstrate their solidarity with the Prophet's family. In many ways the rituals of Muharram are at the very heart of Shi'i piety.

The Role of Ritual in Religious Piety

The study of ritual and performance is crucial to the understanding of Shi'i piety, as it is to the piety of any religion—as ritual is the activity in which the physical and spiritual aspects of religion come together. It provides an expression of religious piety that is apprehensible to all of the senses. In the practice of ritual sights, sounds, smells, and tastes all become vehicles for religious experience. Clifford Geertz defines religion as "a system of symbols which acts to establish powerful, pervasive and long-lasting moods and motivations in men by formulating conceptions of a general order of existence and clothing these conceptions with such an aura of factuality that the moods and motivations seem uniquely realistic."[1] Nowhere does the system of symbols which Geertz designates as religion so fully establish those powerful moods and motivations as it does in ritual performances. It is through ritual that men and women

most completely encounter the symbolic universe that under-
pins and gives shape to their most deeply held beliefs.

I use the term "ritual" to mean a performance involving an encounter with powerful symbols. I assume that participants in rituals believe that this encounter with symbols is—in some way
or other—efficacious. In the context of religious rituals I consider "symbols" to be the component parts of a powerful meta-
language which are used by persons in order to think about the
world in ways that are beyond the range of ordinary language.

Symbols are multivocal, able to stand for more than one thing
at any one time.[2] The multivocality inherent in symbols allows
for the possibility of many different interpretations and experiences of a ritual performance. The meaning drawn from the encounter depends both upon the quality and the direction of the
performance and upon the internal state of the participants.
Each participant brings to a ritual encounter a unique personal
history. In a complex ritual the participant makes choices about
which aspects of the ritual to focus on; choices which are crucial
to the effect of the ritual.

Both cross-culturally—and even within the same religious and
cultural tradition—the uses of rituals may vary greatly. At times
the manipulation of symbols may be almost magical. This is the
case for example for many South Asian Muslims who recite so-
called miracle stories (*mu'jizāt kahānīs*) for the purpose of obtain-
ing material desires. At other times rituals may manifest their
efficacy in the Durkheimian sense that they engender a feeling
of group solidarity through acts of corporate devotion.[3] This aspect of religious performances has been recognized by many
scholars in the field who have been influenced by functionalism
and have focused their attention on the ways in which rituals
build group solidarity.

The primary purpose of certain rituals also may be to focus
people's attention toward a "powerful Other"[4]—as is the case in
the daily ritual prayers of Islam. The participant in a ritual may
see its efficacy as soteriological. From this perspective it may improve the participant's general relationship with powerful beings or God, or it may make up for moral or legal lapses. The
participant also may see the ritual as a "rite of passage" through
which he or she is transformed and made better, either through
a change in social status or through a transformation in spiritual
station or both.

My understanding of ritual draws heavily upon the work of
the late Victor Turner. Following Van Gennep, Turner posed a
tripartite model for rite of passage rituals. According to this

model, the ritual process consists of three stages: (1) separation—in which the initiate is separated from his or her normal role in the social structure; (2) liminality—in which the social status of the initiate is ambiguous; and (3) re-aggregation—in which the initiate reenters society with a new identity. For Turner the liminal realm—the realm of ambiguity where the initiate is betwixt and between, neither this nor that—is the most interesting and important stage in this process. Temporarily freed from his or her structural identity, the initiate is able to encounter and reflect upon the powerful symbols which give meaning to his social reality in an immediate and existential manner. This encounter assists in the initiate's transformation to a new structural identity.

Following Turner, I consider all rituals in some sense or another to be rites of passage because their purpose is to produce some sort of change in the person who engages in them. That rite of passage may involve an external change of status, but it also may involve an internal, invisible change of state or perhaps a reconfirmation of a condition that is expected but not fully experienced or articulated. Even the notion that one becomes better informed about one's religion through participation in a ritual can be seen as a belief about the efficacy of that ritual as a rite of passage, particularly if one believes that such knowledge is somehow transformative.

The participant in a ritual is pulled out of normal time into the liminal realm of symbols and then, after the ritual has subsided, enters back into the realm of normality and structure.[5] Free from the personae imposed by structure, the participant in a ritual is freed in the liminal realm to imagine life as other than it is. Liminality allows participants to enter into what Victor Turner has called the "subjunctive mode"—the realm of "what if" and "what could have been."[6]

Over his career Turner expanded the notion of the liminal beyond the limitations imposed on it by the model of rites of passage. He expanded it to include less explicitly structured activities like religious festivals or pilgrimage journeys. He understood these as liminal or "liminoid" arenas which contain many of the characteristics of the liminal stage of rite of passage rituals in more public and less controlled circumstances. Participants in these liminal activities play out the possibility of a world where structure is in many ways inverted. These types of activities are characterized by equality, humility, and a continuous reference to mystical power as opposed to the emphasis on hierarchy and pride, and the only intermittent reference to the mystical and spiritual which tends to characterize ordinary social reality.[7]

In liminal circumstances this lack of structural identity, coupled with a collective obedience to a higher authority—in the case of the Shi'a the Prophet and his family—produces a sense of equality and an experience of comradeship between the participants which Turner calls *communitas*. *Communitas* "transcends distinctions of rank, age, kinship, position, and in some kinds of cultic group, even of sex." It plays down the socially defined roles of individuals and emphasizes "axiomatic values."[8]

This experience of *communitas* facilitates another important aspect of the liminal realm emphasized by Turner; the communication of *sacra* through exhibitions, instructions, and actions. In the liminal realm "evocatory instruments or sacred articles, such as relics of deities, heroes, or ancestors" are exhibited. Participants are taught and act out the "main outlines of the theogony, cosmogony, and mythical history of their societies or cults, usually with reference to the *sacra* exhibited."[9]

Often this presentation of *sacra* is, as Turner puts it, grotesque and exaggerated. The liminal realm is often replete with monstrous masks and miraculous occurrences. On one level this serves to deconstruct the symbolic content of social structure so as to express the "root paradigms" lodged within it. On another level it is an expression of the subjunctivity inherent in liminality. Liminality allows people to play out and express dimensions of existence which may be absent or latent in their ordinary existence.

The structure of ritual allows for this entrance into the subjunctive realm by creating a space separated out from ordinary reality, a liminal arena where one's attention can be focused on the symbolic "root paradigms" which transcend any particular historical moment by penetrating all of history. The concept of root paradigms, as presented by Turner, is a particularly appropriate tool for the analysis of Shi'i rituals. Turner defines root paradigms as "certain consciously recognized (though not consciously grasped) cultural models" which exist "in the heads of the main actors" in social dramas. These paradigms make reference not only to the current social relationships of the persons who are involved in these dramas but also to "the cultural goals, means, ideas, outlooks, currents of thought, patterns of belief, and so on which enter into those relationships, interpret them, and incline them to alliance or divisiveness." For Turner these paradigms, like symbols, are multivocal. They should not be un-

derstood as mere ethical or aesthetic guidelines. They "go beyond the cognitive and even the moral to the existential domain
and in so doing become clothed with allusiveness, implicitness
and metaphor." He argues that "paradigms of this fundamental
sort reach down to the irreducible life stances of individuals,
passing beneath conscious prehension to a fiduciary hold on
what they sense to be axiomatic values, matters literally of life
and death."[10]

While Turner originally developed this concept in order to explain social dramas, root paradigms are also at the center of religious rituals. As Turner points out, these paradigms emerge
during life crises, "whether of groups or individuals, whether
institutionalized or compelled by unforeseen events."[11] In one
sense all rite of passage rituals are institutionalized life crises in
which the participant is forced to encounter powerful symbols.
This is particularly true in Shi'i rituals in which the participant is
led to identify with intense sufferings to such an extent that they
encounter those individuals—either symbolically or mystically—
who embody the root paradigms of Shi'i Islam.

All of these aspects of ritual are apparent in the performance
of Shi'i rituals of mourning which form the focus of this study.
These rituals which recreate in dramatic fashion narratives of
the events in the lives of the Prophet Muhammad and his
family—particularly the martyrdom of the Prophet's grandson
Imam Husayn at the battle of Karbala—allow for an emotional
encounter with the characters of the sacred history of Islam who
manifest in their actions the root paradigms of Shi'i Islam. They
create a liminal realm removed from ordinary time and space in
which individuals may imagine themselves in the metahistorical
realm of Karbala, whose reality interpenetrates the reality of
day-to-day existence, providing a paradigm against which our
own existence can be judged. There is no doubt that the participants in these rituals see them as efficacious, although different
individuals may value certain aspects of the rituals more than
others. Some Muslims may feel that attendance at religious performances like *majlis* (lamentation assemblies) may result in the
forgiveness of lapses or transgressions. For them the soteriological element of the rituals may come into the foreground. Others may feel that they are simply made better Muslims by the
action of attending lamentation assemblies at which they will
hear lectures about Islamic history or ethics, and thus become
better informed about the nature of their faith. For many participants these performances offer an opportunity ritually to enter
back into the events of a sacred history. This encounter with sa-

cred history—particularly with the drama of Karbala—allows participants to manifest a solidarity with the Prophet and his family and thus with the Shi'i community—for them the "true Islam." They are both internally transformed and have reaffirmed their loyalty to their community.

Although these rituals of Muharram are shared in a communal atmosphere, the experience remains a personal one for each participant, for each one confronts the symbols in a unique manner. The success of the experience depends on how well participants are able to enter into and relate to the Karbala narrative. But the nature of that experience is colored by the character of the experiencer: women bring a different set of experiences to these rituals than do men, old men bring different sensibilities to these rituals than do young children. In fact, each individual brings a unique personality to these events, and thus each event speaks to each person in a slightly different manner.

And yet certain experiences are common to most of the participants in the rituals. As Shi'i Muslims in South Asia they have shared the experience of living as a minority member of a great world tradition in a highly diverse cultural region. This experience is one which is specifically addressed in the rituals of Muharram.

The South Asian Context of Shi'i Islam

This study focuses on the ritual performances of the Shi'i community in South Asia—more specifically the highly diverse and densely populated port city of Karachi, Pakistan. Scholarly studies of Shi'i religion and Shi'i ritual have focused most often on the Muslim communities in Iran. And yet it can be argued that Iran represents an anomalous situation in the history of Shi'ism, as it holds a Shi'i majority. South Asia offers an interesting window on the practice of Shi'ism in a context much more in keeping with the usual position of Shi'i communities, that of a minority surrounded by at times hostile neighbors.

Shi'i ritual performances in South Asia are an extremely rich and complex phenomenon. Part of the reason for their complexity is the complexity of the society in which they take place. A good example of this complexity is Karachi—a city renowned for the intensity of its Muharram performances. The city of Karachi boasts a long history of Shi'i activity and a sizable population of Shi'i Muslims. It is the largest city in Sindh Province and is important both as a port city and as a major industrial center. It is, in fact, the largest city in Pakistan with estimates of its population varying from 4 to 8 million. After the partition of the subcontinent in 1947, Muslims from all parts of India immigrated to Karachi. The small city of Karachi, which then held only 250,000 inhabitants, exploded in population as these *muhājirs* (immigrants) entered into the new state of Pakistan. Among these *muhajirs* were sizable numbers of Shi'a. Certain areas of the city such as Rizvia Society are almost entirely populated with these Shi'i *muhajirs*.

The existence of a Shi'i population in the region, however, goes back well before partition to the earliest periods of the Islamic Empire. Muslim presence in Sindh dates back to the time of the caliphate of 'Ali b. Abu Talib, in the year 49 A.H., when Sindh was an *iqta* (administrative revenue unit) of the early Islamic Empire. In their histories of the region, Shi'i historians cite as evidence of the close relationship between Sindh and the *ahl al-bayt* ("the People of the House") the fact that Imam Zayn al-'Abidin had a Sindhi wife, the presence of Sindhi disciples in the close circle of Imam Ja'far as-Sadiq's disciples, and the protection of exiled members of the family of the Prophet in the courts of Sindhi Hindu princes.[12]

During the 'Abbasid period, due to persecution of the *ahl al-bayt*—who were often the focus of revolutionary activity—many members of the Prophet's family fled from the heartland of the Islamic Empire to what was at that time its nearest border, the region of Sindh. It was sometimes possible for members of the *ahl al-bayt* to find protection in the courts of sympathetic Hindu rulers. One example of this is the case of 'Abdul Ghazi Sahab, one of the important saints of Karachi, whose tomb is located on the beach near Clifton just outside of the city. His tomb is a place of pilgrimage for Sunni and Shi'a alike. Few of his Sunni devotees, however, recognize that the Shi'a consider him a relative of Imam Ja'far as-Sadiq, who had secretly entered Sindh disguised as a horsetrader in order to escape death and mutilation at the hands of the 'Abbasid caliphate. Whereas Shi'i pilgrims remember him as a member of the *ahl al-bayt*, Sunni pilgrims tend to see him simply as a great saint. This is not unusual in South Asia, where pro-'Alid sentiment quite often transcends sectarian differences.[13] At this early time in Islamic history when men like 'Abdul Ghazi Sahab and even in later periods when other *sayyids* (descendents of Muhammad) made their way into Sindh and the Punjab, the distinctions between Twelver Shi'i, Isma'ili, and Sufi Islam were most likely not as clearly drawn as they are now. Many—although not all—of the important saints of Sindh and the Punjab were—and are—*sayyids*. It is still possible to raise a vigorous argument among pilgrims at shrines as to whether or not a particular saint was a Shi'a or a Sunni. After all, the imprint of devotional allegiance to the *ahl al-bayt* on Sufism can be clearly seen in the fact that three of the four major Sufi *tarīqahs* (orders) of the subcontinent trace their origins back to 'Ali. Furthermore, Sufism shares many elements with Shi'ism. Each has a strong narrative tradition replete with miraculous tales. Each stresses the need for a living guide to lead the neophyte to spiritual understanding. Many of the important Sufi shrines of Multan, Hyderabad, and Karachi contain pro-'Alid symbols and markings, and they are at times sites of such 'Alid rituals as mourning for Husayn.

This long history of contact with the *ahl al-bayt* helped to create a strong pro-'Alid presence in the region long before the influx of Shi'i *muhajirs*. The force of pro-'Alid sympathies in Sindh and the Punjab was further strengthened after partition by the influx of *muhajirs* from Lucknow and other important Shi'i centers in India. The fact that many of the great poets of Urdu were Shi'a and wrote poetry about the death of Husayn also helped to maintain pro-'Alid loyalties in the region. In some regions persons who are Sunni in their legal school are Shi'a in many ritual activities and call themselves *mawlai*—the followers of Mawla 'Ali.

The strong presence of Shi'i and pro-'Alid sentiments in India and Pakistan makes it an extremely useful location for the study of Shi'i religion. In this region Shi'ism is not the majority religion, and thus the situation of Shi'i communities is closer to the typical historical situation. Being a minority has forced the Shi'i population to actively defend both their beliefs and practices. Hence there is not only a wealth of printed material available on Shi'i ritual, but the average lay Shi'a is used to and willing to talk about his or her beliefs and the reasoning behind them.

Karachi's rapid increase in population has not been due solely to the influx of *muhajir* populations. Its position as the largest port in the new state, coupled with the fact that it served for a period as its interim capital, led to massive movements of populations from other regions of Pakistan. In Karachi there are now large populations of Punjabis, Pathans, and Baltis, as well as Sindhis and *muhajirs*. Among these migrants there are of course many Shi'a, and they have carried with them their own particular customs and practices. This diversity of customs makes Muharram practices in Karachi among the most colorful and complex anywhere in the Muslim world.

The exact number of Shi'i Muslims in Karachi is difficult to calculate. Government censuses do not ask for sectarian affiliations. Furthermore, communal tensions lead certain Sunni sources to give low estimates while certain Shi'i sources give inflated ones. I find the most reliable figures to be those given to me by an official of the Bilal Muslim Trust who, on the basis of averaging relative attendance figures at various Shi'i religious centers throughout the city on both ordinary days and days of mourning or celebration, estimated that there were about 1.2 million Shi'i Muslims in the city.

This minority community is, in the realm of day-to-day events, culturally indistinguishable from the majority Sunni population. The differences between Shi'a and Sunni are to be found at the level of mythic worldview and in those rituals peculiar to that community which allow for encounters with that worldview. That worldview is rooted in the fundamental assertion of Shi'i Islam which differentiates it from Sunni Islam—the belief that Islam has at its core a personal allegiance to the Prophet Muhammad and his family. The practice of Shi'i piety involves the continual reaffirmation of this belief through narrative and ritual. The following chapters will explore this worldview and address the ways in which the Shi'i community of Karachi encounters the realm of the sacred in two different spheres of ritual activity.

Chapter one details the worldview of Shi'i Islam as it exists in South Asia. Drawing on textual and ethnographic materials, it presents the Shi'i community's self-definition as the Islam of personal allegiance to the Prophet and his family.

Chapter two explores the private and culturally invisible realm of household rituals; rituals which take place in the home, and whose primary participants are usually women. I am here referring to the reading of *mu'jizat kahanis*—miraculous narratives which are the focus of spiritual vows. Although these stories are part of popular culture, they are resonant with the high culture of Shi'ism, as their primary theme is the importance of personal allegiance to the *ahl al-bayt* and the terrible consequences of neglecting that allegiance. These stories provide an excellent window for observing the ways in which ordinary Shi'a enter into contact with the characters of the sacred narratives of their tradition.

Chapter three examines the large public rituals whose participants are primarily men and whose audience is larger and more diverse than that of the above-mentioned household rituals. I refer here primarily to the full-scale performances of ritual mourning for Husayn which take place every year during the month of Muharram and which are the most visible affirmations of personal allegiance in the Shi'i world.

Chapter four describes those performances which took place in Karachi over the first ten days of Muharram 1404 A.H./1983 C.E. The activities at several sites throughout Karachi are presented and analyzed. Chapter five examines the controversial practices of self-flagellation and fire walking associated with mourning for the family of the Prophet.

CHAPTER ONE

The Nature of Shi'ism
in Its South Asian Context

On a warm Thursday evening in Karachi the congregation is just finishing its evening prayers. In the hall adjacent to the mosque, people are gradually gathering around the *minbār*, the staircased pulpit at the front of the room. Some pass through the small room located just to the side of the hall and touch or kiss the relics--some of them made of gold and silver—which have been given as pious offerings to indicate the donors' devotion to the family of the Prophet Muhammad. To one side of the *minbar* a small boy recites poetry in Urdu in memory of the slain Imam Husayn, the martyr of Karbala. Little by little, the room fills with men. Some sit quietly near the rear of the room with tape recorders, preparing to make a permanent record of the evening's performance so that they can ponder more carefully at a later time the things they will hear this evening. Others sit nearer to the *minbar* and, upon taking their seats on the floor, begin to sob almost immediately. As the crowd grows in size, salutary shouts of *"Ṣalāvāt Muhammad wa Al-e Muhammad"* can be heard. A man shouts out *"Nade Haidarī!"* and is answered with a stirring chorus of *"Yā 'Ali!"* Suddenly, from the side of the hall a small man dressed in long coat and lambswool Jinnah cap walks to the *minbar*. Seating himself upon it, he adjusts the microphone and recites a formulaic *khuṭba* in Arabic. He begins slowly and methodically—first reciting a verse of the Qur'an and then explicating it in a purposive manner. As he proceeds, he gradually becomes more animated. As he makes the points of his argument, he gestures with his hands—at times slapping his knees and calling on the crowd to offer salutations to the family of the Prophet. At times he finds himself interrupted by shouts from the crowd of *"Ya 'Ali!"* The tone of his speech grows increasingly more emotional. At a certain point in his presentation his demeanor shifts. He begins to tell a story—the tragic account of the martyrdom of Husayn. Although his audience has heard this tale many times before, its impact has not diminished in the countless retellings. At the first mention of the field of Karbala, some of the men in the audience begin to cry uncontrollably and beat their chests. The sound of women's voices wailing can be heard rising up from the other side of the curtain which divides the room.

The man on the *minbar* himself begins to sob as he speaks of the heat of the desert and the thirst of the innocent children. He praises the courage of the comrades of Husayn and condemns the cruelty of the troops of his adversary Ibn Ziyad. The images are familiar, but they still evoke waves of sorrow from the crowd. The man on the *minbar* begins to speak in the present tense. These are no longer events occurring in a far distant past, but a present reality. One sees the body of the slain 'Abbas, the standard-bearer of Husayn. One hears the parched cries of the child Sakina. Once more the evil Hurmula slays the infant 'Ali Asghar as he is held up in the arms of the Imam. Once more Husayn dies a stranger in a land far from his home. And yet it evokes the same degree of sadness from the crowd as if they were hearing it for the first time. The entire crowd is wrapped in grief. Tears stream from the eyes of the men in the audience. At the conclusion of the narrative the man on the *minbar*—the teller of the tales—collapses in tears before his audience. As the performance ends and the crowd collects itself, those who have come to mourn the sufferings of the martyrs of Karbala have reaffirmed their loyalty and devotion to them. They will also take home with them whatever new insights into their religion they may have learned from the discourse which preceded their tearful encounter with the story of Karbala. To the extent to which the man on the *minbar*—the *zākir*—was able to elicit tears and impart information, he has succeeded in his task.

Mourning Rituals and Their Role in Shi'i Piety

The performance described above, known in South Asia as a *majlis* (plural *majālis*) or lamentation assembly, is one of a large complex of ritual activities in Shi'i piety which center around the act of mourning. Such rituals are referred to collectively as *'azādārī* and are an essential part of Shi'i practice. Although they take place throughout the year, they are most prominent during the ten-day annual observance of the martyrdom of Husayn held during the first part of the lunar month of Muharram. These rituals of mourning for the martyred Imam Husayn and his companions are perhaps the most visible and provocative of all Shi'i religious performances. The nightly gatherings of *majalis* during those ten days are occasions both for the presentation of religious discourses and the shared and public expression of a grief that is central to Shi'i piety. Included among the other acts of *'azadari* performed during this period are elaborate mourning processions (*julūs*). These processions are occasions for the public display of evocative visual representations of Karbala. These include representations of the tomb of Husayn; the Imam's mount, *Zūljinah*; the standard of his brother 'Abbas topped with the five-fingered hand of Fatimah; and the coffins of the Imam and his companions. Such symbols serve as intense reminders of an event which, after nearly fourteen centuries, still triggers passionate devotion in the hearts of believers. For some this devotion manifests itself in acts of physical mourning: the image of men lashing their backs with knives or chains, or walking upon fire and coals in mournful solidarity with Husayn is evidence of the compelling nature of this grief in the context of Shi'i piety.

The intensity of this grief is a reflection of the love and devotion for the Prophet and his family which underlies it. Shi'i rituals of lamentation should not be taken as evidence of an obsession with suffering and sadness per se. The roots of Shi'i ritual are not to be found in a pathological attraction to grief—as is suggested by the sort of media analysis which understands Shi'i Islam as a religion with a persecution complex[1]—but rather in Shi'i Muslims' devotional allegiance to the Prophet Muhammad and his family. This can be adduced from the importance of celebratory rituals and manifestations of piety which are unrelated to mourning. Attempts to define Shi'i piety solely in terms of a religion of revolt or despair miss the point of Shi'i rituals of mourning, which must be understood against the backdrop of the metaphysical assumptions about the family of the Prophet which define Shi'ism as a religious structure.

Shi'ism Defined

Shi'ism is one of the two major schools of thought and practice in Islam. It takes its name from the arabic word *shī'ah* meaning "party of" or "supporters of" and refers specifically to the supporters of 'Ali b. Abu Talib, the cousin and son-in-law of the

Prophet Muhammad. ʿAli is believed by the Shiʿa to have been designated by God and Muhammad as the rightful successor to the authority of the Prophet. The second major school is commonly referred to as Sunni Islam—a shortened form of *ahl al-sunnah wa-l jamāʾah* (the people of the custom and the community). This has emerged as the majority school.

Perhaps because of the numerical superiority of the Sunni school, it has been common in Western scholarship to define the parameters and characteristics of Shiʿi Islam by comparing and contrasting it with the majority Sunni school. This approach denies to Shiʿi Islam its intrinsic sensibilities and identity. Some Islamicists have gone so far as to argue that the majority Sunni school represents orthodox Islam and that Shiʿism—and by extension Sufism, even though this mystical form of piety has normally flourished within a Sunni milieu—is a dangerous heresy which has continually threatened the mainstream of Islamic thought and practice. This has been the stated position of such influential "Orientalist" scholars as Gibb[2] and Goldziher.[3] It can also be found in the writings of important modern Muslim commentators such as Fazlur Rahman.[4] This argument supposes that the intention of God and Muhammad was that the Islamic *ummah* (the community of all Muslims) would organize itself along the lines of Sunnism. While it is possible to understand the motivations and precommitments of Muslim scholars in this matter, it is surprising that so many non-Muslim writers have entered so vigorously into what is essentially a normative theological debate. Perhaps the answer can be found in the spirit of rationalism that permeated scholarship in the late nineteenth and early twentieth centuries—the golden age of Orientalism. It is likely that the Orientalists sought out those elements of Islam which mirrored their own predilections. They turned with particular favor toward those branches of Islam which rejected as irrational and superstitious the miraculous and mystical dimension of religion. For the Orientalists, Shiʿi and Sufi Islam, both full of miraculous narrative, were seen as intrusions into the pure—if somewhat arid—monotheism of Muhammad as propagated by such groups as the Wahabis, the *Ahl al-Ḥadīth*, and the Deobandis. Thus in much Orientalist scholarship Shiʿi and Sufi Muslims are presented as something less than paradigmatic members of the community of Islam and are described and defined by the ways in which they differed from the "true" Islam.[5]

This tendency can be further illustrated by the way in which scholars of Islam incorporated the theological language of church history in setting up categories for the study of a non-

Christian religion. The history of Christianity was written in such a way as to picture an orthodoxy continuously at war with heresies which threatened its unity. Ernst Troeltsch, himself trained in church history and drawing on the work of Max Weber, used the Christian and European categories of sect, cult, and church as the basis of a typology of religious organization. This typology is also prevalent in Orientalist scholarship. While it is possible that these categories may be useful in understanding the development of Christian sectarianism, they cloud the reality of the development of different schools of thought in Islam. Such a position assumes that Sunnism always existed as an "orthodoxy" against which "sects" such as Shi'ism struggled for adherents—a position which is historically inaccurate. And yet this is the position held by a great number of Islamicists, who define Shi'ism oppositionally by demonstrating how it diverges from the "true" Islam.

Obviously, such an approach is unacceptable for any objective description or analytical exploration of Shi'ism. Research into Shi'i thought and practice either through the study of textual materials or through ethnographic methods must take into account the ways in which the members of that community define themselves. Shi'i Muslims do not primarily define themselves oppositionally; they define themselves first and foremost as Muslims, and they consider their forms of piety to be an authentic—to their minds, the most authentic—response to the event of the Qur'anic revelation. Like all Muslims, they find justification for their practices in the Qur'an and in the lives of the Prophet, his companions, and family. They define their beliefs in positive terms—a belief in God and his Prophet that is supported by and coupled with a belief in the doctrine of *imāmat* (divinely designated leadership). A consequence and characteristic of this belief is an emotional devotion to the cause and persons of the *ahl al-bayt* (the household of the Prophet).

One useful way of distinguishing between Sunni and Shi'i piety has been suggested by Professor Karrar Hussain.[6] It relies on the fact that Islam as a cultural phenomenon can be best defined as a series of responses to both a man—the Prophet Muhammad—and a book—the Holy Qur'an. It is a response to what Marshall Hodgson has called "the Qur'anic event,"[7] an event which is seen by all Muslims regardless of their "sectarian" affiliation as the crucial occurrence in the history of the world. The crucial distinction between the Shi'i and Sunni schools of Islam can be discovered most clearly in their respective attitudes toward the relationship between "the Man" and "the Book."[8]

These attitudes are reflected in the familiar *ḥadīth* (report concerning the Prophet) of "the pen and ink." According to this *ḥadith*, when the Prophet was upon his deathbed, he said: "Prepare ink and paper that I will have a letter written for you which will be a cause of guidance for you and prevent you from being misled." ʿUmar, the future second caliph of the Islamic state, replied: "His illness has run out of hand and he is delirious." He then added: "For us the book is sufficient."[9]

From the Shiʿi perspective such a statement verges on blasphemy. According to Shiʿi prophetology, for the Prophet at any time to be out of his senses is an impossibility, as his station demands that he always be fully conscious. Furthermore, the Shiʿa declare emphatically that the book is in no way sufficient. Shiʿism has argued consistently for the necessity of a living interpreter of the Qurʾanic event.[10]

As Karrar Hussain has argued, for the Shiʿa the proof of the verity of the Qurʾan lies with the Prophet. The Qurʾan is the word of God because Muhammad has declared it to be so. As Hussain, himself a Shiʿa, stated during a series of public lectures on the Qurʾan during Ramadan in 1983: "I have no way of knowing that the Qurʾan is the book of God, except that the Man has told me that it is. And he has never lied to me."

He has further argued that the existence of the Qurʾan is historically preceded by that of the Prophet. At the time when ʿAli, Abu Bakr, and Khadijah accepted Islam, there were but a few verses of the Qurʾan in existence, and thus it could not have been the Qurʾan which was the focus of their allegiance. Their allegiance was first to the man Muhammad and only secondarily to the book which he was revealing. According to this argument, it was the exceptional character and personality of Muhammad which provided them with proof of the verity of the book.[11]

For the Sunnis, however, this argument is reversed. The Qurʾan is its own proof by virture of its *iʿjāz* (miraculous uniqueness). The proof of the verity of the Prophet's claim to be the messenger of God is the fact that he is designated as such by the Qurʾan. Thus, in Sunni Islam "the book" takes a degree of primacy over "the man."[12] There is in this an important distinction between the positions of Sunni and Shiʿi Islam. For the Shiʿa, the proof of the verity of the book lies in the man, whereas for the Sunni the proof of the man lies in the book. To put it in a slightly different way, for the Shiʿa it is evident that the Qurʾan is the book of God because the Prophet has said that it is, whereas for the Sunni it is clear that Muhammad is the Prophet of God because the Holy Qur'an has so designated him.

Thus, Shi'ism can be defined as the *school of thought in Islam which stresses personal allegiance and devotion to the Prophet and his family as the most crucial element and sign of one's submission to the will of God.* The method of distinguishing between the two major schools of Islam on which this definition is based is nonjudgmental. It is based upon the intrinsic natures of the two schools rather than on a simple comparison of the minority to the majority school. Most importantly, when tested in the field by interviewing Muslims of both persuasions, it became clear that both Sunni and Shi'i Muslims found this to be a fair and inoffensive way of distinguishing between the two schools.[13]

The Consequences of Personal Allegiance in Shi'i Islam

This emphasis on allegiance to "the man" has important consequences for Shi'i thought and practice—including Shi'i ritual. For the Shi'a, to be a Muslim is to offer allegiance to a person as well as to a message. This view of Islam as a personal allegiance facilitates the generation of sacred narratives about the persons to whom allegiance is due. The personal histories of the Prophet and his *ahl al-bayt* have become important as sources of spiritual training and focuses of ritual activity. Therefore, any understanding of Shi'i thought and practice must begin with an examination of Shi'i attitudes toward the *ahl al-bayt*—in particular, 'Ali, Fatimah, and the Imams—which underpin the entire system.

A central principle of Shi'i Islam is the importance of devotional allegiance—both individual and communal—to the person of the Prophet. This allegiance is understood both in political and spiritual senses and includes allegiance to those understood to be the legitimate successors to the Prophet's authority. Shi'i Islam believes in the necessity of a living guide for the Muslim community. This is the basis of the theory of *imamat*: that after his death the Prophet had intended 'Ali, his son-in-law and cousin, to succeed him and that after 'Ali authority would be designated to certain of those from among his descendants through Fatimah, his daughter and sole source of grandchildren. It is further held that 'Ali's right to succession was usurped by Abu Bakr and 'Umar, the first two caliphs of the Islamic state.[14] Western writers have tended to emphasize the political dimension of these events. While their political importance

should not be denied, in the minds of many Shi'a the argument
with the Sunni position does not focus on the issue of the political office of the caliphate. Political authority is indeed a part of
the problem, and for Sunni Muslims it may be the central issue.
But for the Shi'a the central problem is not that of the early Muslim community's rejection of 'Ali's right to the caliphate but
rather its rejection of his inherent station as Imam. In Shi'i
thought the Imamate is a spiritual station which remains an intrinsic characteristic of the person of the Imam whether or not it
is recognized by anyone else. That 'Ali should have been the
caliph, and would have been if the people had chosen wisely
and in accordance with the wishes of God and his Prophet, is
not questioned by the Shi'a. The caliphate was indeed his due.
But in the final analysis his acceptance of the role of caliph is left
to the will of the people, whereas his role as Imam is a matter of
designation (naṣṣ) both by God and the Prophet and can be neither questioned nor removed. For the Shi'a the Imamate is
something much greater than a mere political office. It is an office of miraculous power and carries with it both mystical and
soteriological dimensions.

   It should be emphasized that the Shi'a do not understand the
concept of Imamate as something external which has been
tacked onto Islam. They offer evidence for their position from
both the Qur'an and *hadith* literature—just as the Sunnis do for
their religious positions. Part of their argument is based on Surah 2:124 of the Qur'an, in which God promises that he will
make of Ibrahim and his descendants Imams. They argue that
this not only justifies the existence of the station of Imam but
that it proves the station of Imam to be higher than that of
prophet because Ibrahim was already a prophet at that time
when God promised to make him an Imam, and surely God was
not intending to lower Ibrahim's status. This commonly held attitude should not be taken as an indication of *ghullūw* (extremism); the Shi'a do not place 'Ali at a level higher than
Muhammad, as Muhammad is said to contain both prophecy
and Imamate in his person. But 'Ali's excellence is thought to be
second only to that of the Prophet. Like the prophets, 'Ali and
the Imams are thought to be *ma'ṣūm* (protected from error). They
are the guides of the community, possessing extraordinary and
esoteric knowledge and wisdom. The metaphysical status of 'Ali
and Muhammad is made especially clear in the famous *hadith* in
which the Prophet declares that he and 'Ali shared a preexis-
tence before the creation of the universe. According to this *hadith* the Prophet was reported to have said that God had created

a light before the creation of the world and that he and 'Ali were taken from that light. The light was then placed into the loins of Adam and passed down uncorrupted through the lineage of Ibrahim until it was divided between Abu Talib and 'Abdullah — the respective fathers of 'Ali and Muhammad. This light was then rejoined when 'Ali married the Prophet's daughter Fatimah. It then was split again with the birth of her two sons, Imam Hasan and Imam Husayn.[15] For the Shi'a the Prophet and his family are more than simply human beings as they represent the existence of a preexistent prophetic light in the world. Thus, the usurpation of 'Ali's right to the caliphate is seen as an implied rejection of that prophetic light.

This light imagery is an important part of Shi'i narratives. Of particular importance is the famous *Ḥadīth Kissa'* (*hadith* of the cloak) which Shi'i families sometimes use ritually as a way of invoking the *ṭufail* (intercession) of the *ahl al-bayt*. In this narrative the Prophet calls together the four closest members of his family — 'Ali, Fatimah, Hasan, and Husayn — one by one under his cloak. The angel Jibra'il appears and declares that he has come because he was attracted to the brilliant concentration of light on the earth which could be seen all the way up in the heavens.[16] These five "Persons of the Cloak" collectively as well as individually are the center of much devotion in Shi'i piety. In South Asia they are known as the *panjatan pāk* — the pure five — and they are symbolized by the ubiquitous Fatimid hand in which each of the five fingers represents one of the five *ahl al-bayt*.

Devotion to Muhammad and the *ahl al-bayt* — in particular, the People of the Cloak and the Imams (and to some extent anyone who can show a genealogical connection with 'Ali and Fatimah) — is thus a central, if not the central motif, of Shi'i piety. Shi'ism is the primary vessel for that element of Islamic piety which Marshall Hodgson has designated as "'Alid loyalism." Hodgson defines 'Alid loyalism as

that varied complex of special religious attitudes associated with loyalty to the 'Alids (descendants of 'Ali) — not only reverence for the 'Alids themselves, but certain exalted ideas about Muhammad's person and the supposition of a secret teaching he transmitted especially to 'Ali and so on — whether these attitudes appear among Jama'i Sunnis or among those who, by explicitly rejecting the *jama'ah*, identified themselves as Shi'is in the proper sense.[17]

Although 'Alid loyalism is most obvious in Shi'i piety, this concept is also crucial for any comprehensive understanding of Islam—either Sunni or Shiʿa—in South Asia. In Pakistan and North India, and particularly in Sindh and Multan, devotion to the ʿAlid cause and to ʿAlid personages is not limited to the Shiʿi community but can also be found among Sunni Muslims. This is especially true among those Sunnis influenced by the Sufi tradition. Furthermore, ritual acts of piety associated with devotion to the *ahl al-bayt* are frequently to be found in non-Shiʿi contexts.

Devotion to the *Ahl al-Bayt* in Shiʿi Piety

Devotion to the *ahl al-bayt* which is inherent in the concept of ʿAlid loyalism is thus understood as the central motif of Shiʿi piety on which all other aspects of piety can be said to rest. The lives of the fourteen *maʿṣūmīn* (the Prophet, Fatimah, and the twelve Imams) are held up as examples for the rest of humanity. Furthermore, the *ahl al-bayt* represent real individuals who may continue to influence peoples' physical and spiritual lives.

It may be objected that by raising devotion to the family of the Prophet to a central position in Shiʿi piety I am belittling the importance of Shariʿah, or Islamic Law, in Shiʿism. I do not mean to imply that Shariʿah is unimportant in the lives of Shiʿi Muslims (or that antinomianism is rampant among the South Asian community where I did my field research). As Hodgson has indicated, Shariʿah-mindedness—the sense of allegiance to an autonomous body of religious law—is a crucial element of Twelver Shiʿi piety.[18] However, on the basis of my own field observations and interviews, I would argue that devotion to the family of the Prophet constitutes the bedrock of Shiʿi piety. While it is undoubtedly true that obedience to the Shariʿah is an important part of piety and that the *ʿulamā*, or religious scholars, because of their knowledge of that law, play an important role in South Asian Shiʿism, the fulfillment of legal obligations can be seen as one result of devotion to the Prophet and his family. One follows the law as an expression of one's devotion, but love (*muḥabbat*) comes first. For example, it is commonly held that devotional rituals of an emotive nature—such as mourning for Husayn—can, in some instances, make up for lapsed Shariʿah obligations.[19] On more than one occasion during field interviews I was told, in reference to my own religious situation, that it was not so important whether or not I was nominally a Muslim as long as I held the *ahl al-bayt* in love (*muḥabbat*) and respect (*iḥtirām*).

The Importance of Narrative in Shi'i Piety

One source of the popularity and vitality of Shi'i forms of piety can be found in the strong narrative dimension inherent in 'Alid loyalism. Just as the Prophet is the proof of the Qur'an because of his character, the Imams inspire allegiance because of their personalities and virtuous actions. 'Alid loyalism focuses its attention on the human component of the Qur'anic event, emphasizing loyalty to "the man" Muhammad and by extension to his descendants. The meaning of life, the intention of religion, and the proper modes of behavior for human beings can be sought not only in explicit revelations from God to human beings through a prophet who is understood merely as a channel for divine revelation, but also in the sacred and mythological history of Muhammad and his family—a history replete with miraculous events and wondrous occurrences. It is a history rich with compelling drama and high tragedy. In the context of ritual and narrative the sacred heroes and heroines of Islam can be encountered in the performance of acts of extreme compassion, bravery, and sacrifice. These exceptional people are held up as paradigms of behavior. The Prophet and his family are understood as having lived lives full of incidents which are meaningful signs for those possessing the spiritual insight to read them. For Shi'i Muslims the root paradigms of Islam are most clearly articulated in narratives about the *ahl al-bayt*.

The importance of this narrative dimension is difficult to overestimate. As Abdulaziz Sachedina has noted, the formal theology of Shi'ism is almost identical with that of the Mu'tazilites.[20] But Mu'tazilism was too dry and arid to appeal to more than a small intellectual elite. It is not primarily theology which attracts people to a religious movement. The theological ideas of the Mu'tazilites survived, but they needed an emotional vehicle to carry them. That vehicle was the dramatic nature of Shi'i narrative which, wedded as it was to the lives of people who were not only companions of the Prophet but his blood kin as well, allowed the people who told and remembered those narratives to enter into a vicarious experience of intimate allegiance to him.

The Role of the Miraculous in Shi'i Narrative

A good part of the power of these narratives arises from the nature and status of their protagonists as they are understood in the Shi'i community. Because of their exceptional character—the fact that they were all *ma'sum* and in some sense participants in the prophetic light—the Prophet and the Imams are thought to be capable of performing miracles. The performance of these miracles is not relegated to some past history; the Imams are believed in some sense to be still living and available to believers. One reason for this belief is the complementary belief that all of the Imams were martyred. As the Qur'an assures Muslims that martyrs do not die but instead live in a paradisical state, it is commonly believed that their *tufail* can be sought and that by this intercession—which sometimes can be obtained simply by being in proximity to symbols of their power and authority—not only spiritual but mundane difficulties can be removed by miraculous means. Thus, the possibility of encountering the miraculous is an important element of Shi'i piety.

The lives of 'Ali and Muhammad provide the Shi'a with a rich source of these narratives, many of them embued with the wondrous and the miraculous. These narratives are available both in bound editions and in inexpensive pamphlets which can be purchased in the bazaars around Shi'i religious centers. They also find their way into the content of *qawwālī* (Sufi music) and *na'ats* (devotional songs about the Prophet). A great deal of this literature concerns 'Ali—his exceptional abilities, his compassion toward his enemies, his dealings with the invisible world of the *jinn*, his miraculous birth and childhood, and his special and extremely close relationship with the Prophet. Much of this literature carries about it the fragrance of popular devotion and folk religion. For this reason some of the more educated Shi'a with whom I had conversations denied the authenticity of much of it—particularly that which imparts a supernatural quality to the Prophet himself, such as accounts that he left no footprints on sand but did leave them on stone or that he was constantly shadowed by a cloud. But more often than not the sources for these narratives can be found in the Persian and Arabic writings of accepted authorities such as Shaykh Mufid and Allamah Majlisi.

Miraculous occurrences are a part and parcel of the Shi'i vision of the universe. One of the common terms for miracles is *kharq-i 'ādat*, which means "a break in the habitual."[21] The role of the miraculous in Shi'i narrative is often connected with the recurrent theme of persons seeking or recognizing the need for giving allegiance to the Imam. In such narratives the Imams demonstrate their authority through miracles. Such a break in the normal patterning of events is given to prophets and other holy personages as a proof of their claims to religious authority. Whereas prophets and Imams can work actual miracles, Sufi saints are deemed capable of *karāmāt*, a lesser form of this type of occurrence.[22]

Once again, the source of this belief is to be found in the Qur'an and *hadith* literature. The Qur'an itself is replete with miracles of earlier prophets; for example, Jesus' speech in the cradle and the parting of the Red Sea. And, although there has been a tendency to discount the miraculous elements of Islam among nineteenth- and twentieth-century Islamic reformers, who claim that *the* miracle of the Prophet is the incomparable Qur'an itself, such early biographies of the Prophet as that of Ibn Ishaq contain accounts of miracles. Tabari's history is also full of miraculous signs in the lives of the prophets and Imams.

It is not surprising that such stories are focused upon by later Shi'i writers. Majlisi devotes an extremely long chapter to the miracles of the Prophet in his Persian work *Ḥayāt-ul Qulūb*,[23] a primary source for the *majlis* reciters of Pakistan. Mufid includes a lengthy chapter on the miracles of Imam 'Ali in his *Kitāb al-Irshād*.[24]

Shaykh al-Mufid lists categories of miracles and also gives as a reason for the existence of such phenomena that in them "normal human behavior is transcended and in it there is a great wonder and an illustrious miracle to the minds of men."[25] These miracles are thus seen as evidences for the verity of the claims of the Imams to spiritual authority. This is particularly apparent in his chapter on 'Ali in *Kitab al-Irshad*. Mufid credits 'Ali with perfect knowledge, which he possessed even as a child. In the manner of the Islamic Jesus, he is shown as preaching from the cradle. Mufid notes his exceptional military prowess, including feats of strength and bravery which (he argues) could only emerge from a divine source. Mufid even assigns to the miraculous the fact that 'Ali's reputation as a great and good man has survived despite constant Ummayyad propaganda against him. Most importantly, he notes the ability of the Imams and prophets to know "hidden things." Included in this category of miracles is 'Ali's knowledge of the treacherous deception of his former supporters Talha and Zubayr and the hidden deformity of a man from among the Kharijites.[26]

Knowledge of this kind is common in stories about the Imams who would, when approached by enemies who had come to curse them, reveal to them events in their past which they could not possibly have known by rational means. Such stories often end with the conversion of the enemy to the cause of the Imam. As Michael Gilsenan has pointed out in his study of Egyptian Sufism, this ability to know the hidden events of a person's life is one proof of the power of a saint. Such knowledge of what is hidden in a social sense is a metaphor for knowledge of what is hidden in a religious sense.[27] And, of course, the Imams are said to have esoteric knowledge of the Qur'an which is thought to have been passed on from the Prophet himself.

The primary function of the miraculous as outlined by Mufid is to demonstrate the authority of the Imam. The ability to work miracles is taken as evidence of spiritual authority. Perhaps foremost among these abilities are the special cognitive powers of the Imams which allow them to understand the hidden meanings of things. These are represented in stories of the miraculous abilities of the Imams to know secret things. Such stories provide a means for reflecting upon the relationship between the exterior (*ẓāhir*) and the hidden (*bāṭin*). In them mundane secrets become metaphors for a greater form of hidden knowledge. Furthermore, the account of a miracle may have both inner and outer meanings, allowing for a multivocality which enhances the power of the miracle story.

Miraculous Narratives as Breaks in the Rational

An important element of miracle tales is the creation of a literary reality which facilitates belief in the possibility of a nonrational order which transcends the logical categories of day-to-day experience. In fact, this creation of a "subjunctive realm"[28] in which the improbable is imagined and experienced is a major motif in almost all of Shi'i ritual piety.

Within such narratives, a miraculous act is often preceded by an illogical and threateningly irrational activity which is either alleviated, explained, or inexplicably known by the Imam— although the event occurred far from the Imam's physical proximity and was thus hidden from him. This type of occurrence is particularly common in the ahistorical *mu'jizat kahanis*, or miracle stories, which are commonly used for the making of spiritual vows called *mannats*. Often the protagonists of these stories initially find their physical situation miraculously and inexplicably changed for the better—often from poverty to wealth through the blessing of a holy personage. But by forgetfulness or unthankfulness—generally the omission of a promised pious action—conditions become reversed in the extreme. The new situation often constitutes a break in the predictable structure of reality which proves to be extremely disorienting.

For example, in one such miracle story a man and his wife awake to find their home destroyed and their children dead. They further discover that whatever food they attempt to eat becomes putrid before it reaches their mouths. In another story a couple who have rejected the miraculous power of the *ahl al-bayt* eventually find themselves jailed by a king who believes that they have murdered his son (as a melon which they had in their possession has miraculously assumed the shape of the young prince's severed head). In the end it is only through the intervention of the *ahl al-bayt*, who remind these unfortunate couples of unfulfilled actions and advise them of means to fulfill them, that things are restored to normal.[29]

These situations possess many of the characteristics which Turner ascribes to liminality. Miraculous occurrences provide an arena in which one is forced to think in terms removed from those of the normal day-to-day world of ordinary social relations. The witness to a miracle is forced to focus upon transcendent realities. In the context of Shi'i Islam, these greater realities are connected with claims of spiritual authority. When one accepts the authority of the Imams—which ultimately comes from God—then one's life proceeds predictably and satisfactorily. But forgetfulness produces a state which makes the world thoroughly irrational; it is only by the intervention of the Imams (again in miraculous fashion) that the true nature of reality—that is, the proper nature of authority—can be reflected upon and proper allegiances can be restored.

The Relationship between 'Ali and Muhammad as a Paradigm in Shi'i Narrative

Stories of the special relationship between 'Ali and Muhammad constitute an important source for Shi'i narrative. This relationship is a paradigmatic one for the community. If one of the functions of miraculous narrative is to allow the believer to step outside of his or her day-to-day reality in order to reflect upon the deeper meaning of things in the form of powerful symbols, then one of the most ubiquitous and powerful of these points of reflection is the relationship between the Prophet and 'Ali. As Shi'ism is the religion of personal allegiance to the Prophet, 'Ali is the paradigm for all subsequent Islamic behavior in that he is the perfect servant of the Prophet.

The clearest statement of their relationship is to be found in the story of the event at Ghadir Khumm. The circumstances of this event are known to all Shi'a and the day of its anniversary is an occasion for community celebration. The narrative states that while returning from his final pilgrimage to Mecca the Prophet stopped at the well at Ghadir Khumm and asked the crowd accompanying him: "Am I not closer to you than you are to yourselves?" The crowd answered in the affirmative, and the Prophet said: "I leave you two things that if you hold to them you shall not err. One is the book of God and the other is my *ahl al-bayt*." He then called 'Ali up in front of the crowd and said: "Whoever I am the *mawla* of, this man 'Ali is his *mawla*. Oh God, befriend whoever befriends him and be hostile to whomever is hostile to him and support whomever supports him and desert whomever deserts him."[30]

The translation of the word *mawla* is problematic. It means both "servant" and "master." It also means "friend." For the Shi'a this event is evidence that the Prophet indeed had intended for 'Ali to be his political successor, for to simply swear friendship to him publicly in such an ostentatious manner would have been unnecessary. The narrative implies that there is a strong connection between obeying 'Ali and obeying God—equating the state of being God's friend with that of being the friend of 'Ali.[31]

The intimate relationship between 'Ali and the Prophet is delineated even more clearly in the story of the night on which the Prophet made the Hijrah from Mecca to Medina. This narrative is a favorite one of readers of *majlis*, and it is often embellished with greatly emotive language. According to this narrative, before the Prophet embarked for Medina, a plot had been hatched by the Quraysh to assassinate him. The angel Jibra'il informed the Prophet of this plot, and the Prophet went to see 'Ali. Muhammad told him of the nature of the plot—to murder him in his sleep—and requested that 'Ali should sleep that night in his bed in order to conceal his departure. As recorded by Majlisi, 'Ali's reaction is significant. He first asks if this action will in fact ensure the safety of the Prophet. Having been assured of this, 'Ali laughed, thanked God for the privilege of risking his own life for that of the Prophet, and fell to the ground in adoration. He then rose and said: "Go wherever God has commanded; let me be your sacrifice. Order what you please and on my life I will do it; and in this and in every other matter I supplicate the grace of God." Majlisi then notes that Muhammad compares 'Ali's willingness to sacrifice himself to that of Isma'il. Thus the love between 'Ali and Muhammad is shown to be congruent to that between Ibrahim and his son.[32]

The Shi'a believe that the Qur'an refers to this event in Surah 2:208: "There is also a man who sells his soul for the sake of those things which are pleasing to God." This aspect of 'Ali, that he is a man who has sold his soul to God, is one that is used very effectively in the oral performance of *majlis*. In *majlis* 'Ali is put forth as a paradigm for the proper attitude of submission to God's will. He has sold his soul to God by having offered his life in loving devotion to the Prophet. By giving himself to the Prophet he has sold himself to God. As one *zakir* puts it, 'Ali— who has normally *shab bedār* (one who seldom slept)—"sold his *nafs* (soul) to Allah and thus on this one night slept peacefully and without fear." 'Ali dedicated his spirit solely to God, and "what greater jewel is possible than this—bringing his will fully and totally into accord with God's will."[33]

At this point the *zakir* from whom I have taken this account almost takes this line of reasoning to the point which some might misconstrue as *ghulluw* or 'Alid extremism when he says: "Before [this night] it was the *nafs* [soul] of 'Ali, but after that night of the Hijrah this *nafs* no longer remained 'Ali's. Rather the *nafs* of 'Ali became the *nafs* of Allah; where it was the hand of 'Ali it has become the hand of Allah. Where it was the tongue of 'Ali it has become the tongue of Allah; where it was the eyes of 'Ali they have become the eyes of God. . . . Who is like this 'Ali . . . whose intention are God's intentions?"[34]

Although this passage is related in a Shi'i work, the close connections between Shi'i spirituality and Sufism can be clearly seen. This transformation of the *nafs* through dedication to the Prophet can be seen as the model for Sufi practice in which the *nafs* of the neophyte is transformed by devotion to the shaikh— who in one sense serves as a metaphor for the Prophet—so that the *nafs* of the devotee is brought into the proper relationship with the moral order of the universe as intended by God. It also should be noted that in the Sufi path *vilāyat-i murshid* (devotion to the spiritual master) ultimately leads to *vilāyat-i rasūl* (devotion to the Prophet) and ultimately to *vilāyat-i khuda* (devotion to God).

This understanding of the symbolic power of the relationship between God, the Prophet, and 'Ali is difficult to overestimate. If Muhammad is God's beloved and the center of the spiritual hierarchy on Earth, then 'Ali as the finest example of devotion to the Prophet becomes a model for all Muslims. A proper understanding of the relationship between these two men becomes an essential element in the lives of those wishing to live a deep spiritual life. Again their mutual relationship is structurally like that of the Sufi shaikh and his disciple in the condition of *fanā fī-shaykh*, in which the self of the disciple is annihilated in the self of the master.

The clearest example of this for the Shiʿa is to be found in the incident at Mubahila, which is referred to in the Qurʾan (Surah 3:61). According to the Qurʾanic narrative, the Prophet challenged the Christians of Najran to a spiritual contest calling the curse of God upon the liar. They agreed to meet at Mubahila on the next day. The Prophet was told by God to bring his sons, his women, and his self (*nafs*). The story ends with the Christians backing down and asking to be allowed to keep their own religion. The story is important for the Shiʿa because Muhammad appeared with Hasan and Husayn, his sons; Fatimah, representing his women; and ʿAli, as his *nafs*. Accordingly, Muhammad equates his own self with ʿAli, and ʿAli is henceforth known as *nafs-i rasul* (self of the Prophet). According to Shiʿi sources commenting on this event, the Christians were so moved by the divine radiance emanating from the *panjatan pak* (the pure five—Muhammad, ʿAli, Fatimah, Hasan, and Husayn) that they were afraid to risk debating the Prophet.[35]

Two other stories indicative of this special relationship between ʿAli and Muhammad are particularly well known and used in the Shiʿi community. One concerns the miraculous birth of ʿAli. According to tradition, ʿAli was born inside the *Kaʾbah*, the holiest shrine of Islam. After his birth the Prophet entered the holy structure and, upon touching his tongue to ʿAli's, ʿAli recited the *shahādah* (confession of faith) or (according to some) a verse of the Qurʾan. Thus, ʿAli is identified with Jesus, who is depicted in the Qurʾan as speaking revelations in the cradle.[36]

An even more popular story among South Asian Shiʿa is the narrative of the siege of the Fort of Khaybar. The following version is an amalgam of several versions in both English and Urdu, oral and written.[37]

Involved in an extremely difficult and lengthy siege at the Jewish fort of Khaybar, the Prophet—who was suffering from a severe headache—gave his standard to Abu Bakr, who was repulsed from the walls of the fort and forced to retreat. He then passed the standard to ʿUmar, who could do no better. The Prophet then said: "Tomorrow I shall hand over my standard to one who loves God and his Prophet and who is the beloved of the Lord and his Prophet and who is a fearless charger who never turns his back upon a foe. At his hands, the Lord will give victory." Of course, all of the Prophet's companions were anxious to be so honored. 'Ali was apparently out of the running for this honor, as he was suffering from ophthalmia and thus was temporarily blind. However, when he awoke the Prophet sought out 'Ali but could not find him. He was informed that 'Ali was a great distance away and unable to see. But 'Ali was summoned and appeared before the Prophet (some say that this was caused to happen miraculously). The Prophet then took 'Ali's head in his lap and applied his saliva to his eyes as a balm. At that instant his eyes were miraculously healed. 'Ali took the banner and armed with his sword, *Zūlfiqār*, stormed the citadel and defeated the inhabitants of the fort. At one point 'Ali singlehandedly removed the door of the citadel, which seven other persons later could not move, and used it as a shield. From above an angel was heard to announce: "There is no hero but 'Ali and no Sword but *Zūlfiqār*."

Because of this victory 'Ali was given the title "Mushkil Kusha," which means "remover of difficulties." 'Ali is thought by many to be the remover of difficulties both mundane and spiritual. The formulaic call *"Ya 'Ali Madad"* ("Oh Help, 'Ali") is commonplace not only in speech but also in written form on objects such as necklaces and bumperstickers. It is even repeated—in South Asia—by many Sunni Muslim as well, for 'Alid devotionalism often transcends the ordinary divisions between Sunni and Shi'a.

The Self-Understanding of the Shi'a
vis-à-vis the Larger Islamic World

I have attempted to define Shi'ism on its own terms as that religious school of thought in Islam which emphasizes the personal relationship between the believer and the Prophet. The accompanying emphasis on narrative as a way of learning proper Islamic values and behavior and the metaphysical character of the family of the Prophet are important characteristics of Shi'i Islam which are independent of its relationship with the larger Islamic world. Shi'i piety, however, emerged amidst struggles for power in the Islamic world, and there are ways in which the Shi'a understand their faith in an oppositional fashion.

'Alid loyalist attitudes have been greatly influenced by the history which forged the early Islamic community. They represent one way of interpreting the social drama which began when the Prophet came down from Mount Hira for the first time and began to preach his message, which implied not only a change in spiritual direction but also in social and economic loyalties. The majority of the Quraysh—the leading tribe of Mecca, of which Muhammad's clan of Banu Hashim was a prestigious but economically weak part—were caught on the horns of a dilemma. As Hodgson has pointed out, loyalty to this new entity of Islam consisted of two elements—a loyalty to the message and a loyalty to the messenger himself.[38] As the Prophet gained important converts and the number of Muslims increased, it was at least theoretically possible (and from the Shi'i perspective this is exactly what happened) that the Quraysh, in recognizing the attraction and power of the message, could simply have adopted the Qur'an as a central focus of piety and left the Meccan social system and its hierarchies basically intact.

But for many, loyalty to the message meant loyalty to the messenger as well. Particularly during the early portion of Muhammad's career, when the Qur'an was but a few verses and there was no way one could speak of a full-fledged Shari'ah law, membership in the community was determined to a large degree by allegiance to the person of the Prophet. It might be possible for the Quraysh to tolerate the message and coopt it to fit their own ends, but the Prophet as a leader represented a distinct threat to the Meccan system.

A period of crisis reached its peak with the event of the Hijrah. The Quraysh had grown fearful enough of the Prophet's authority that, regardless of the social consequences, they deemed that he should be killed. The Prophet thus set out to found a new community in Medina and began a period of struggle which culminated in the conquest of Mecca and the final reaggregation of the Muslims to the larger Meccan community, with the Quraysh accepting the Prophet's authority over them.

With the death of the Prophet, however, the old tensions reasserted themselves. The lines were drawn between those who emphasized the authority of the man and those who emphasized the authority of the book. Some Muslims went so far as to argue that in the absence of the Prophet zakāt (almsgiving) was no longer mandatory, as they had given allegiance only to him. In the Shi'i view of history the initial breach between the Quraysh and the Muslims was never truly healed. The Muslims of the Quraysh, after the death of the Prophet, attempted to organize the Muslim ummah around the Qur'an and the Sunnah not only of the Prophet but of the companions of the Prophet as well, thus cloaking their own political decisions with an air of religious legitimation. The Prophet was merely the supreme model of the proper follower of the message. The center of piety was to be the Qur'an, and allegiance to the Prophet was relegated to a lower status than allegiance to the Qur'an. As the Shi'a look back on this period of Islamic history, the rights of Banu Hashim, in particular the right of 'Ali to the caliphate, were denied in spite of the explicit wishes of the Prophet. Banu Umayyah—the Prophet's former enemies—were given preference, and the *ahl al-bayt* were oppressed or ignored.

It is here that the importance of mourning in Shi'i piety becomes crucially important. The importance of the mourning does not lie in the act of mourning itself but rather in the enormity of the crimes against the *ahl al-bayt*—as they are understood by the Shi'a—coupled with the innocence of the victims. The rejection and persecution of the *ahl al-bayt* is seen as a rejection of Islam itself. Fatimah, 'Ali, and the Imams became symbols of a trust betrayed.[39] The stories of their individual sufferings under what are seen to be unlawful usurpers became the substance of narratives recited in *majlis* which still inspire a mixture of grief and outrage; the Imams are seen as persons who remained true to their ideals even when ignored or abandoned by their friends. The chiliastic idea that a hidden Imam would return and bring about a just social order in a corrupt world became a rallying point for later Shi'ism, and 'Ali became a symbol of the oppressed and maltreated hero as well as an example for those who may have felt similarly ignored by the powers that be.

No other drama of this period of early Islamic history has so captured the imagination and ritual activity of Shi'i Muslims as the martyrdom at Karbala of Imam Husayn, the last living grandson of the Prophet and the last of the People of the Cloak who was killed by the official forces of the Islamic state. This event is understood by the entire Shi'i world as one of the definitive actions in all of world history.

Karbala is remembered through the recitation of narratives and the performance of ritual. The events of Karbala are central to Shi'i piety and therefore are focuses of intense ritual activity. The ritual approaches to the narrative of Karbala can be broadly broken down into two categories; those which are public and those which are more private and take place inside the home. Each of these two types of rituals will be dealt with separately in the succeeding chapters. Both types of rituals are clearly linked to the central attitudes of Shi'i piety. First of these is the belief that the Prophet had decided and designated that his proper successors were to be found among his descendants—in particular, ʿAli and his lineage through the Prophet's daughter Fatimah. This succession is not purely political in its nature but also metaphysical. This can be seen in the belief that Muhammad and ʿAli were created before the creation of the universe from a divine light. Connected with this is the belief that the special creation of ʿAli and Muhammad from this spiritual light and their especially close relationship with God has endowed them and their spiritual descendants with special abilities and powers. Furthermore, the miraculous abilities of the Imams are not something confined to a long dead past; rather, as the Imams are martyrs and thus still living, human beings have access to their power. Finally, there is the belief that the Prophet passed down a special form of knowledge to the Imams and that this knowledge allows the Imams to see what is hidden, both in a spiritual and a material sense.

Thus, narratives about the *ahl al-bayt* are an important element of Shiʿi piety. A consistent theme in these narratives is that of humanity's rejection of "the Truth"—whether that rejection is the result of greed, ignorance, or simply forgetfulness and weakness. Ultimately, the rejection of the claims of the *ahl al-bayt*—replete with murder and betrayal, and culminating in the occultation of the last of the twelve Imams, who will return as an eschatological figure when human beings are finally ready to accept him—constitutes for Shiʿi Muslims a rejection of the Prophet and of Islam itself. In the virtuous and heroic conduct of the *ahl al-bayt* in the face of every imaginable difficulty, Shiʿi narrative presents the believer with a dramatic, evocative, and compelling paradigm of behavior.

As stated above, the most famous and most emotionally powerful of these narratives is that of the tragedy of Husayn at Karbala. The bare bones of the story are simple enough. Husayn, the grandson of the Prophet, is called from Medina to Kufa by men who claim to be his supporters against the tyrannical despot Yazid b. Muʿawiyah b. Abu Sufyan. Yazid had demanded that Husayn offer to him an oath of allegiance, but Husayn refused. Husayn learned that Yazid planned to have him killed while he was in Mecca; so, in order to avoid bloodshed in the holy city, Husayn with his family members set out for Kufa in Iraq. In the Iraqi desert near the town of Karbala, Husayn and his small band were met by the forces of Yazid, under the command of Ibn Ziyad. Husayn was cut off from water and deserted by all but his closest friends and relations. His supporters in Kufa deserted him as well under pressure from Yazid's men. Husayn offered to go back to Mecca or to disappear into the frontier, but Ibn Ziyad would accept nothing less than his oath of full allegiance to Yazid. One by one Husayn's companions—vastly outnumbered—went bravely to their deaths. His half-brother 'Abbas, while attempting to bring water for the child Sakina, was brutally murdered—his hands cut off to prevent him from carrying water back to the camp of Husayn. The infant son of Imam Husayn, 'Abdullah—better known as 'Ali Asghar—was shot by an arrow while the Imam, under a flag of truce, requested water for the innocent child. Finally, having watched all but one of his male relatives and companions—his own son 'Ali, who was ill in the tents of the women—go to their deaths, the Imam was cut down in combat, alone and thirsty in a strange land. His body was brutally trampled and his corpse left ignominiously naked in the desert, unburied. The women were paraded uncovered through the city of Damascus. The head of the last remaining grandson of the Prophet was carried into the city atop a pole. That such a thing could happen within living memory of the Prophet shocked the conscience of the Islamic world. That such a thing could happen at all still shocks the hearts of Shi'i Muslims, and in the yearly remembrance of this tragedy in the month of Muharram the Shi'a encounter the events of Karbala in a dramatic fashion.

It is not surprising that these events should constitute the central focus of the most important public rituals of Shi'i Islam. The remembrance of Husayn is performed with variations in the different cultural regions where Shi'i Islam established itself; yet, although each region has brought its own sensibilities to bear, the underlying emotion remains the same.

Devotional allegiance to the Prophet and his family, which is seen so clearly and forcefully in the Muharram rituals commemorating the battle of Karbala, finds articulation in numerous ways. Devotional allegiance has communal, familial, and personal dimensions. The following chapters examine some of the ways in which Shi'i Muslims demonstrate their love for the people of the Prophet in both public and private arenas.

CHAPTER TWO

Household Rituals:
The Uses of Miraculous Narratives

In the first chapter we have established the importance of the Imams and the Prophet in Shi'i Islam, both as historical and metahistorical personalities, as foci of allegiance. In the context of Shi'i piety they are understood as powerful spiritual entities who, rather than being relegated to an existence in some far distant historical past, are instead thought of as living presences whose intercession (*tufail*) can be sought even today. They are metahistorical personalities whose paradigmatic virtues have been revealed in history but whose spiritual existence is not bounded by mere historicity. The Prophet and Imams are understood to inhabit a spiritual realm parallel to that of normal waking consciousness, but it is a realm which humanity may contact at times.

One important means of achieving contact with this spiritual world is the performance of ritual. In a very profound sense all Islamic ritual involves the possibility of encounter with the divine. As Hodgson has so eloquently noted, the act of prayer (*namāz* or *ṣalāt*) in Sunni and Shi'i Islam at one level is a mystical action, for in repeating the words of the living God as they were heard by the Prophet, worshippers are in some sense able to recreate the experience of the Prophet as he himself first heard those words.[1] The ritual of prayer is an attempt both to emulate the historical actions of the Prophet and to taste something of the transcendent experience of Muhammad.

Islamic ritual includes both public and private acts. Although Islam stresses community, even shared and prescribed forms of devotion have a powerful individual dimension. One of the great strengths of Islam is the extreme mobility of its ritual actions. Prayer is compact and simple, requiring only a clean space

35

for its performance. It can be done by a single individual in iso-
lation. However, the spatial structuring of the act of prayer—
with the worshipper facing inward toward the spiritual center of
the community at Mecca—and the fact that it is done at prescribed times present the performer of *namaz* with a communal
dimension as well. Prayer is at once a solitary observance and
one which links worshippers with the larger community of Islam.

This communal aspect of Islamic ritual is seen most clearly in
the *jum'ah* or congregational prayers which occur on Fridays. In
these prayers the men of the community come together behind
one Imam and pray in unison. But it should be remembered that
the act of prayer is not contingent upon the presence of a community. It is theoretically possible—although not optimal—to be
a Muslim alone. (This was the case with the great Sufi figure
Uways al-Qarani, who converted to Islam merely on the evidence of hearsay about the Prophet.)

In much of traditional Islamic society women have much less
access than men to the public side of Islamic practice. Their
realm of activity is largely that of the household and their existence is in many ways one of living in a universe which is separate from but interconnected with that of men. Therefore, it is
not surprising that the personal dimension of Islam may be
stronger among women, whose access to public rituals is limited
by the culture of male dominance. Although it is not forbidden
in the Qur'an or Shari'ah, South Asian women generally do not
attend Friday prayers or many of the other functions of the
mosque. (This is perhaps less true in the Shi'i community,
where women do take an active part in the religious life of the
imāmbārgāh—the building used for Shi'i activities.) Possibly for
this reason women take part in a wide range of household rituals which form an important part of their religious life. That the
home should be the center of religious life for Muslim women
should not be surprising. The domestic paradigm is strong in Islam, and in many respects men and women live in separate
realms which intersect only in the home and in certain public rituals. The world of women is not easily accessible to men but is
known of by them, although such knowledge may be shrouded
in hazy understanding.

The most common household rituals, aside from the women's
majalis, which are similar in content and structure to those of
their Islamic brethren, are the recitations of miracle stories (*mu-
'jizat kahanis*). These stories are among the most ubiquitous
pieces of literature in the South Asian Muslim world. It is important to note that the reading of *mu'jizat kahanis* is not an act of

devotion specified by the Shari'ah. To the best of my knowledge it is not to be found in the Sunnah of the Prophet. However, these stories form an extremely important part of popular piety in Shi'i Islam in South Asia, particularly among women. They are clear examples of the power of 'Alid devotional ideas in South Asia and the ways in which people in the privacy of their own homes respond to the verities of Shi'i piety. They are also among the clearest examples of the concept of Islam as personal allegiance in Islamic popular culture and show the way in which that concept informs the lives of ordinary people.

The *mu'jizat kahanis* are evidence of the ways in which 'Alid devotionalism maintains a hold on the daily affairs of believers. As I have argued in the preceding chapter, for the Shi'a the Imams are not merely characters of some ancient historical moment. Instead, they are living, spiritual entities whose presence and assistance can be evoked by various ritual activities. The aid of the fourteen *ma'sumin*—Muhammad, Fatimah, and the twelve Imams—can be sought for either mundane or spiritual assistance. One of the most common ways of invoking the presence and aid of the Imams is by reciting sacred narratives. In a very real sense the recitation of these tales recreates the characters and brings them into the world through the organ of the imagination.

The recitation of *mu'jizat kahanis* is usually linked to the making of *mannats* or spiritual vows. Generally it is the case that a favor is asked of the holy person and the intention is made to read a particular story—for instance, the story of Bibi Fatimah or 'Ali Mushkil Kusha—along with the distribution of sweets— when the request has been granted. Sometimes the story is read beforehand, with the assumption that the vow will be fulfilled. In any event, it is commonly believed by people of many different economic, ethnic, and educational backgrounds that reciting these stories is efficacious.

Interestingly, many Sunni women also make use of these same stories. One Sunni woman told me, for example, that she used to read the *kahani* of Imam Ja'far as-Sadiq until she heard the rumor that the reason for its being read is to celebrate the death of the Caliph Uthman. (The rumor is untrue, although it is commonly believed by many people.) The point here is that the stories are considered efficacious not only by the Shi'i community but by many members of the general Muslim population of South Asia.

The origins of the *mu'jizat kahanis* are unclear. One possibility is that there is a link between these stories and the making of *mannats* and the indigenous Hindu tradition of *vrats*. *Vrats* are ritual readings of texts associated with fasting in the Hindu devotional tradition of *bhakti*. Usually there is a *pūja* (devotional offering) performed and the reading of a text associated with the particular *vrat*. They are available in cheap manuals in markets nearby to temples and are written in colloquial Hindi or dialect.[2]

Similarly, the *mu'jizat kahanis* are written in simple Urdu, which is easily understood by most literate people. They are available in inexpensive paperbound editions at bookstalls near shrines and *imambargahs* or at festivals and fairs. Although they can be found in more than one published edition, they are remarkably similar to each other in form and vocabulary. Lately collections have become available which gather stories related to many of the important figures of Shi'i metahistory into one volume.

While there are stories for many of the *ma'sumin* as well as other figures, such as Zainab and 'Abbas, certain stories are more popular than others. Part of this may have to do with the age, and thus accepted authenticity, of the various texts. It is commonly held that the *Janāb-i Sayyidah ki Kahānī* is very old but that the now increasingly popular *Das Bībiyan ki Kahānī* (The Story of the Ten Women) is relatively recent—perhaps having come into existence only since Partition. For many Muslim reformers these stories are suspect and are most probably non-Islamic, but the act of making *mannat* is less controversial. At one point I was an active participant in a *mannat* rather than just an observer. When I was returning to the United States from Pakistan at the end of 1983, some of my Pakistani friends came to my flat and tied around my arm a ribbon with a rupee sewn inside of it. I was told that I would be guaranteed a safe trip home by this action but that on my return I would have to distribute a rupee's worth of sweets and arrange a reading of the story of Bibi Fatimah. Upon my return I arranged for this, but rather than the Bibi Fatimah story, the person who read the story read a Persian translation of what he considered to be the more authentic *Hadith Kissa'*.

Whatever the authenticity of the stories, they play an important role in the practical piety of many Shi'i Muslims. Unlike the larger public performances of Muharram, which are visible to the larger non-Shi'i community, they take place solely within the community and within the walls of the household. They may involve only two or three people or, in the case of the story connected with the *kundah niyāz* (ritual performed in the memory of Ja'far as-Sadiq), a larger number of members of the local

Shi'i community. But, in any event, these rituals do not face out into the larger community of general Islam. They are meant to reinforce certain attitudes and ideas within the community, but they do not reveal in a direct and provocative way the differences which separate the Shi'i and Sunni communities from each other.

This chapter will focus on four of the most important of these narratives. First is the *Bībī Fāṭimah ki Kahānī* or *Janab-i-Sayyidah ki Kahani*, perhaps the most famous and widely used of the *kahanis*. Second is the more recent *Das Bibiyan ki Kahani*, which is particularly interesting because of its portrayal of women both in Islamic history and in contemporary South Asia. Third is the story associated with Hazrat 'Ali, the story of Mushkil Kusha. Fourth is that associated with Imam Ja'far as-Sadiq and the yearly *niyaz*, whose origins are connected to him.

The basic argument presented here is that although these materials are apocryphal they nevertheless fulfill functions and teach lessons which are inherent in the theology and imamology of Shi'i Islam. As one *maulvi* (religious leader) put it to me, it may be true that the reading of the *kahanis* is not part of the Shari'ah, but it nevertheless encourages people to come together to offer prayers and food, activities which are all central to Islam. Thus, the *kahanis* should be understood and examined in light of the religious context in which they are used. Within that context they resonate with the religious verities of the more classically authentic tradition. Furthermore, these stories must be understood as the center of household rituals. These rituals facilitate the creation of a liminal space in which women can reflect upon their own lives in light of the root paradigms that are at the center of the *kahanis*.

Janab-i Sayyidah ki Kahani

This story is also called *Bibi Fatimah ki Kahani* and its title refers to the daughter of the Prophet, Bibi Fatimah, who is one of the fourteen *ma'sumin* and "the mother of all of the Imams" after 'Ali, her husband. In a collection of *mu'jizat kahanis* entitled *Mu-'jizāt wa Munajat*, the *ādāb* (proper courteous behavior) required for hearing the story is given.[3] It says: "Light incense, cover your head, sit down courteously and consider that you are at this time in the presence of the sinless Sayyidah. Refrain from foolish and frivolous conversation. Refrain from laughing. Listen to the miracle which is being related with a trusting and pure heart. And then with respect eat the sweets which you have gathered for distribution."

Thus, it is obvious that the story is to be read in a ritual context and with an air of seriousness that involves the belief in the spiritual presence of the Prophet's daughter.[4] This is followed in the text by the recitation of the story.

OUTLINE OF THE STORY

The story begins with the Qur'anic phrase, *Bismillah ar-Rahman ar-Rahīm* (In the Name of God, the Merciful and the Compassionate). The story consists of interlocking miracle tales. The following version is not a literal translation but rather a rendering based on three separate versions.[5]

It is reported that one day the wife of a goldsmith was, in her usual manner, filling earthen pots of water at a well when suddenly she heard a commotion. The cause of this commotion was that her son had fallen into the kiln of her neighbor the potter and it was certain that he had burned to death. Hearing this dreadful news, she fell into a dead faint. A crowd gathered and found her unconscious from grief. While in this unconscious state, the woman saw a veiled woman approach her who said, "Oh, fortunate one, do not grieve! God is all powerful, even to the point that he can raise the dead. It is a certainty that he will do so. Make a vow that if God, through the intercession of Janab-i Sayyidah — Fatimah — delivers you from this sadness and misfortune and your child is restored to you safe and sound, then you, after making prostrations of thanks will hear the *kahani* of Janab-i Sayyidah Fatimah."

Accordingly, the wife of the goldsmith made such a vow while in the unconscious realm ['*alam-i be-hosh*]. When she returned to consciousness and opened her eyes, she saw that her son was standing safe and sound next to her by the miracle of Janab-i Sayyidah and the power of God. The people saw this with amazement. (At this point in the story the reader is asked to offer salutations to the Prophet and his family.)

The woman was terribly happy to see her son alive and immediately offered prostrations of thanks. Then she brought two dirhams' worth of sweets and having placed them in a clean place, went to her neighbors and told them, "God has fulfilled my desire through the intercession of Fatimah. I have vowed to hear the story of Bibi Fatimah. Consequently, it is also proper for you — as my neighbors — to leave here and recite for me the story of Fatimah. If you do so, I would be grateful."

Her neighbors said, "We have no free time" and "We haven't got time to waste." Hearing this she became melancholy and left to return home. Taking the sweets, she went crying away from that inhabited place in the direction of the desert, in the hope that she might meet some servant of the Lord and arrange for that person to read the *kahani* and thus fulfill her obligation.

After some time had passed, the same veiled woman who had appeared to her in the unconscious state appeared to her in the waking
realm. She said, "Oh woman, do not cry! Spread your *chador* [cloak]
and sit down and I will tell you the story. Listen attentively and offer
salavats to the *ma'sumah* [Fatimah]."
Then she read:

In the city of Medina there lived a Jew whose daughter was getting
married. All of the Jews decided together that if they invited the
daughter of the Prophet of the Muslims, then (God forbid) the
Prophet would be humiliated, because Janab-i Sayyidah would
come wearing old and torn clothing. According to this decision,
the Jew appeared in the presence of the Prophet and said, "I claim
the right of friendship and therefore I request that your blessed
daughter Janab-i Sayyidah should come to my humble household
for the marriage of my daughter. If you give her your permission to
take part in the wedding, then my dignity will be increased."

The Prophet replied, "Fatimah's lord and master [*mālik-o-mukh-
tār*] is now Hazrat 'Ali Ibn Abu Talib. Thus you should bring him
your request."

Having heard this the Jew presented himself to 'Ali [*Janāb Amīr*]
and made his request. Ali replied, "Janab-i Sayyidah has authority
over herself in this matter."

Therefore, the Jew presented himself at the door of the *ma'sumah*
and said, "Oh daughter of the Prophet, my daughter is getting
married. It is my desire that you should come and take part in the
wedding. In that way my dignity shall be increased."

From behind the door she answered, "I will obtain permission
from 'Ali [*Janab Amir*], and then I will give my answer."

The Jew replied, "I have already presented myself to your father,
the Messenger of God, and your husband, the Lion of God. They
both have given authority in this matter to you."

Having heard this, Janab-i Sayyidah became somewhat distressed. At that moment, the Prophet (the Seal of the Station) came
in and saw that his daughter was perplexed. He asked her why she
was so melancholy. She replied, "Oh dear Father, a Jew has come
desiring my participation in his daughter's wedding. What do you
command?"

The Prophet replied, "Daughter, do as you wish."

Janab-i Sayyidah replied, "Dear Father, my participation in this
wedding would not be befitting of your dignity. When I go to the
wedding, all kinds of laughter will fly about because their women
will be wearing costly clothes and the finest jewels, and I have only
this old and tattered cloth which I have patched here and there."

Having heard this, the pure Prophet said, "Oh my dear daughter, if it is God's will, then you should go even in this condition."

Thus Janab-i Sayyidah, in the face of this, made preparations to go.

In order to prevent His beloved from being ridiculed in such a manner, at the very moment when Janab-i Ma'sumah made the intention to go to the wedding, God, by his high command, sent virgins of paradise [*hūrīs*] laden with fine clothes, jewels, and ornaments to her; and they bedecked the beloved of the Prophet with a robe of honor and authority [*khilat*] and with the jewels of paradise. And then, as soon as Fatimah (the Mistress of the Two Worlds) mounted the palanquin, several *huris* on the left and right and several on the front and back took up the handles of the palanquin, in the manner of the humblest of servants. Then, taking the form of men, they set out in the company of the Jew in the direction of his house. From the direction in which Janab-i Sayyidah's entourage was passing the atmosphere became perfumed. People were dazzled and asked the Jew, "Whose procession is this, and where is it going?"

The Jew answered in a boastful style to each one who was inquiring, saying, "This is the procession of the beloved daughter of the Prophet of the Muslims, who is coming to my house to take part in my daughter's wedding."

When Janab-i Sayyidah arrived at the house of the Jew amidst all of this pomp and dignity, his entire house became illuminated by her light, and a fragrance such as no one had ever before smelled spread to every corner of the house. All of the Jewish women who were there fell unconscious from envy after having seen the glory and dignity of Janab-i Sayyidah. After a little while all of these women regained consciousness. But the bride did not regain consciousness. The women saw the bride and were astonished because she had died. Accordingly, in a short while the house of the wedding became a place of mourning. Janab-i Sayyidah was also perplexed. But, having given comfort and consolation to each of them, she said, "Pray to God. Everything is within his power. To him the raising of the dead to life is no great matter."

All of the Jewish women said with one voice, "We have never until this day seen a corpse raised back to life. What bride, having died, will come back to life?"

Then Fatimah called for a pot of water and performed ablutions, and offered two *rak'ats* of supplicatory prayers, and raised her hands to make a *du'ā*. And she said, "Oh my God, I am the daughter of the Prophet."

Then (in the form of poetry) she continued: "You have given to Fatimah the name 'the Truthful.' For the sake of the Prophet, do not now betray my name." She then continued, "Oh, my God, People will say that the Sayyidah came and caused the death of the bride and turned this wedding house into a house of mourning."

Not a moment had passed before Fatimah's *du'a* was accepted and the bride rose up reciting the *kalimah* [the shahadah, the recitation by which one accepts Islam]. And she said, "I bear witness that God is one without partners and that your father is the true and final Prophet of God. Please, instruct me in Islam."

In this way, with a sincere heart this woman became a Muslim. Having seen this miracle of Janab-i Fatimah Zahra, five hundred more men and women became Muslims, and the court bid her adieu with great ostentation. And they gave her as a servant one of the Jewish women who had become a Muslim, whose name was Umm Habibah. When she returned home and related this tale to her father—the Prophet of God—he became very happy and offered a prostration of thanks.

After this she recited a second *kahani* in this fashion:

THE SECOND PART

In a city there lived a king. This king dearly loved hunting. One day he told his wazir, or first minister, to prepare the hunting equipment. The wazir did so, and when everything was ready he informed the king. The king and the wazir set out for the hunt, and the king's daughter and the daughter of the wazir also set out with them. They arrived at a forest, where they set up their tents. Some of the people of the camp lay down in order to rid themselves of exhaustion. Some of them began to eat breakfast. All of a sudden, a violent storm appeared with such a force that huge trees were pulled up from the earth and flung about. Because of the dust and darkness, nothing could be seen even close at hand. In this violent world, no one was aware of the whereabouts of anyone else. No one knew the whereabouts of the tent of the king. When the storm had lost a little of its force and the scattered people once again began to gather together in one place, the search for the princess and the daughter of the wazir began in earnest, as they had become lost. The king and the wazir, because of their fatherly love, were terribly upset.

After a very long period of time they still did not achieve their objective. In the end, with unsatisfied hearts they were forced to head back to the palace. The entire palace was thrown into lamentation from this news of the loss of the girls, and the king's subjects were also caught up in this grief. By coincidence, after the king's hunting party had headed back, a king from a neighboring kingdom had come to hunt in the same forest. That king gave orders to his wazir that he should seek out some water because he was suffering from thirst. The wazir set out in search of water, and when he arrived at the top of a mountain he came upon two lovely and beautiful girls. These were the lost princess and the daughter of the wazir who had become separated from their fathers and their caravan.

As it happened, when these girls became separated from their fathers, they found themselves on the top of this mountain. They had become very upset. It was apparent that they were in a terrible situation. Both girls cried with such force from the violent pain of this apparently perpetual separation (from their families) that they became unconscious. In this unconscious state they saw a veiled woman approaching them. With extreme kindness she said, "Oh girls, fear not! Make an intention that when you are again reunited with your fathers you will hear the story of Bibi Fatimah."

Thus, the two girls according to these instructions took a solemn oath. When they regained consciousness, having spoken with one another about their experiences while they were unconscious, they confirmed their vow [*mannat*] and awaited the grace and mercy of God.

It was then that the aforementioned wazir searching for water came and found them. When he saw these two abandoned girls atop this mountain, he was very astonished. He asked, "Oh girls, Where do you live? Tell me of your family. And tell me how it is that you came to be atop of this high mountain."

The two girls with tears in their eyes after telling him the entire story told him of their lineage and station. After being made aware of the status of the girls, he immediately went to his king and told him the entire story. The king, having heard this story, was greatly moved and gave an order to the wazir. He said, "If it pleases the two girls, I want them to come to me. Go to them immediately and bring them to me."

According to the instructions of the king, the wazir along with some more men and some horses went to the girls. He left the horses at the foot of the mountain and went to the top of the mountain and requested, "Oh girls, please come with me."

The girls agreed and descended with the wazir to the bottom of the mountain. Having placed them on horses, he brought them with dignity to his king who brought them all to his palace.

By means of a royal emissary the first king was informed that his lost daughter along with the daughter of his wazir were at the house of the neighboring king. He sent out his first minister, along with gifts for the other king's palace. By means of a letter, he made clear his desire that the girls should be returned to him.

When the king received this letter, he sent a reply which read: "Your children are well and are with me as a trust, but it is my wish that you would give your daughter in marriage to my son and your wazir's daughter in marriage to my first wazir's son. It would be for me an occurrence of great happiness which will increase our affection for each other."

Accordingly, the first king, after much thought and attention, accepted. Thus both girls with dignity and care, were returned to their fathers.

Now an appointed day was fixed, and in both households the things of the wedding were beginning to be prepared. The final event of this time arrived when both girls were married according to religious custom. After this the brides departed and set out for the boy's house. At the same time, when all of the other items of the dowry and bridal vestments had been loaded, the *lūṭa* [water pot] from the *shādī* [wedding] which was very valuable, had been left behind. According to the custom of that time, it was extremely necessary to leave with the *luta*. On the road it became evening. Because of the coming of nightfall, the marriage procession stopped in a protected place. At this time it became necessary to find the *luta*, but it could not be located. It became clear that it had been left behind. Thus the wazir sent out a special horseman to bring back the *luta*.

When the horseman arrived, what did he see? Where the palace had been there was now an empty field. There was no throne, no crown, no king, no army—nothing. Only the *luta* was left in the field, with no one watching over it. The horseman wanted to lift up the *luta*, but it was impossible because, as he reached out his hand to grab it, a dangerous serpent stuck out its tongue from inside of the *luta* and struck, attempting to bite him. The horseman having jumped back, persisted. He tried to get the pot, but he could not. Each time he did so the serpent obstructed him. Under compulsion, he headed back in the direction of his kingdom. Through the agency of the wazir, this occurrence reached the ear of the king. The king was astonished and a little while later, after thought and reflection, became filled with fear. He went to the girls and said, "I know that you are sorceresses or evil spirits who have taken the form of women for the purpose of practicing strange magic. At this moment I shall imprison you and certainly tomorrow I shall execute you." The king was again filled with anger and indignation and returned to his tent, and both women were imprisoned.

When the girls found themselves in this state, they became faint with grief. They embraced one another, and they cried greatly and began to speak. "We do not understand what has happened. Yesterday there was a wedding and we were made brides, and today in a prison we are made prisoners. Now tomorrow the lamps of our lives shall be extinguished. We do not know what black sin has been committed by us, in whose retribution this penalty is being inflicted upon us. My Lord, forgive us!"

Having said this they cried so intensely that they fell unconscious. In the unconscious state, they saw the same woman who had come to them on the mountain top. She appeared and in perfect kindness said, "Girls, you made a vow on the mountain that when you again met your fathers you would hear the story of Janab-i Sayyidah. You were reunited with your mothers and fathers but you did not hear the *kahani*, and for this reason misfortune has befallen you. Now it is good fortune that you should hear this story in this prison. God will make your difficulties easy by the intercession of Fatimah."

The girls asked, "In this prison where can we find a dirham with which we can obtain the sweets for hearing the story? And then who will bring them?"

The woman said, "Do not be afraid. In the hem of your garments you will find two dirhams. You will see a person going out from the rear of the tent. There is a bazaar nearby: he will bring the sweets."

Having said that, she disappeared. The girls regained consciousness. They told one another of their experiences in the unconscious world. Then the princess saw that two dirhams had appeared in the hem of her garment. Both of them became very happy. In the morning, from the rear of the tent an aged man was going out. Having seen them he spoke to them and asked them what they wanted. Then he brought two dirhams of sweets and gave them to the girls. Then the two girls in this prison read the story one to another, and then they made a *du'a*. Suddenly the king's executioner arrived there, and both girls were led in the direction of the place of execution, where both said with one tongue, "First we should go to the king so that he can speak to us."

The girls were presented to the king. They asked the king to send a person once again to their homeland to see if things were not set right, and, if not, then they were willing to be killed. He sent his horseman, who was very honest, to the palace of the girls' fathers so that having gone there he could inquire as to the conditions there. Accordingly, when he went there he saw that the king's palace and crown and throne appeared as before. He was astonished beyond limits and, having completed his task, he told the entire occurrence to the king. At that time the king went to the girls and asked, "What magic is this? I am completely astonished. I want you to remove this astonishment."

At the king's request, the girls told the whole truth of their story: how they had arrived on the mountain, how they had become unconscious, how they had made a *mannat* to read the story of Janab-i Sayyidah, how they had forgotten their vow when they met their mother and father, and how they had not fulfilled it. And they said, "Now that we have heard the *kahani*, this censure which has fallen upon us has ended, and we have been made safe."

Accordingly, the king believed them and then, having released the girls, restored to them their dignity and respect, and, laughing happily, headed off for his own country.

Having read the *kahani* to the wife of the goldsmith, the great woman vanished. The goldsmith's wife returned to her house, and what did she see but that the houses of all of those people who had refused to hear the *kahani* were on fire.

In this manner God by the intercession of Janab-i Sayyidah, fulfilled the wish of the goldsmith's wife. In this way the Lord of Both Worlds will fulfill the heart's desires of believers in the name of the family of the Prophet. *Amin* and *Amin*.

[The *kahani* then says:] The *kahani* is finished; only one thing now remains and that is that after the reading of the *kahani* and before the distribution of the sweets it is necessary to recite the *ziyārat* of Janab-i Sayyidah.

ANALYSIS

This story forms the central focus of a ritual. This ritual follows the tripartite form of separation, liminality, and reaggregation suggested by Turner and Van Gennep. In order to read the story the participants must first set apart from ordinary reality both themselves and the space in which the story is to be read. The actual reading of the story corresponds to the liminal stage of the ritual process. The interlocking tales of the *kahani* are full of fantastic and miraculous occurrences. They present the deepest verities and root paradigms of Shi'i piety in a powerful and dramatic way. At the end of the reading, following the recitation of a *ziyarat* for Fatimah, the women share food before returning to their ordinary routines and thus "reaggregating."

Before the reading of the *kahani*, a special spatial-temporal arena must be created. It is clear that one should be *pāk* (ritually pure) before the recitation, as prayers are necessary as a part of it. One should perfume the arena in the manner of Sufi shrines. Most importantly one should "courteously . . . consider that you are at this time in the presence of the sinless *sayyidah*." This evocation of sacred space is also evident at the culmination of the ritual which ends—as do other Shi'i rituals—with the reading of *ziyarat*, which is a symbolic visitation to the graves of the *ahl al-bayt*. These actions facilitate the purpose of the recitation which is to hear with an open heart the miracle story and through this action to evoke in some sense the presence of Bibi Fatimah.

The actual reading of the story is the heart of the ritual. The story itself blends the fantastic with the historical, or rather what could be called the metahistorical. As pointed out in the preceding chapter, the fourteen *ma'sumin* are, in the minds of the Shi'a, living presences who are able to assist people in their daily activities. The narration of events in which Fatimah participates helps to bring an image of Fatimah into the mind of the hearer and thus re-creates Fatimah in the minds of the listeners.

Such stories are generally read by women. Thus, it is not surprising that the protagonists in this story are women and that their problems resonate with the kinds of problems which women confront in South Asia. The central setting for the narratives are weddings which are for many women, particularly those living in some degree of *purdah* (segregation), a major arena of public interaction. Most importantly, the stories reflect the interaction of Fatimah in the lives of women who are clearly South Asian; thus allowing Indian and Pakistani women to identify directly and immediately with these narratives.

The folk and household elements of these stories have caused many Shi'a and other Muslims to deny their authenticity. One reason for this is the general tendency to downplay the miraculous in contemporary Islam. Even among those who accept the importance of the miraculous in Islam there are those who are troubled by the lack of a classical basis for these tales. After all, many tales of the miraculous are to be found in the classically accepted accounts. Thus, some Muslims question the value in relying upon apocryphal tales which at the very least, are *jādū* stories (fairy tales) and possibly Hindu accretions.

This argument neglects, I think, an important aspect of these stories. In their structure and content such tales resonate with the greater cultural tradition. That is, they display the same root paradigms of virtue and morality that are found in the literature of the classical tradition. The reading of the *kahanis* in the context of these rituals allows women to identify with the sufferings of the *ahl al-bayt* and thus to encounter the root paradigms of their faith.

The *kahanis* develop themes and metaphors in the events of their narratives which clearly vibrate at a resonant frequency to the events of the history which form the basis of Shi'i piety. In the emotional and existential domain of ritual they bring to the fore the root paradigms of that tradition by presenting the important symbolic metaphors of Shi'ism. Images of separation of family members from each other, of marriage houses turned into mourning houses, and of people forgetting former vows of fealty clearly find their basis in Shi'i religious history. These and other themes of 'Alid loyalism are clearly delineated in the plots of the interlocking stories of the *kahanis*. In this way the stories are manifestations of Shi'i piety and in that context they function to reinforce attitudes essential to it. Furthermore, by going beyond the historical limits of the early Islamic period and showing how the *ahl al-bayt* function in different historical periods, they reinforce the belief in the continuing efficacy of devotion to the *ahl al-bayt*.

The *Janab-i Sayyidah ki Kahani* is a particularly powerful example of this. Throughout, it makes use of incidents and symbols which resonate with the symbols and occurrences found in the classical sources of both Shi'i and Sufi piety, although these occurrences take place in another environment.

The overarching frame story of the *kahani* concerns the wife of the goldsmith. The goldsmith is an important metaphor in Islamic mystical writings. It is used, for example, in the first book of the *Mathnawī* of Rumi. In Rumi's narrative a prince spied a fair young maiden and tempted her away with promises of gold. She soon fell sick, and none of the court physicians could cure her. Finally, a physician came from heaven itself and discovered that she was ill from the love of a goldsmith. The physician married the woman to the goldsmith and, after six months of harmony and bliss, he gave the goldsmith a poisonous draught, after which he began to decay and lose vitality. Thus, she lost her attraction to the goldsmith and was reunited with the king.[6] One interpretation of this story has the king representing the *rūḥ* or spiritual dimension of the human personality and the goldsmith representing the *nafs*—in this instance the baser animal side of a person. The physician represents the role of the Sufi shaikh who, by his knowledge, shows the woman—who represents the *murīd* or spiritual disciple—the reality of the world and thus turns her back toward the king and in the direction of God. Thus, the goldsmith's wife is in some sense the metaphor for the spiritual aspirant, and her experience becomes a model of the spiritual quest.[7]

An important aspect of the story is that it deals with knowledge gained in the realm of the unconscious. The phrase "world of the unconscious" (*'alam-i be-hosh*) is used consistently throughout the story. It is in this realm, having shut out the normal waking state, that one can make connection with spiritual helpers such as the Imams and the other notables of the metahistorical Shi'i world. One important way of reaching this realm is through lamentations or grief. The goldsmith's wife is driven into this realm by grief from the loss of her son in the furnace of the potter. The image of the furnace is a Qur'anic one and refers to Ibrahim being thrust into the fire by Nimrod, only to emerge unscathed.[8] This fire becomes a metaphor for hell.[9] Through the intercession of the daughter of the Prophet the boy is saved from the fire, implying as well that devotion to the Prophet's family assures one of salvation from damnation. This is clearly shown at the end of the story when the woman discovers that the houses of those persons who had refused to hear the story had been destroyed by fire. Devotion to the *ahl al-bayt* saves one from fire, whereas rejecting them leads to fiery suffering. This resonates with the role assigned to Fatimah in Shi'i eschatology. She is described as "the one who will save her followers from hell-fire," which is also a literal meaning of the word "Fatimah." Grief is also important in the second story. There is the grief of the first king and wazir at the loss of their daughters. The two young girls in the last story grieve not only for their separation from their beloved family but also for the hopelessness of their situation. In each of these cases not only does their grief allow them a connection with the invisible realm but also the apparent hopelessness of their situation allows them no other recourse but God (and his designees).

In all of this there is a strong Shi'i resonance. The goldsmith's wife is rendered unconscious by grief and her resultant lamentations. This state of unconsciousness, however, is no mere void but rather an opportunity for an encounter with the members of the Prophet's family (in much the same manner as it is believed that mourners for Husayn encounter Zainab and Fatimah at the *majlis* where their tears are gathered to be brought before God). *Mātam*, the rhythmic breast beating which is done in commemoration of the suffering of the martyrs of Karbala, is understood by many of the people who perform it to be a kind of *zikr* or meditation. Mourning has an immediate spiritual benefit and is a means of encountering the spiritual world.

Although the veiled woman is not directly identified as Fatimah, it becomes apparent that this is indeed who she is. Again, in clear resonance with the larger cultural tradition, Fatimah makes the same argument to the goldsmith's wife which the Prophet Muhammad had made to the Quraysh—that God can physically raise the dead. This argument was consistently ridiculed by the Meccan polytheists, and several chapters of the Qur'an make reference to this. Thus, belief in the ability of God to raise the dead is connected with accepting the veracity of the prophetic utterance.

The woman made a vow in the unconscious realm that when God delivered her from her misfortune she would read the story of Fatimah. She awoke to find that her son indeed was alive and well. All of the people of the town were amazed. This accords with the Shi'i theory of miracles, since the purpose of such miracles is to prove the authenticity of the claims of the holy family. They also serve a complementary function in that they establish the special station of the *ahl al-bayt* with God, who has endeared them to such an extent that he will grant their recommendations. They are understood as those who are favored by the divine being. At this point in the story the reader is asked to call for salutations on the Prophet and his family, thus affirming with the woman and the people in the story the greatness of the Prophet's family.

There would, however, be no drama in the story if this was all that there was to it. At this point another important theme is brought into play. This is the theme of humankind's forgetfulness and ingratitude toward God and the holy family, which is worked out in the rest of the story. The woman finds that no one wishes to read the story to her and she will thus be unable to fulfill her vow. This recalls the times when ʿAli was let down by his followers or the Kufans' betrayal of Husayn. It fits the pattern in Shiʿism, which Hodgson notes, of ʿAli becoming the symbol of a trust betrayed.[10] Once again the goldsmith's wife is miraculously aided by the same woman she saw in her dream, but this time the realm of the unconscious penetrates into the waking world. The veiled woman then recites the story for the woman.

The story she recites involves the attempted ridicule of the Prophet by the Jewish community of Medina. Although the proper *adab* (courtesy) is followed in the making of the invitation and Fatimah is approached through her father and husband, it is the unity of will of the holy family which is emphasized. The Prophet sends the Jew to ʿAli who then sends him to Fatimah herself. This brings out the Shiʿi belief that the prophetic light is one, and thus the will of all of the *ahl al-bayt* is the same. Through this series of actions the centrality of Fatimah and her pivotal function becomes obvious and Fatimah is held up as the central axis of the *ahl al-bayt*.

The poverty of ʿAli and Fatimah is an important motif in Shiʿi piety and an important aspect of this *kahani* and others. Many stories in the classical tradition tell how Fatimah gave away even the last scrap of food in their household to beggars. Her poverty is in some sense a badge of honor. Thus, her concern is not for herself but rather for the dignity of her father. Yet, despite this, Muhammad advised her to go.

It is here that the theme of miraculous interventions is once again picked up. God sends the virgins of heaven to her and he bedecks her in the robe of authority and creates such an atmosphere of glory around Fatimah that not only is the entire house illuminated by her presence—in a probable reference to the prophetic light—but the entire wedding party is rendered unconscious by the presence of the miraculous. The death of the bride (analogous once again to the death of the son of the goldsmith's wife) becomes an opportunity for Fatimah to demonstrate both the ability of God to resurrect the dead and the special relationship between God and the *ahl al-bayt*. Her prayer to God is that if God does not resurrect the bride, it will bring dishonor upon her and her father. Thus, the bride is resurrected and immediately accepts Islam and takes instruction from Fatimah. In contrast to the situation of the neighbors of the goldsmith's wife, the crowd is truly impressed and five hundred people are converted. This amplifies the special relationship between the Prophet and God, that God so loves Muhammad that he will intercede in history for him.

It also amplifies God's love for Fatimah, which is a very important theme in Shi'i piety. In fact, one of the titles of Fatimah is *Mahbūb-i Yārdān* (the Beloved of God). It is also through this story that we learn how Umm Habibah became a servant in the household of the Prophet, since she was given as a servant to the Prophet's household as a result of all of these occurrences. Thus, in the manner of Eliade, the myth takes on a cosmogonic function explaining the origin of an historical situation. At the same time, the myth's authenticity is reinforced by the bringing in of an historical fact to validate the story itself.

The Shi'i dimensions to this story are many and profound. Fatimah portrays the paradigmatic virtues of Shi'i women and thus is held up as the queen of women. Although she is terribly modest and scrupulously observes *purdah*, she is self-motivated and is a person in her own right. The power of the family of the Prophet and their special relationship to God is shown throughout. On a deeper level, the expression of grief as a way of coming into contact with supernatural forces is also emphasized in this portion of the narrative.

The second part of the *kahani* may be a later accretion. I have found two versions. The older one is much simpler than the first and only tells the bare bones of the tale, without the embellishment found in the later versions. Once again, although the story is in many ways a kind of fairy tale, it resonates with Shi'i theological and mystical ideas. A common scenario in this type of tale involves members of a family becoming separated from each other by a violent and inexplicable occurrence. Again, the classical Sufi image of the soul as one separated from its beloved is apparent in the image of the two young girls alone on the mountaintop. But that separation is to be allayed through the efficacy— once again—of the *ahl al-bayt*. Through the grief of this separation (which again mirrors the grief which the survivors of Karbala are understood to have felt at the loss of their family members), the girls make contact in the realm of the unconscious with the *ahl al-bayt* in the person of Fatimah from whom they learn that they are to make a *mannat* which they renew in the waking world. The girls — perhaps serving as metaphors for the human soul — forget their vows as they become entangled in the things of the world. This results in the disruption of their fathers' land and their imprisonment, and it is only when they once again are filled with sorrow and enter the unconscious realm that they again encounter Fatimah and remember their vow, which results in the successful resolution of their difficulties.

In both stories motifs familiar from the story of the battle of Karbala are presented out of context in a synchronic rather than diachronic arrangement of the Karbala narrative. The motif of death on a wedding night, which is a parallel to the story of Qasim's wedding — an important event in the Karbala narrative which will be discussed in more detail later in the text — and the motif of women in prison and the woman prisoner confronting a king recalls Husayn's sister Zainab confronting Yazid in Damascus after Karbala. Such motifs are common in the *kahanis* and increase the resonance of the stories with the larger tradition.

Thus the *kahani* presents, in an immediate and direct ritual context, a lesson in Shi'i verities. Not only are moral paradigms portrayed, but the efficacy of mourning, the importance of the remembrance of God, and the power of the *ahl al-bayt* are all made clear. The destruction by fire of the house of those who rejected the command of Fatimah implies what will happen in the afterworld to those who cast aspersions upon the *ahl al-bayt* or reject the efficacy of faith in them. Thus, the final lesson of the *kahani* is the importance of allegiance to the *ahl al-bayt*.

In looking at the *kahanis* it should be remembered that they are primarily a part of the religious activity of women. In fact, some people informed me that they felt that it was improper (*be adab*) for me as a male to be reading certain of the tales. The importance of these stories in the religious lives of women derives from several sources. Like weddings, they allow women to engage in social activities which otherwise might be denied to them. Whereas a husband might deny his wife the right to have her friends and relatives over for tea, he cannot easily disallow a congregation for the performance of a pious action (a point reinforced in the *kahani* in the account of the divine retribution witnessed upon those who had rejected the *kahani*).[11] The *kahanis* allow women an opportunity to take part in the manifestation of

'Alid loyalism and to recognize their important role as women in Islamic piety. The protagonists of the story are women and the sufferings they incur are sufferings universal among and particular to women. The activities which the protagonists engage in are familiar to South Asian women. This encourages the women to identify with the story, thereby allowing their own desires and readings of the *kahani* to become a part of the fabric of the story itself.

Das Bibiyan ki Kahani

The elements described above are probably most evident in the popular *Das Bibiyan ki Kahani* (The Story of the Ten Women). In this story, two brothers are living in the same town. One is wealthy, the other poor. To alleviate his poverty the poor brother tells his wife that he will go off to a distant land to try to obtain work. (This, of course, mirrors the social situation in much of Pakistan, where large numbers of men are taking jobs far away from their homes either in large urban areas or as guest workers in foreign countries, particularly in the Arab Emirates.) The woman, of course, was distressed and wondered how she would survive. The woman, who was very pious, went weeping to the house of her husband's brother and requested that he help her. The husband's brother offered her a job as a servant in the house. He entrusted her to his wife, who was to feed her out of what remained after the meals were finished and to assign duties to her in the household. She was terribly mistreated by her sister-in-law, assigned all the work of the household to do, and given barely enough to eat. In her humiliation and distress, she prayed to God to send her husband back to her. Crying, she fell asleep. In her dream she encountered a veiled woman who told her that her husband would soon return to her and that on Thursday she should read *Das Bibiyan ki Kahani*. At this point in the story, the Qur'an is quoted as saying that Maryam (Mary, the mother of Jesus) was chosen by God and was sinless. From this the reader is assured of the high stature of Maryam in Islam. The reader is then told that in Islam four women possess such high status. These are Fatimah, who holds the highest rank, and after her Sarah, the wife of Ibrahim. After her is Asiyah, the wife of the Pharaoh, because she practiced the religion of Moses and Harun even though it resulted in her death. The fourth is Hagar who, even when abandoned in the desert without water, did not lose her faith in God.[12]

The reader is then told of other women who did not leave their faith even though it brought them discomfort in this world. These include Zainab, her sister Umm Kulthum, Sughra bint al-Husayn, her sister Hazrat-i Kubra, and Sakina bint al-Husayn. The *kahani* is thus to be read in the name of these ten women—Mary, the four named by the Prophet and the Qur'an, and the five women involved in the tragedy of Karbala.[13]

The story which the woman is to hear concerns the immediate family of the Prophet. It emphasizes the ascetic lifestyle of the Prophet's family and their hospitality and generosity. The story relates that one day 'Ali invited the Prophet to his house for dinner, although his family had very little food. Even though they had only four *rōṭi* (pieces of bread) they gave one to their servant before dividing the rest among the *panjatan pak*. On the succeeding nights Fatimah, Hasan, and Husayn each in turn asked the Prophet to dine. After the last of these nights their servant Fizza met the Prophet at the door and respectfully asked him to dine as her guest as well. The next day the Prophet arrived, and 'Ali was distressed as he had not been told that Fizza had invited him and thus had not been able to make arrangements for the dinner. Fizza said that she was not worried as she trusted in God. She went to the corner and prostrated herself, asking God to help her feed his beloved—the Prophet. Miraculously, a tray of food from paradise appeared. She immediately offered prostrations of thanks and brought the tray to the Prophet. The holy family ate, and the Prophet asked where the food had come from—although he in fact already knew the origin of the food by means of a dream. She replied, "In our house God does not refuse even the requests of a servant."[14]

The veiled woman told her to read this story for ten days at a prayer carpet, having performed ablutions (*wuzū*) and having made a *niyyat* (proper intention). When her husband returned, she was to make special sweet cakes (*laḍū*) and write upon them the words "*das ladu*" (ten *ladu*) and offer them in the names of the ten women. The poor woman asked the veiled woman who she was and who the ten women were. The woman revealed herself as Fatimah and said that the other nine were the ones mentioned above. Fatimah then guaranteed that whoever keeps their memory will have their desires fulfilled. She then reassured her that her wishes would be fulfilled in ten days. Having awoken from her dream she went back to her own neighborhood and gathered people to hear this story, as it was Thursday night. On the tenth day her husband did return.[15]

It is interesting to note an element of class consciousness being articulated here. The woman returned to her poor section of town and read the story to the people there, implying that those who suffer are in some sense close to God. In fact, the entire story is an explanation of suffering. The great and famous women of Islam had all suffered, and thus one's suffering is not necessarily to be seen as a stigma. Rather, the poor and oppressed can be seen as following in the footsteps of the *ahl al-bayt* who through their asceticism showed a solidarity with the poor.

When the husband returned, he brought with him a good deal of wealth. The woman immediately went back home and made the *ladu*, as instructed by Fatimah in the dream. She attempted to share the *ladu* with her wicked sister-in-law, but, in contrast to the poor people of her own neighborhood, she refused to have anything to do with it and unceremoniously threw her out of the house.[16]

When the wicked sister-in-law (referred to as haughty [*maghrūr*], a particularly nonvirtuous epithet) woke up the next morning she found that her children were all dead and that all of her possessions had vanished. The husband and the wife began to lose their minds because of this catastrophe. And after a while they discovered that they were out of food and were hungry and decided to go to the house of the husband's sister. They were forced to travel on foot and their feet became blistered. On the way they tried to eat things which were growing along the roadside but as soon as the food reached their mouths it turned into inedible garbage. When they arrived at the sister's house the people of her household had already eaten, but the sister gave orders that if any food remained it was to be given to them. As they had been hungry for several days they were happy to see the food, even though it was only leftover rice. But once again the food became inedible when they tried to consume it. They now were certain that they would starve to death. The husband and the wife then went to see a king (*badshāh*) who was a friend of the husband to seek a remedy for their problem. The king offered them his hospitality and brought them food, but it became rotten and full of worms as soon as they touched it. They both became worried that the king would become distressed by the fact that the food had become rotten and would accuse them of sorcery, so they buried the food and had the servant who had brought it carry away the the tray. The wife went outside into the courtyard and sat down. At this same time she saw the queen and the princess bathing. They removed their necklaces and hung them on a peg. The peg opened up and swallowed the necklaces. The princess and the queen both saw this, as did the woman, who ran to her husband quite upset. Frightened that they would be blamed, they secretly left to avoid imprisonment or execution. They rested at a riverbank and the husband asked rhetorically what fault they had committed to deserve such blame. The wife admitted that it surely must be her fault. She admitted that she had refused the *tabarruk* (blessed food) of her sister-in-law and that she had told her that she would not eat such "brick and stone" food. She admitted that their difficulties appeared after this sin. The husband commanded his wife to beg forgiveness for her sin. Upon hearing this, she bathed herself in the river and prayed for help from Fatimah. As they had nothing else, the husband fashioned cakes from the sand. By the miraculous intervention of Zainab and Umm Kulthum, the sandcakes were transformed into sweetmeats. They each recited *darūd*, ate five of the cakes, and offered thanks to God. They returned home to find everything back to normal and their children alive. And they were all very happy. In the last paragraph the reader of the story is exhorted that just as the holy women had forgiven the sins of this woman they shall also forgive the sins of all women and fulfill their hearts' desires.[17]

This story clearly resonates with the root paradigms of the high culture of the Shi'i tradition. It clearly delineates the results of unthankfulness to God and disrespect for the *ahl al-bayt* while confirming the saving power of holy family and its willingness to forgive. It also emphasizes the populist elements of Shi-'ism, condemning the wealthy who abuse the powerless. Interestingly, the rich and the poor are seen quite literally as brothers. The proper attitude toward servants is shown by the *ahl al-bayt* who give the largest portion to their servant and only dine themselves afterward—unlike the husband of the wealthy sister-in-law who feeds his servant out of what remains. The haughty and wealthy are made to feel hunger and derision so they may understand the foolhardy nature of their arrogance. Material well-being is shown to be fragile and in need of support from faith, which alone is constant.

Finally, this story reconfirms the importance of women in the history of Shi'i piety. Women come away from this story realizing that, far from being outsiders living on the fringes of Islam, women have been at the center of the faith. Their importance is verified by the Qur'an, by the Prophet, and by the historical role of women at the battle of Karbala. The story teaches that women are to follow in the footsteps of those other women who have suffered for their beliefs. It clearly places the women who read this story into the fabric of a continuing chain of feminine piety going back to the origins of Islam.

The Story of ʿAli Mushkil Kusha

Until now we have focused upon miracle tales dealing primarily with the concerns of women. In these stories the spiritual aid has come from Fatimah—and there are other miracle stories which involve, for example, Zainab. But the ultimate human helper is, of course, ʿAli. The phrase "*Ya ʿAli madad*" is often repeated by Sunni and Shiʿa alike. As stated in chapter one, ʿAli is called "Mushkil Kusha" or the "remover of difficulties," in reference to his exploits at the battle of Khaybar. The story of ʿAli Mushkil Kusha is one of the most prominent of the *kahanis*. It is commonly read on Thursday nights usually (again) by women, although men may take part. Often women will use this story to make a *mannat* for a boon for their husbands—such as that they shall find employment. The story appears in different formats. Idries Shah has included a version of this story in his collection, *Caravan of Dreams*,[18] with the implication that it is a Sufi teaching tale. He does not, interestingly enough, identify Mushkil Kusha as ʿAli, even though the great majority of his readers outside of the Muslim world have no idea that it is the first Imam who is referred to in the title of the story. Although in the introduction to his version of the story he makes reference to the use of the story in "an event," he does not make clear the kind of things for which the story is used or the commonplace, nonexotic quality that it has in the South Asian context, where almost everyone, not just Sufi shaikhs, know of the existence of this tale. But, interestingly, he records that the tale is an example of a specific kind of story which contains elements from the realm of "higher events" and can communicate to the mind the nature of these higher events.[19] Whatever he means by this, it is clear that the story is more than a mere fairy tale; in reality it is a powerful vehicle for experiencing the higher verities of the system of Shiʿism in a way which might be considered subliminal or even esoteric.

The story is as follows:[20]

In an Iranian city there lived a woodcutter who was very poor. He sold wood to keep himself and his small children alive. One day he said to his daughter, "Go to the neighbor's house and get a light for my cigarette." When she went to light the cigarette, she saw that the neighbor's wife was roasting a liver. The girl very much desired to eat some of the liver, but the woman did not pay any attention. The girl, having come outside of the door, put out the cigarette and again went inside to light it. She did this thinking that perhaps this time she would give her some of the liver to eat, but again she did not give her any. Having become disappointed she returned home, so late, however, that half of the cigarette had burned away. When the father took the cigarette he said, "Daughter, did you smoke half of this cigarette yourself?"

She replied, "No, Father dear, the neighbor was roasting a liver, and I wanted some very much. Therefore, I repeatedly put out the cigarette and went back to relight it so that perhaps the wife would give me some of the liver to eat. But she did not give me any. Oh Father, tomorrow it is necessary that you should bring me some liver."

The father replied, "Daughter, we have no money in the house, even to buy a single match. Where can I get a liver?"

The girl continued, "No, dear Father, tomorrow you will certainly bring liver."

The father said, "O.K. Daughter, for two days you will not eat. I will gather together two days' worth of wood and sell it and thus bring you liver."

The daughter agreed. The woodcutter went into the forest, gathered together wood and set it aside. The next day when he went into the forest he saw that the wood which he had gathered had burned and become ashes. Having seen this he became very sad and cried so intensely that he became unconscious. While in this unconscious state he saw a veiled man standing there. [Here the reader is enjoined to offer *salavats* (blessings) to the Prophet and his family.] Lifting up several stones from the earth he said, "Take these. When you accept these, then say *Fātiḥah*[21] in the name of Mushkil Kusha."

When the woodcutter regained consciousness he saw that those very stones were in his hands. He placed them in his pocket and returned home. Having returned home he concealed himself behind the door. When his daughter saw that her father's return was delayed, she went outside and saw her father concealed behind the door. She said, "Dear Father, come inside."

The father said, "Daughter, I am ashamed to come to you. I went out, having made a promise that I would bring you some liver. But all of the wood burned and became ashes."

The daughter said, "Father, you should come inside. God will provide us with much."

When it became evening, the woodcutter reached into his pocket, took out the stones, and gave them to his daughter so that she could give them to his children to play with. Having taken the stones, his daughter went over to one room and spread them out. In the early morning, when the wife of the woodcutter rose for prayers, she saw that the room was exuding light upon light. Frightened, she went out and told the woodcutter, "Our entire room is on fire in all directions."

The woodcutter awoke and saw that there were shimmering jewels in the room. [Once again the readers are asked to offer *salavats*.] He threw a cloth over them. In the morning he took one of the rubies and went to a jeweler. He said, "Buy this ruby and give me the price of it."

The jeweler, upon seeing this excellent ruby, became bewildered. He told the woodcutter, "Bring sacks from your house. However much you can lift having filled them, you may take away. This is the value of the ruby." So he took away as many sacks as he could carry. And he purchased the land where Mushkil Kusha had given him the stones [*salavat*]. He had a splendid palace built on that land where he began to spend a life of extreme ease and indulgence. One day the woodcutter said to his wife, "Now, it is obligatory that I go on the *Hajj* [pilgrimage to Mecca]. While I am gone on the *Hajj*, you must offer *Fatihah* for 'Ali Mushkil Kusha every month."

After several days the wife of the woodcutter said to her daughter, "Go and bring seven kinds of sweets on which we will read *Fatihah* for Mushkil Kusha."

The daughter said, "Mama, now that we have become very noble, we don't need to read *Fatihah* over different kinds of sweets."

The mother remained silent. After a few days, the mother and daughter went to a bath house to bathe. While they were there, there was suddenly a clamor that emptied the bath house, because the king's wife and daughter were on their way to the bath house. Eventually everyone left except the wife and the daughter of the woodcutter. They said, "We are more noble than the queen. We won't leave."

Just then, the emperor's wife and the princess arrived in the bath house. They had already heard of the existence of a very noble and wealthy woodcutter. When the daughter of the woodcutter came out of the bath house, the princess saw a very valuable necklace of pearls around her neck. The princess asked, "Where did you get that necklace?"

The daughter of the woodcutter said, "Come, we shall be companions. You take this necklace, and I will go to my house and put on another one."

The princess replied, "We have made you our companions as well, therefore you should come to our house."

One day the daughter of the woodcutter went to meet the princess. The princess was bathing. When the princess came out from the bath she said to the servant, "Bring my necklace from its peg."

The servant looked on the peg for the necklace but it was gone. The servant said, "There has never been a theft here until today. This is the work of your friend."

Eventually, news of this reached the king. He interrogated the woodcutter's wife and daughter and they answered, "When we were poor we did not steal. Why should we steal now that we are rich?"

But the king was not satisfied. He issued a command, that both the mother and the daughter should be thrown into prison and that a wall should be erected in front of their house. Meanwhile, when the woodcutter was on his way to perform the *Hajj*, some bandits met him on the road and stole everything from him. So, he turned back without having performed the *Hajj*.

When he returned, he saw a wall standing in front of his house. He asked, "Where are the people of my house and why is there a wall in front of my palace?"

Some people told him the entire story. The woodcutter came to the king and said, "If they weren't thieves when we were poor, why would they become so now?"

The king refused to accept this. The woodcutter said, "If they are not to be freed from prison, then I should also be imprisoned, because it is not honorable that my wife and daughter should be imprisoned while I remain sitting at home."

Accordingly, the woodcutter was also imprisoned. When it became night, the woodcutter, having spoken to his wife and daughter, asked, "After I left, did you continue to offer *Fatihah* for Mushkil Kusha?"

They said, "No."

The woodcutter said, "Enough. This is the punishment for your transgression."

Therefore, they spent the whole night offering repentance and crying. While they slept they saw in their dreams a veiled man approaching. [At this point the reader again is asked to offer blessings upon the Prophet and his family.] And he said, "You have forgotten to make your offering, therefore, divine reproach has descended upon you."

The woodcutter said, "I have no money to offer *nazr* [religious offering]."

He replied, "Lift up your mattress. Take out 5 paise from under it. Having acquired the sweets with this money, offer the *nazr* and your difficulties will disappear."

In the morning when the woodcutter woke up, he lifted up his mattress and took out the five coins. While he was standing near the door of the prison, a young man approached on horseback. He said to him, "Boy, bring five paise' worth of sweets."

He replied, "Old man, you have become a prisoner, and now you want to eat sweets. Today is my wedding, so I am going to the bazaar to purchase *mehndhī* [henna for painting decorations upon the hands of the wedding party] and the other necessary things. Therefore, I cannot do work for you."

The boy, having said this, had proceeded only a few steps when he fell from his horse and died. When the boy's father learned that the young boy had died, he passed by the door to the prison crying.

The woodcutter asked him, "Bring me five paise' worth of sweets." The man said, "Even though my son has today died on the day of his wedding I shall do this task for this prisoner."

He brought the sweets to the woodcutter, who offered them in the name of Mushkil Kusha. He asked the man, "Why are you so sad?"

He said, "Today my son was to be married but he has died." The woodcutter gave some sweets to him and told him, "Having dissolved this in water, place some of it in your son's mouth."

Accordingly, the man did just this. As soon as the drop of water entered the body of the boy, he rose up reciting the *shahadah*. [Again the reader is asked to offer blessings.]

At the same time, when the king had sat down to eat, he saw a beautiful bird coming with the missing necklace in its beak. The bird returned it to its peg.

The king, having seen this, was astonished and said, "In this there is surely some hidden mystery."

He went to speak to the woodcutter. The woodcutter explained the entire circumstances to the king. The king became very happy. He placed his crown at the feet of the woodcutter and said, "Now my father and I are your sons. As long as we live we shall do your service." [*Salavat.*]

He prayed to God that in the same manner in which he had eased the difficulties of the woodcutter, he should dissolve all of the difficulties of faithful men and women by the right of the Imams. [At this point there are blessings offered in Arabic.]

This is not the only version of this story. An older version of the tale also concerns a poor woodcutter.[22] Every day he would go into the jungle and gather wood which he would then sell in the bazaar for money for food and return home in the early evening. One day he was unable to gather a bundle of wood and decided that if he returned home with no money for food it would terribly upset his children who would cry from hunger, and so he decided to spend the night in the forest and then in the morning gather enough wood to buy food. Thus, he spent the night in the jungle. In the middle of the night a rider approached him from the direction of Mecca and asked him who he was. He replied that he was a poor woodcutter who was always having to go into the woods to gather wood for money for food, but that today it was his misfortune not to have gathered enough wood so that he was instead spending the night in the jungle. After that he would return to them in the morning and feed his hungry and thirsty family. The mysterious rider gave five paise to the man and told him to purchase certain kinds of sweets and to offer them in a *Fatihah* in the name of Mushkil Kusha. He told him that God would remove his poverty by means of this *Fatihah*. The man took the coins and miraculously found himself transported back to his hut. When the morning came he woke up his wife and they purchased the sweets and read the *Fatihah* and ate until they were full and were very happy. The next day, in accordance with his usual practice, he took up his tools and went out into the forest. He came across the dried branch of a *pīlū* tree. Taking the name of ‘Ali, he split the bush asunder onto the ground and uncovered a hidden treasure. He took a few rubies from the treasure and, offering thanks to God, went first to the bazaar and bought food and then gathered the rest of the treasure and eventually purchased the entire forest, in which he erected a fine palace. He built *musafar khānahs* and *nigārkhānahs* (buildings in which travelers can rest) in various places and staffed them with servants doing all kinds of work. He became very wealthy and famous. One day a king went on a hunting expedition in those very woods. He became thirsty and sent out an order that a servant should be sent for water. A servant set out and went in all four directions and began to search for water. In the distance the servant saw a walled city. Moving quickly he arrived and, having seen the entrance to the walled city, he went inside. There he saw an elaborate well and at it an attendant distributing water and servants engaged in different kinds of labor. The attendant gave the servant some water who then took a cup of it to the king. The king wanted to know who had built this well, and the servant told him that there was a woodcutter who had colonized the city and that he had built facilities for travelers in different places. He said that this woodcutter had given gifts and money to the needy, and that his city was nearby and that this was where he had brought the water from. The king was amazed and desired to see this city and this woodcutter so he gave an order that the woodcutter, along with his wife, should come to him. His commander and first minister advised him that it was not proper to invite such a person but perhaps things would change and he would be summoned. They returned home, and the king told the story of these happenings to his wife, who insisted that they be invited. So they were. The woodcutter and his wife appeared at the court of the king and offered rubies as gifts. The woodcutter went outside but his wife remained with the wife of the king.

Here the story mirrors the plot line of the other version. A necklace is lost, and the two are thrown into prison, where in a dream the same masked rider appears to them and tells them that they have neglected to offer *Fatihah* for ‘Ali and that this is the reason for their current difficulties. They have no money, so the masked rider tells them where they can find the money under their mattress. The couple attempts to find someone who would help them to acquire the sweets necessary for the *Fatihah*. They first encountered a woman who refused because she was too busy preparing the wedding of her son. A second woman approached in the company of her son's funeral procession. As the story puts it, upon hearing the name of 'Ali she immediately left her necessary work to help the couple. Following this, she returned home to find her son alive and the woman who had refused to help found her child dead. This woman then went to the other woman to ask how her son had come back to life. She informed her how she had brought the necessary items to read *Fatihah* for 'Ali and had then found her son alive. Hearing this, the other woman, with a contrite heart made a *niyyat* (intention) that if her son was restored to life she would also read *Fatihah* for 'Ali. At that very moment her son was restored to life. Miraculously, the queen's jewels were returned, and when the king sent for the prisoners they were found to be unfettered. They told the entire tale to the king, who clothed them in robes and led them in honor out of the city. The king instituted the practice of reading *Fatihah* for 'Ali every Thursday throughout the kingdom. From then onward the king was always victorious in battle over his enemies, conquered many lands, and acquired great wealth. The story concludes by granting the assurance that whoever reads *Fatihah* every Thursday will be greatly blessed and that it is not possible in such a short space to list all of the possible blessings attained from this action.

ANALYSIS

This story contains many of the same elements found in the previous tales but adds others as well. It is important to note that in the entire corpus of miracle *kahanis* the same motifs occur. Bridegrooms die and are resurrected by faith in the *ahl al-bayt*. The wealthy and proud are reduced to poverty. Other motifs are also common in these stories. One is that of the hidden treasure. The woodcutter finds a hidden treasure whose wealth is immeasurable. This is a possible reference to the famous *hadith qudsī*, in which God reveals: "I was a hidden treasure and desired to be known; therefore I created the creation that I might be known."[23] Thus, on one level the hidden treasure may refer to the knowledge of God. This treasure is a source of light—a substance whose metaphoric significance in Shi'i piety has already been discussed.

In the second version of the story the woodcutter uses his wealth to establish places for travelers to rest and to distribute water. Of course, the distribution of water is a common Shi'i image related to the thirst of the martyrs of Karbala, but it is also a common Sufi image whose origins predate Islam and is a metaphor for the distribution of spiritual blessings and knowledge.[24]

Cities populated with servants of one who has found the treasure of God may refer both to the disciples of the shaikh in Sufism or to those doing the work of the Imams—perhaps a reference to the *da'wa* of the Isma'ilis.[25] This imagery is coupled in the second version with the image of a man establishing places for travelers which resonates with the standard Islamic image of the spiritual disciple as a *salik* or traveler.

The motifs of ungratefulness and haughtiness are important in this story. The story emphasizes the dependency of human beings and the fragility of our good fortune. In the midst of all this, only devotion to the *ahl al-bayt* can give people a degree of security. To believe that people are inherently deserving of their positions in the world is to become egotistical and to court disaster, as was the case with the wife and daughter of the woodcutter.

The remembrance of 'Ali both through grief and in the midst of grief is emphasized at several points in the story. The clearest example is the dichotomy between the woman who is too busy with the wedding of her son to concern herself with *Fatihah* for 'Ali and the woman who leaves what is her "necessary" work at the very mention of the name of Mushkil Kusha. This is the crucial element of the story; that personal allegiance to the Imams not only conveys spiritual benefit but it also carries with it a material benefit. Likewise, the neglecting of that allegiance results in terrible troubles. All of the various motifs reminiscent of Karbala and other aspects of imamology point toward this understanding.

The *Niyāz* of Ja'far as-Sadiq

The last of these miracle narratives which we shall examine is the one associated with the *kundah niyaz* of Imam Ja'far as-Sadiq which takes place on the twenty-second day of Rajab every year. The story itself is interesting, not only because it reamplifies themes found in the other miracle tales but also because it affirms and gives validity to a ritual which for many persons has lost its historical significance—the aforementioned *kundah niyaz*.

On this day Shi'i families prepare a kind of sweet dish called *kīr* in clay pots called *kundah* and invite people over to share it as a *niyaz* (food offered in the name of a holy person). The reasons behind this are not commonly known and are to some extent controversial. Some in the community are under the impression that the ritual celebrates the death of Uthman—the third caliph of Islam. (One young Sunni woman told me that she stopped reading this *kahani* because of this rumor.) Others told me that it was simply established as such by Imam Ja'far as-Sadiq for no particular reason. I later discovered that the twenty-second day of Rajab is the date of the death of Mu'awiyah b. Abu Sufyan, and although some felt that the establishment of the *niyaz* on this day is mere coincidence, it appears likely that there is an historical connection.[26]

One young Shi'i *zakir* and intellectual told me that this *niyaz* comes under the category of *tabarra-i a'māl* or *tabarra* of works, as opposed to *tabarra-i zubān* or verbal *tabarra*, such as the ritual cursing of the first three caliphs. This aspect of the *niyaz* is not spoken of openly in front of Sunnis, and many Shi'a are unaware of the hidden significance of the *niyaz*. It is not known by all Shi'i Muslims but is passed on to some members of the community by means of oral tradition.

The miracle story connected with the *kahani* is not always read as part of the *niyaz*, but it helps to emphasize the importance of the *niyaz* as an act of Shi'i piety. The story contains similar characters and incidents to those presented in the previous *kahanis*. Once again, the story concerns a poor woodcutter who every day went into the forest to gather enough wood to eke out an existence for himself and his family. As in the *Das Bibiyan ki Kahani*, the husband told his wife that he would go to another place to look for work. The story continues:[27]

When the husband arrived in a new city, his condition did not improve very much. For twelve years his situation remained the same. His poverty and worry did not lift and he was unable to send support to his wife and children. Finally, because of her poverty, the wife took a job as a sweeper in the palace of the wazir and was able to feed her children. One night she dreamed that she saw herself sweeping in the palace of the wazir when Imam Ja'far as-Sadiq entered the courtyard with some of his companions. He turned his attention to his companions and said, "Do you know what the date is and which month it is?" With great courtesy the companions said, "Today is the twenty-second day of Rajab." Then the Imam said, "If anyone who is surrounded by any difficulty or is afflicted by any calamity, with a contrite heart makes one and one-quarter *ser* of *pūrīs* (if possible, sweet *puris*)[28] in two clay pots and gives them in my *niyaz* on the twenty-second day of Rajab, by the time of the morning prayer Allah will hear their request and grant it." At that moment she opened her eyes and made an intention (*niyyat*) to offer the *niyaz* and then, according to her intention, she did just that.

At the time of the morning prayer, at the same moment when the wife of the woodcutter was distributing the *niyaz*, her husband had climbed into a tree and was cutting wood; suddenly his axe slipped from his hand and fell to the ground. He climbed down from the tree and just as he went to pick up his axe he saw something shining buried in the ground. He dug it up and found a big treasure. He took some of the wealth and covered the rest of it up. Little by little in a short time he had removed the greater portion of the treasure. He prepared for his journey home and set out with great pomp and pride.

When he arrived home he built his children a splendid house. He prepared them the things that they would need for a comfortable life, and they passed their time in ease. One day the woman told her husband the story about the *nazr* of the Imam. When he learned that she had made her *mannat* on the same day on which he had found his hidden treasure he was very moved and became very faithful and agreed to always remember that day.

One day the wife of the wazir climbed out on her balcony and saw in the distance a splendid palace where there were also servants. She pointed out the house to a servant and asked whose it was. She replied that it was the house of the woman who had once been a sweeper in the palace of the king. The wazir's wife sent a message asking the woodcutter's wife how she had risen from poverty, and the woodcutter's wife responded by telling the whole story. The wife of the wazir could not accept this. She decided that it was a lie. "Where did her husband steal the treasure which has made him wealthy?" she wondered. "She has concealed this from me." At the same time that this idea had come into the wretched heart of the *begum*, a terrible misfortune befell her husband, a famous first wazir.

The assistant wazir of the king of the time was his enemy. He took this opportunity to slander him to the king. He charged that the first minister was a traitor and had embezzled a great deal from the treasury. The king called for an accounting and, when it was not correct, he stripped the wazir and his wife of all of their property and cast them out of the palace. While on the road, they bought a melon and bound it up in a towel so they could sit down later and eat it.

On the morning of the very day on which the wazir was exiled, the prince had gone out hunting. By evening he still had not yet returned. The king became very upset. The same wazir who had been the reason for the explusion of the first wazir said to the king that the wazir, perhaps for reasons of enmity, had harmed the prince and this was why he had not yet arrived. Hearing this, the king sent out an order that the wazir should be arrested. The horsemen of the king went out in all directions and brought the wazir into the presence of the king.

Up until this time they had not eaten the melon and it was still rolled up in the towel. The king asked what was in the towel and they answered that it was a melon. But when they opened up the bundle they found inside it the head of the prince. The king became terribly angry upon seeing the head of his dead son and gave the order that they should spend the entire night in prison, and then in the morning they should be executed.

They were both locked in the prison. The wazir said to his wife, "I don't understand how this sudden calamity befell us. What kind of sin merits this kind of punishment?" After much thought the wife said, "The woodcutter's wife said that it was because of Imam Ja'far as-Sadiq's *nazr* that she obtained her treasure, and I absolutely refused to accept it and thought it a lie." The wazir realized that this was the source of their difficulty and commanded that they beg the Imam for forgiveness and show repentance.

Thus, they spent the entire evening in prayers for forgiveness. They made *niyyat* for the *nazr* of the Imam. God accepted their repentance. In the early morning the prince returned home and presented himself to the king. The king clasped his son to his chest. He demanded to know why he was so late in returning. The prince replied that the hunt continued until late, and thus they had stayed the night in a garden.

Following this, the king sent for the two persons in prison and they looked into the bundle and saw a melon. The king was absolutely amazed. The wazir told the king about the woodcutter, and the woodcutter was sent for. They told the entire story from beginning to end, and as the king heard it faith entered into his heart. The first wazir once more assumed his duties, and the traitorous wazir was removed and cast out of the city.

In an older version of the story the woodcutter and his wife live in Medina, and it is in the wazir's house that the wife takes refuge. The most important difference in these two versions is that she learns of the *kundah niyaz* when the Imam himself (in real time rather than in the unconscious realm) comes into the house of the wazir and she overhears him.[29]

ANALYSIS

As with the other stories, this one is read as the central focus of a ritual. This ritual is linked to a particular day of the calendar and can have a large number of participants. The requirements of the *niyaz* are given in one of the collections of *kahanis*. These requirements of the *niyaz* of Imam Ja'far as-Sadiq are as follows:

On the twenty-second day of this blessed month the *niyaz* of Imam Ja-'far as-Sadiq is done in almost every home. Because of ignorance people do not know the prescribed time and *adab* of the *niyaz*, which they have never heard. Therefore in order to acquaint you people with it we will tell you the method of the *niyaz*.

On the twenty-second of Rajab, awake at 3:00 A.M. (which is the morning of 22 Rajab). Having cleaned and straightened the house, spread out a clean white cloth, *dari*, or rug which you have acquired. You should light candles or incense in your house and make yourself ritually clean and perfume yourself. Having taken water in a clean container, add to this water 1 1/4 *ser* of flour and this amount of sugar and knead it. Then fry them in a quarter of a *pao* [a quarter of a *ser*] of *ghee*, having made them into 14 *puris* or fried cakes. Then divide them into clay pots which you have first washed out with the clean water. Place seven in each pot and by lighting more incense or candles make more light and fragrance. After the morning prayer [*namaz*], read the miracle story which is in this book or hear it. After that give the *niyaz* of Imam Ja'far as-Sadiq and ask for your wish. *Insha Allah*, God will fulfill it. After this feed all of the faithful (who are present).

All of the things which are used in the *niyaz* should be kept facing the direction of the *qiblah* [facing toward Mecca]. And you should face the *qiblah* also. At first you should read *darūd* three times. Then, raising your hand you should say this: [Here there is inserted a long formulaic passage which reads] "In order to further promote the victorious sacred and pure spirit of the Chief of the Universe, and the best among the creatures of God, the Mercy of the Universe, the praiseworthy among human beings Hazrat Ahmad [the noble] Muhammad [the chosen one], Peace be upon him and on his progeny." This is the holy *nazr* of Imam Ja'far as-Sadiq. On presenting this sincere offering, three times at the beginning and the end read the *darud*, then three times *surah al-hamd* and three times *surah al-akhlās* and then make your *du'a*.[30]

I am told by some persons that it is traditional to place a ring in one of the cakes and that it is good fortune to find it. Although the written versions of the story that I was able to find did not make mention of it, *kir* (rice pudding) is usually distributed as the central part of the *niyaz*. The *puris* are merely used to eat the *kir*. Often the *niyaz* is given without the reading of the story, as was the case with a *kundah niyaz* which I attended.

The story itself is much like the other stories we have examined. The motifs of hidden treasure and poverty alleviated by the miraculous intercession of the *ahl al-bayt* have already been discussed. It is interesting here that the *madadgār* (helper) is the sixth Imam rather than 'Ali or Fatimah and that the woman simply overhears from him the necessary actions for her to perform, and yet they are still efficacious. In this story the efficacy of the Imams is not denied verbally or through actions but simply through thought and this thought leads to catastrophe. In a more metaphysical dimension the story argues that without faith in the Imams things appear other than they are. A melon appears to be the head of the prince; an honest wazir appears dishonest. Thus, one message in this story is that knowledge of the reality of things requires faith in the *ahl al-bayt*.

Conclusion

While examining these stories, it is important to keep in mind their ritual context. It is the direct and existential characteristic of the performance of ritual, and the liminal environment that it creates, which allows for the encounter with the root paradigms of Shi'ism. They are not simply didactic tales but they carry coded within them much of the lore and wisdom of the tradition. They are not simply read silently; they are read aloud to someone in an area that is set aside and made pure. They culminate in the distribution of blessed food (*tabarruk*). Their purpose is to evoke the presence of the *ahl al-bayt*. In that sense these narratives have a great deal in common with the mourning performances of Muharram, which also evoke the presence of spiritual realities while simultaneously educating their performers and observers in the verities of Shi'i Islam. But, unlike those rituals, to be discussed in chapter three, these are more personal and less intense. Possibly that is because the miracle stories merely echo and resonate with the events of the Karbala narrative, which are in some sense the definitive events of Shi'i Islam and constitute its root paradigms, while the Muharram performances are immediate evocations of those events.

CHAPTER THREE

Public Performances:
The Ritual Encounter with Karbala

In chapter one I defined Shiʻi Islam as the Islam of personal allegiance and stressed the importance of "the man"—the Prophet and the Imams—vis-à-vis "the book"—the Qurʼan. This personal allegiance is articulated and reaffirmed in ritual actions throughout the Islamic calendar. For the Shiʻa, history is crucial because those to whom allegiance is due acted out the drama which is the guide to proper conduct in the crucible of history. The importance of history in Shiʻi piety can be seen by looking at the Shiʻi ritual calendar.[1] Important Sunni festivals and public feast or fast days are few. There are the two ʻĪds, Ramadan, the Hajj, and perhaps ʻĪd Milād-i Nabī (the birthday of the Prophet). But for the Shiʻa the calendar is full of important days of commemoration. These include not only the death and birth anniversaries of the Prophet, the Imams, and other notable figures, in particular, Fatimah and ʻAbbas, but also important events in the life of the Prophet. Most notably these include the meeting with the Christians at Mubahila and the naming of ʻAli as mawla at Ghadir Khumm. Beyond this, the Shiʻa are aware of the history of the Prophet and his family as crucial. The most crucial of all these events, however, is the martyrdom of Imam Husayn at Karbala.

These events are not simply historical but are metahistorical. They are archetypal and in some sense stand outside of real time and are parallel to it. Commemoration of these events allows Shiʻi Muslims the opportunity to reaffirm their allegiance through emotional actions of devotion. The devotion of Shiʻi Muslims to the family of the Prophet takes its most striking and visible form in the public performances associated with the month of Muharram commemorating the martyrdom of Imam

71

Husayn. The South Asian *'ālim* and *zakir*, 'Ali Naqi Naqvi, has said of the opening of this month of mourning:

The mournful crescent of the month of *Muharram* has already appeared on the horizon. The carpet of mourning for the oppressed sufferer of Karbala has been spread in every home. Century-old wounds which have established themselves in the hearts of the pure and faithful Muslims have reopened. Each people according to its own religious beliefs is expressing this grief. In Karbala, he who became an innocent martyr was oppressed to such an extent that his suffering has drawn the sympathy of the whole world. Even God has busied himself in the expression of this mourning, and he has made the skirt of the horizon eternally bloody with redness and continues to bear witness to this blood of injustice.[2]

It is not surprising that an event to which such a cosmic dimension of tragedy has been associated should find itself articulated in the form of public rituals. The death of Husayn is no mere martyrdom but is a turning point in human history. One's allegiance to Husayn is seen as the primary proof of one's obedience to God. For the next ten days and beyond the streets of Shi'i neighborhoods change in atmosphere. Cassette recorders blare out *marthiyahs* (poems of mourning) for the martyred Husayn. People begin to dress in black. Nightly, the *imambargahs* fill with people who have come to hear the recitations of the story of these martyrs who, in the context of Shi'i thought and practice, have given their lives for all of Islam and all of humanity. Because of its size and its religious and cultural diversity, the city of Karachi is the scene of some of the most intense and provocative mourning ceremonies in all of the Shi'i world. These performances are the subject of this chapter.

Azadari as a Complex of Ritual Performances

The complex of activities that are performed during the month of Muharram comes under the general heading of *'azadari*. *'Azā* in Arabic comes from the same root as a word meaning to console or to take patience. It means a "ceremony of mourning." The related word *ta'zi'at* is used to mean an expression of grief, sorrow, or condolence. Idiomatically, the word *'azadari*, which combines *'aza* with the Persian suffix *dari*, is used to express specifically the "sorrowful and mournful feelings that arise with the memory of Hazrat Imam Husain." The complex of activities involved in *'azadari* include "mourning congregations, lamentations with the beating of the breast, and all sorts of actions that seek to express the emotions of grief and anguish."[3]

The four primary forms of ritual activity associated with *'azadari* are *majlis, julus, ziyarat,* and *matam. Majlis* refers to lamentation assemblies where the stories of the martyrs of Karbala are recited for the purposes of remembrance and the evocation of grief. The religious specialists who recite *majalis* are called *zakirs.* The task of the *zakir* is to evoke the atmosphere of Karbala in the context of an expository sermon designed for the religious edification of the community. *Julus* refers to processions of mourning in which sacred objects related to the family of the Prophet are carried through the streets and neighborhoods.

Ziyarat (literally, "visitation") is the term generally used to refer to pilgrimage. In the context of Muharram performances *ziyarat* has three meanings. First it refers to the visitation of sacred objects that are located in the *Husayniyya* of *imambargahs.* Second it refers to special formulaic Arabic salutations made at the ends of other rituals, such as *majlis,* which are symbolic of actual visitations to the graves of the *ahl al-bayt.* The *ziyarat* is done by first facing the *qiblah* and reciting *salāms* and then turning toward Mashad in Iran and back toward the *qiblah.* Three Imams are greeted in the *ziyarat.* First there is Imam Husayn, who is greeted while facing the *qiblah,* because it is believed that one should say this *ziyarat* facing Mecca. Second is Imam 'Ali Rida who is buried in Mashad, Iran. Third, one addresses Imam al-Mahdi while facing the *qiblah* because his residence is believed to be in Mecca. Finally, *ziyarat* also refers to a specific ritual performed on the twelfth day of Muharram. This is analogous to the standard ritual performed by Muslims of reading the entire Qur'an on the third day after the death of the deceased and distributing food in the dead person's name. This is done every year since it was not done at the time of Husayn's martyrdom.

Matam (literally, "funeral ceremony") is the physical act of mourning the death of the Imam. It may be done simply by beating the chest with the hands (*hāth ka mātam*), but in more intense forms it may involve flagellation with knives or chains (*zanjīr ka mātam*) or walking on fire (*āg ka mātam*). These last types of *matam* will be discussed more fully in chapter five. For now, let us turn our attention to an examination of *majlis, julus,* and *ziyarat*— the primary public ritual performances associated with *'azadari.*

From the above it is clear that *'azadari* involves the performance of a complex of rituals. These acts of ritual mourning constitute a crucial element in the religious lives of the South Asian

Shi'a. In the ritual arena of *majlis* and *julus*, the participant not only confirms his own religious beliefs but publicly reveals them to those outside of his community. Mourning *julus* is no mere ceremonial procession and the *majlis* is no mere recitation of facts. Rather, each is an emotional encounter with a world of symbols.

In calling *'azadari* performances "rituals," I refer back to my definition of ritual in the introduction as *a performance involving an encounter with powerful symbols*. *'Azadari* rituals allow for reflection on the most powerful symbols of Shi'i piety—the *ahl al-bayt* and the martyrs of Karbala. In these rituals the characters of the sacred drama of Karbala are evoked and serve as metaphors for the root paradigms of Shi'i piety. As in any really good secular drama, the metaphors in sacred dramas are multivocal, able to stand for more than one thing at any one time.[4] This multivocality allows different individuals to have different interpretations and experiences of a ritual performance. The quality of the *zakir* and the personal history of the person listening to him may both have an impact on the way in which the *majlis* is experienced.

'Azadari allows for an emotional encounter with the characters of the sacred history of Islam—who for the Shi'a have a metaphysical as well as an historical significance. Such rituals as *majlis* offer an opportunity for the ritual recreation of Karbala which allows the Shi'a to experience and display a grief for the Prophet and his family. Through the public and communal expression of this grief the participants in *'azadari* rituals demonstrate their allegiance to the Prophet and his family and their solidarity with the Shi'i community and its history. As a minority community both in South Asia and within the larger Islamic *ummah*, this public affirmation of solidarity is a crucial element of *'azadari* rituals. The *'azadari* rituals speak simultaneously to the community itself and to its critics in ways which maintain the unique character of Shi'i Islam.

The Shi'a as a Minority Community

Any discussion of Shi'i mourning performances in South Asia must address the fact that the Shi'a exist as a minority in a complex religious environment. Because of the public nature of these performances, they impinge upon the religious lives and sensibilities not only of the Shi'i community but of the larger Sunni community as well. Despite the strong and visible Shi'i presence in Karachi, it should not be forgotten that the Shiʿa are a minority community (as they are throughout most of South Asia). Their beliefs and practices are controversial vis-à-vis the Sunni majority of the region. And yet in most things, Shiʿi and Sunni Muslims are culturally indistinguishable from each other. They wear the same clothing, practice the same art forms, and, except for differences in what outsiders might consider minutia, perform the same types of rituals.

There is, however, a fundamental conflict between these two schools of thought in Islam. This conflict revolves around each school's understanding of the role of the Prophet and his family, both in the history of Islam and in the metaphysical structure of the cosmos.

As argued in chapter one, the Shiʿa understand Islam to be not only an allegiance to a set of ideas or laws (whose primary source is the Qurʾan) but also *a personal allegiance to the bearer of the message—the Prophet Muhammad*. In Shiʿism this interpretation of Islam as a personal allegiance carries with it the belief in *nass* or designation. According to this doctrine, the Prophet designated his son-in-law and cousin ʿAli as his spiritual and political successor. (In fact, this designation is seen to be linked to an archetypal cosmogonic event in which Muhammad and ʿAli were both created from the same primordial light before the creation of the universe.)[5] In turn, ʿAli and his progeny designated a line of Imams coming to an end with the Imamate of the current Imam Mahdi. In the Shiʿi version of history each of these Imams—beginning with ʿAli—was rejected by the larger community. All of them (except for the last, who remains in protected seclusion as a repository of the messianic hopes of the community) were ultimately martyred. For the Shiʿa the sufferings of these persons are evidence for the very rejection of Islam by the majority of the Muslims. In this view of history not only did the majority of humanity reject those persons to whom the granting of allegiance was an essential element of membership in the Islamic community, but these same persons who called themselves Muslim went so far as to murder those who were closest to the Prophet. For the Shiʿa the expression of grief and sorrow over the sufferings of those who were beloved of the Prophet is a way of demonstrating solidarity with Islam as truly intended by God and his Prophet, and also of separating themselves from those who claimed to be Muslim and yet committed acts of violence against the Prophet's kin.

Thus, while Sunni and Shiʿa may be said to be at one level culturally indistinguishable from each other, there are important theological differences between the two schools. These differences are emotionally charged. For the Shiʻa, many of the close companions of the Prophet, who are understood by the Sunni community as important links with the founder of the Islam, are seen as disreputable usurpers who purposefully disobeyed the intentions of God and the Prophet. The Shiʻa are thus seen by the Sunni as disrespectful of the Prophet's companions and by implication of the Prophet himself. Furthermore, and possibly more importantly, many Sunnis feel that this emphasis on personal allegiance borders upon *shirk* or associating partners with God. Their devotion to ʻAli is understood by them as something akin to idolatry—in much the same way as certain Muslim reformers see the devotion of Sufi *murids* to their pirs as *shirk*. The result is sometimes a harsh antagonism. Unfounded rumors are rampant in the Sunni community. For example, some erroneously believe that the Shiʻa use a distorted Qurʼan or that no Shiʻa ever names his son Muhammad because they believe that ʻAli is greater than Muhammad.

These tense ideological differences normally remain invisible. But participation in certain ritual practices of mourning will immediately identify a person with one school or the other. While it is true that the Sunni and the Shiʻa differ on other points of ritual, these are primarily matters of jurisprudence which are only indirectly related to fundamental issues of theology and soteriology. For example, most Sunnis pray with their hands folded, while the Shiʻa pray with their hands outstretched, and the Shiʻa break their fasts a few minutes after the Sunnis during Ramadan. Most of these rituals, however, are done either in private or in the presence of coreligionists. The performances associated with Muharram are of a different order. The public nature of these mourning practices rips a hole in this stasis of invisibility. Furthermore, in these performances the fundamental differences in worldview which divide the two communities are brought to the forefront. The tension between the two schools is heightened by the mutual misunderstanding of each side's interpretation of the events being commemorated and at times communal violence may erupt. These rituals are thus the most important of all those in the Shiʻi calendar, not only because of the importance of the historical events which they remember but also because they annually bring to the fore the crucial differences between Sunni and Shiʻa which are normally—if somewhat uncomfortably—buried.

The Two-Sidedness of 'Azadari Rituals

The provocative nature of Shi'i rituals reveals another important dimension of 'azadari of which most Shi'i Muslims are well aware. This element of 'azadari was pointed out to me by a Shi'i gentleman in Rizvia Society in Karachi. As he noted, all rituals — and he referred both to rituals of 'azadari and other rituals of Islam — have two dimensions. The first is the benefit which accrues to the person actually performing it. Thus, if a man prays or fasts there is a certain amount of spiritual benefit which accrues to him on the basis of that action. But each action faces outward as well as inward. There is also the effect of the ritual on others who observe it. Thus, if a man through a ritual action demonstrates an extremely striking example of piety or devotion, he may give evidence of the verity of his beliefs to those who do not share them (or may be hostile to them).

This element is crucial in the rituals of Muharram, for in these rituals the community not only is looking in on itself but also is pulling back a curtain and revealing in a dramatic and emotional fashion the real distinction between themselves and those who are against them. The rituals of Muharram, however, are not an invitation to hostility but rather are an invitation for outsiders to join them. They are an attempt by Shi'i Muslims to demonstrate both to themselves and to others the superior nature of their religious claims.

'Azadari as a Focus of Controversy

The long-standing religious complexity of South Asia has led to a vigorous and open, if at times heated, religious debate. Not only has there been a continual interaction between the majority Hindu population, itself highly diverse, and the Muslims of South Asia; but also among different kinds of Muslims who have varied ethnically, linguistically, religiously, and socially. Turks, Iranis, and indigenous converts might belong to different Islamic legal schools. Sufism was and still remains an important feature of Islam in South Asia, and different *tariqahs* have vied with each other for disciples. Sunni rulers of Turkish extraction who followed the Shafi'i *mazhab* (legal school) depended upon Irani nobles, who were often Shi'a, to rule over both Hindus and Muslims of the Ḥanafī *mazhab*. Elements of folk religion have been tolerated to varying degrees by the common populace. There has also been the presence of Christianity as the religion of the colonial Raj. The rise of "fundamentalism" has further expanded the inherent diversity of the situation.

Historically, each school of thought has attempted to prove the verity of its own claims and discredit the claims of its rivals. This situation has produced a great deal of readily available printed polemical materials arguing over the issues of this or that religious school of thought. This is particularly true of materials arguing for or against the Shi'i religious position vis-à-vis that of the Sunni Muslims, as the position of each respective school poses a direct threat to the cherished opinions of the other's faith. The presence of these materials makes South Asia in many ways the perfect laboratory for the study of Islam.

It is an empirical fact that the performance of 'azadari has been maintained over a long period of time in Islamic history. Its history has been a focus of reflection for Shi'i scholars of South Asia. The Shi'i community has produced important works of scholarship on the subject of the history of 'azadari. As with other Shi'i writings, there is a dual purpose to this literature. On one level its purpose is to demonstrate and reinforce the permissibility of the performance of Shi'i rituals in an environment where there is considerable hostility to such rituals. Histories of 'azadari written in Pakistan and North India attempt not only to describe the development of 'azadari but also to demonstrate the ways in which such practices are connected with the larger realm of Shi'i practices in the context of the Islamic world as a whole. Part of this attitude arises from the fact that the greatest single concentration of Shi'i Muslims lives in Iran, where the most important centers of Shi'i learning are to be found. Most of the important *mujtahids* and *āyatullahs* of the Shi'i world are from Iran. And yet few if any South Asian Muslims have forgotten that there was a time when Lucknow in Uttar Pradesh was a major center of Shi'i learning. There is a great deal of pride among South Asian Shi'a concerning the accomplishments of the Shi'a of the subcontinent. The fact is many of the Muharram performances of Shi'i Muslims of South Asia are distinctive to the region. Many Shi'a are anxious to demonstrate the acceptability of these performances to the larger Shi'i and Islamic worlds.

The authors of these histories make every attempt to demonstrate the permissibility of these performances to the larger Sunni population. Probably the most universally respected of the Shi'i histories of 'azadari (or at least the one most commonly recommended to me) is 'Azadari ki Tarīkh by Sibtul Hasan Fazil Hansawi, a highly respected scholar, who was the curator of Arabic and Persian manuscripts at the Aligarh Muslim University.[6]

While I am not qualified to attest to the historical accuracy of his arguments, they remain an excellent primary source for the community's understanding of its own history. It is significant that Sibtul Hasan begins his book by bemoaning the attacks made upon the practice of 'azadari. Similarly, 'Ali Naqi Naqvi, a mujtahid of India and a prominent zakir, in his book Azadari: A Historical Review, is primarily concerned with demonstrating the permissibility of 'azadari to the larger Islamic community.

The controversy between Shi'i and Sunni Muslims remains powerful in contemporary Pakistan. In Karachi there are several "brands" of Islam as well as secularists, Christians, and a small minority of Hindus. Given this religious diversity, it is not surprising that there is a great deal of dialogue among people concerning questions of religious practice and belief. During the period of my field research in 1983 I lived in a boarding house in Rizvia Society. Although the area is almost entirely Shi'i, the tenants were almost all Sunnis. Almost every night they and I would enter into long discussions about the theological and ritual differences between Sunnis and Shi'as. Much of this debate centered around the question of the permissibility of Shi'i mourning practices.

The question of the permissibility of 'azadari is not new to South Asia. During the seventeenth and eighteenth centuries the region saw an upsurge of Muslim revivalist and revitalization movements. While these movements varied in content, many shared an antipathy for what they considered to be bida' (innovation). These groups opposed any religious practices which they deemed not to be a part of the practice of the Prophet or his early companions. Many of these movements had anti-Shi'i tendencies. A classic example was that propounded by Shah Waliullah Dihlavi, whose approach to jurisprudence is more fully articulated in such later movements as the Deobandi school. According to the followers of Shah Waliullah, matam is not permissible. His disciple and son, Shaikh Abdulaziz Muhaddith Dihlavi, wrote a series of fatwas (legal decisions) on the subject of matam in which he criticized Shi'i mourning practices. The basic thrust of these fatwas is that such activities as julus and majlis are bida' and as such should be avoided, if not altogether prohibited.[7]

These attitudes are still found, particularly in neorevivalist movements like the Deobandis and the Ahl-i Hadith. Thus, it is not surprising that there would be a fierce debate not only in works intended for the scholarly community but also in pamphlet materials—much of it cheaply bound and inexpensively available—and in *majalis* containing the kinds of argumentative information which a minority community needs to defend itself and its positions to the larger community. Much of this literature is concerned with proving to the Sunni community the permissibility of those rituals which are understood to be violations of Islamic law.

The Permissibility of *'Azadari*

Since the Shi'a live in a complex and heterogeneous social environment, surrounded by a large Sunni population that disagrees with their practices, it is important to understand their arguments regarding the permissibility of *'azadari*. These arguments can be divided into two major types. One is soteriological in nature and is based upon Shi'i sources. The primary audience for these is Shi'i. The other type of argument is that which attempts to prove the permissibility of the Shi'i practices of *'azadari* in the Sunnis' own terms. This allows for a justification of their actions but also functions as an argument for the superiority of their position. Ultimately, the Shi'a wish to argue that the performance of *'azadari* is not merely permissible but should be a fundamental focus of Islamic practice for all Muslims. As 'Ali Naqi has written:

Leaving aside the Shi'a and the Sunnis who recite the *shahadah* of the pure Prophet and claim the love of the oppressed Husayn, the Hindus and the Parsis also take part in this mourning and recollect and commemorate the oppressed martyr of Karbala. But it is regrettable that among those who profess Islam, [there are] some [who] in the name of human conscience, appear to be expending all of their energies in order to prevent the expression of this suffering. But this is quite another thing, that this attempt is like trying to paint upon water and in the face of God will come to nothing.[8]

He continues:

From the point of view of the general body of the Muslims, first of all [in determining] whatever thing is such that one's head will bow before it are the Qur'an, the sayings of the Prophet, or—after that—in the customs of the noble companions, and the way of action of the *tabi'in* [companions of the companions]. If only one [example] of a thing is found among these, then that is enough to demonstrate the validity of an opinion. Then, what about a situation in which all of these sources line up side by side so as to prove something.[9]

The kind of arguments which *'ulama* like 'Ali Naqi make in their *majalis* and in their writings are designed to be read by Shi'a who will then use these arguments in dialogue with Sunni Muslims. Thus, it is not unusual for Shi'i writers to use only accepted Sunni authorities when they are presenting their arguments for the permissibility of *matam* and *'azadari*.[10] By so doing, they are attempting not only to justify their actions to the larger community of Islam but to demonstrate to them that the Shi'i position is in fact the most truly Islamic one and thus to bring non-Shi'i Muslims into the fold.

The following arguments are taken from an article by the aforementioned *'alim* and *zakir*, Ayatullah 'Ali Naqi Naqvi. Naqqan Sahab, as he is known, is one of the most influential *zakirs* in the region and is in great demand for *majalis* during Muharram. Unlike many *zakirs*, 'Ali Naqi was trained as a member of the *'ulama* in the *madrasahs* (religious schools) of Iraq. His writings on these issues are of a particularly high intellectual caliber and are indicative of the types of arguments made within the community for the permissibility of *'azadari*.

As the Qur'an is universally accepted by all Muslims as authoritative, 'Ali Naqi first of all looks for a justification of mourning performances in the holy book. He cites as Qur'anic evidence for the permissibility of weeping the fact that the Prophet Ya'qub's eyes "turned white with weeping and grief" because of his separation from Yusuf. The argument is that, as Ya'qub is a prophet and he mourned publicly, it is permissible for us to do so. In fact, to be opposed to weeping in the face of this would be to deny the authority of a prophet of God—a fundamentally non-Islamic position.[11] The purpose of this kind of argument is to put Sunnis on the defensive. As Sunnis accept the authority of the Qur'an and of all of the prophets mentioned in the book, they are forced to explain why they oppose the practice of mourning as *bid'a* when it is part of the Sunnah of a Qur'anic prophet.

A second form of universally accepted authority in the Islamic world is the Sunnah of the Prophet, which consists not only of his speech and actions but also of his *takrīr* (unspoken approval). By using examples from out of the accepted Sunni corpus of *hadith* in which the Prophet either mourned or allowed mourning, 'Ali Naqi presents his Shi'i audience with the kinds of argumentation intended to place its Sunni opponents in an uncomfortable intellectual position. He notes several instances in which the Prophet is reported to have cried aloud with grief. These are presented as a justification of mourning for Husayn.

The most prominent of these incidents has to do with the death of the Prophet's uncle, Hamzah, at the battle of Uhud. It is reported that when the Prophet came upon the slain body of Hamzah he cried, swooned, and recited lamentations. Furthermore, when he came upon Hamzah's sister, who was weeping, he too became overcome with tears. 'Ali Naqi has said of this incident: "To say after this that crying and lamenting are contrary to religious law is to appear to be opposing the actions of the Prophet."[12]

It is also noted that the Prophet wept aloud at the death of his infant son Ibrahim and said: "My eyes are filled with tears and my heart is grief-stricken; still we are saying no such thing as would offend God when we say 'Oh Ibrahim, it is a heartfelt grief we feel for you.'"[13] It is further reported that Ibn Auf chided the Prophet for behaving in this manner, and that the Prophet replied: "Oh Ibn Auf, this is a sign of the heart . . . the eyes are meant for crying and the heart for grieving."[14]

While this discussion shares the basic nature of the above-mentioned Qur'anic argument, it also reveals another dimension of argument more fully in keeping with what are primarily Shi'i concerns. Immersed in this argument is a subtle verification of the basic assumption of Shi'i jurisprudence that ultimately all shar', or revealed law, must be in accord with aql, or reason. Thus, the argument is not only that matam is legitimate for all Muslims, whether or not they are Shi'a, because it is a part of the Sunnah of the Prophet. It is also argued—in this case by the Prophet himself—that matam is legitimate because it is perfectly natural and reasonable. In this argument the naturalness and reasonableness of mourning is emphasized. Eyes are made for crying, as the Prophet himself points out. For 'Ali Naqi, Husayn's suffering draws the sympathy of the whole world because it is the natural tendency of human beings to show sympathy with the oppressed—an argument he has worked out more fully in his major work, Shahīd-i Insāniyat. Thus, mourning is absolutely natural—a fact which is proved by the evidence of non-Muslims such as Hindus and Parsis commemorating Husayn's martyrdom. It then should be no surprise that the Prophet would give evidence regarding the acceptability of mourning, given the Shi'i position that shar' accords with reason.

Another important incident is that reported by Abu Hurayrah, who states that the Prophet cried to such an extent upon visiting the grave of his dead mother that he also caused others around him to cry.[15] As mentioned above, a particularly important incident in the history of Islam for the Shi'a is the death of

Hamzah at the battle of Uhud. It is important as an analogue of Karbala because it involved the brutal death of a beloved member of the Prophet's family who died while fighting for Islam and whose body was desecrated by the enemy. The act of desecration was incidentally performed by Yazid's grandmother, Hind, the wife of Abu Sufyan. The Prophet is reported to have arranged a mourning assembly for Hamzah's death when he discovered that since he had died far from home no one was crying for him. The Prophet had the women come into his house and read *marthiyah* (mourning poetry). ʿAli Naqi comments on this:

It is worthy of deep reflection that Hamzah had passed away while away from home. And no one cried, so the Prophet had the women of the Ansar cry and weep and recite lamentations, and the custom was enacted that when some relative died first of all Hamzah was cried for. So then if some oppressed [person] on becoming a martyr [dies] while traveling; if we should cry and weep for him as his relatives are unable to cry, where is the blame? . . . the reality is this, that the suffering of Hamzah is next to nothing when held up before [that of] Husayn. The martyr of Karbala endured the epitome of sufferings. And certainly in the heart of the Prophet, Husayn was so much loved that in this also he was greater than Hamzah.[16]

Thus, mourning for Husayn is shown to be permissible as it is analogous to mourning for Hamzah. But these are primarily arguments from a Shiʿi scholar specifically designed for use in argumentation with Sunnis. They are designed to demonstrate the permissibility of ʿazadari. But for the Shiʿa ʿazadari is not merely permissible, it is an important mark of one's Islam. The sadness involved in the tragedy of Karbala is for the Shiʿa unavoidably evocative of grief. This is because the death of Husayn is not merely a martyrdom. It would be enough for one to grieve over the death of a loved one. This is evident from the example of Hamzah. But Husayn is more than an ordinary man. As one Shiʿa in Karachi told me, the difference between the attitudes of the Shiʿa and the Sunni concerning the death of Husayn comes down to the fact that for the Sunnis Husayn is a great hero who gave his life for Islam, but for the Shiʿa Husayn is the grandson of the Prophet, and this we can never forget. As the grandson of Muhammad, he was the beloved of Muhammad, and much is made by the Shiʿa of the special love that the Prophet had for his grandchildren. As Muhammad was the most beloved of God, the tragedy of Karbala attains a cosmic proportion. Husayn was a bearer of the same light from which 'Ali and Muhammad were created before the very creation of the world. Thus, the death of Husayn—the last of the *panjatan pak*, the people of the cloak—at the hands of those who claimed to be the followers of the Prophet signifies the turning away of humanity from God and the Prophet. The stories of the barbaric behavior of the troops of Yazid after the killing of Husayn—for example, that they celebrated his death by anointing their eyes with Husayn's blood as *sormah* (a cosmetic for darkening the eyes)[17]—are indicative of the fact that the murder of Husayn was more than a mere political killing but was rather a total rejection of God's guidance. In Shi'i narrative it is an action which not only humanity but all of nature mourns. It is an action which God and the Prophet foresaw and this foreknowledge colors all of history with a sense of sorrow.

Given the enormity of the event in the metaphysical system of the Shi'a, it is not surprising that one's reaction to the events of Karbala are of extreme importance with regard to one's relationships with God. It also has a bearing on one's status in the afterlife. Mourning becomes a sign of solidarity not only with Imam Husayn but with all of the prophets and with God. That solidarity reaffirms the personal allegiance which is the thread connecting all Shi'i piety.

The Shi'i Argument for *'Azadari*

These arguments from 'Ali Naqi are designed for a Sunni audience. They attempt to convince that audience on the basis of the textual and historical sources held as sacred and authoritative by that population that the Shi'i view of Islam as a personal allegiance is the true one. The arguments are designed to give ammunition to Shi'i Muslims in the ongoing dialogue with the Sunni community, not to convince the Shi'i community who already accept the validity of *'azadari* and the claim of 'Ali to the Imamate and who would, in any event, be unwilling to accept an *hadith* passed through Abu Hurayrah, a companion considered unreliable by Shi'i jurists.

Shi'i Muslims recognize another argument for participation in *'azadari* practices, which in some instances takes precedence over all other considerations. That is the soteriological dimension of these practices. Because of the cosmic dimension of the tragedy of Karbala, weeping for Husayn is taken as a sign of true Islam. By crying, each person shows his or her allegiance to the true designees of God and the Prophet. Furthermore, unless one's heart is not hardened, one cannot help but cry. And the inability to cry over such a heinous crime may be taken as evidence that one is spiritually lost.

The act of crying for Husayn is salvific. Ja'far as-Sadiq has said: "Anyone who remembers us or if we are mentioned in his presence and a tear as small as a wing of a gnat falls from his eye, God would forgive all his sins even if they were as the foam of the sea." He has also said: "There is no servant whose eyes shed one drop of tears for us, but that God will grant him for it the reward of countless ages in Paradise."[18] It is both a sign of remembrance of the sufferings of the family of the Prophet and a show of solidarity with the *ahl al-bayt*. The crying itself is powerful and allows for an immediate encounter with the figures of Shi'i narrative. It is commonly believed that Fatimah and Zainab appear at the *majalis*, that after the *matam* they gather the tears of the mourners in their skirts, and that on the Day of Judgment they will present these tears to God as proof of the sincere faith of that person.

'Azadari' is practiced at intervals throughout the year. On nearly every Thursday there is a *majlis* in the major *imambargahs* of Karachi. *Majlis* may be organized for special occasions or for special merit. They are also held on the death anniversaries of the *ahl al-bayt*. But *'azadari* during the month of Muharram has special significance. The prescribed actions for this period and the meanings behind them are outlined in the *Tuḥfat ul-'Awām*, which is basically a handbook for "the common people," as the title suggests, for ritual actions. Besides being a guide for prayer, fasting, and the *Hajj*, it also contains descriptions of superogatory *a'māl* (actions), such as special Qur'anic verses to be recited during the regular prayers, or *ziyarats* to be recited.

In the chapter entitled "The Actions of Muharram" these actions are discussed under four headings. The first concerns the permissibility of fasting during the *'Āshūrā* period. It states that if anyone fasts or makes supplicatory prayers to God on the first day of Muharram, then God will accept these actions in the same way in which God granted the Prophet Zachariah's request for progeny with the birth of the Prophet Yahya. It notes that because on the third day of Muharram the Prophet Yusuf was delivered from the bottom of a well whoever keeps a fast or makes supplicatory prayer on this day will have his difficulties eased by God. However, on the ninth or tenth day of Muharram one is advised not to fast because on these two days Banu Umayyah kept a fast in order to make auspicious the killing of

Imam Husayn. It is noted that there are a great number of *hadiths* from the *ahl al-bayt* to this effect. It further goes on to state on the basis of an *hadith* from the eighth Imam that whoever stays away from his worldly concerns on the ninth and tenth days of Muharram (and instead engages in acts of prayer and mourning), God will cause his worldly concerns to prosper. But whoever considers it to be a time of blessing and thus engages in worldly affairs or stores up goods in his house, on the Day of Judgment God will consider him to be among the people of Ibn Ziyad and 'Umar b. Sa'd. Rather, one should spend the entire day in mourning because the shedding of conscious tears for Husayn will bring about the forgiveness of one's great sins.[19]

It is interesting to note the style of argument here. As *Tuhfat-ul 'Awam* is designed solely for the use of Shi'i Muslims, its style of discourse is not like that mentioned above in relation to polemic literature. The sources quoted for the verification of the ritual actions are *hadiths* from the Imams, which for the Shi'i community have unquestionable authority. Mourning for Husayn is given such great importance that the Imams have argued that to do it will result in the forgiveness of sins. Conversely, to attach no importance to the period of time in which Husayn's martyrdom occurred (or worse yet to consider it auspicious) is to court damnation. On the Day of Judgment such persons will be resurrected alongside the killers of the Prophet's grandson. Thus, one's choice of action regarding participation in mourning for Husayn is made somehow equivalent with the moral choice made by those who were actually at the battle of Karbala—to stand with or against Husayn. And that choice will be mirrored in the afterworld.

This style of argument is continued in an *hadith* connected with Imam Musa al-Kazim, which states that, if one wishes to share in the blessings of those who gave their lives as sacrifice at Karbala, then whenever he remembers the calamities of Imam Husayn he should cry and say, "Oh, I wish that on the day of 'Ashura I could have been a companion of the martyrs of Karbala." A person who does this can receive the salvation of a martyr. This *hadith* reinforces the above-mentioned argument by equating a passionate and mournful wish to have been alongside the Imam with the actual act of having been there by equating the spiritual reward of the two actions. With this *hadith* the first section of the chapter ends.[20]

The second section deals with the fundamental practices of *Shab-i 'Ashura* (the evening of 'Ashura). In this section it is reported on the authority of Imam Ja'far as-Sadiq that if anyone

PUBLIC PERFORMANCES

87

recites the *Ziyarat* of Imam Husayn on the eve of *'Ashura* it is as if he was an actual companion of the martyred Imam. And, it continues, if anyone remains awake all night and spends the entire night in tears, mourning, and the performance of pious actions, it is equivalent to the pious actions of all of the angels and this mourning has attached to it the spiritual blessings of sixty years of good actions. The reason for this is that Imam Husayn, when he was surrounded by his enemies at Karbala on the eve of his martyrdom, spent the entire night awake in the performance of religious actions and in preparation for his martyrdom. Thus, whatever believer says four *rak'ats* of prayer in a prescribed manner on *Shab-i 'Ashura*, God will forgive his sins of fifty years past and fifty years to come.[21]

The manner in which these prayers are to be said is as follows. In each *rak'at* worshippers must recite after *surah al-hamd*, *surah-i qul huwa'llahū ahadun* (Surah 112) fifty times.[22] According to another tradition it is reported that the four *rak'ats* should be read with two *salams*. In the first *rak'at*, after *surah al-hamd*, the worshipper should recite *āyat-ul kursi* (the Throne Verse) ten times. In the second *rak'at* he should recite *surah-i qul huwa'llahu ahadun* ten times, in the third *rak'at* he should recite ten times *surah-i qul-a'ūdhu bi-rabbi'l-falaqi* (Surah 113), in the fourth *rak'at*, *surah-i qul a'ūdhu bi-rabbi'n-nasi* (Surah 114). And then, after *salams*, he should recite one hundred times *surah-i qul huwa'llahu ahadun*. These involved actions demonstrate the believers' willingness to have been companions in martyrdom at Karbala and give evidence of their sincerity.[23]

These *surahs* are all significant. Surah 112, 113, and 114 all begin with the word *qul*—the imperative of "to say." "*Qul huwa'l-lahu ahadun*" means "Say, God is One" and is thus also known as *Surah-i Tauhid*. "*Qul a'udhu bi-rabbi'l-falaqi*" means "Say, I seek protection of the Lord of Daybreak"; and "*qul a'udhu bi-rabbi'n nasi*" means "Say, I seek protection of the Lord of Men." These *surahs* are commonly read in the act of *Fatihah* as a benediction over the fruits or sweetmeats which are distributed.[24] The last two of these are especially connected in the minds of Shi'a with Hasan and Husayn.

The third section deals with actions related to the actual day of *'Ashura*. The text states that it is clear that the day of *'Ashura* is a day of absolute sadness. It states that the enemies of the Shi'a have forged *hadiths* about the excellence of *'Ashura* or the benefits of fasting on this day, but these are simply fabrications.[25] (This is substantiated in Shi'i histories in which it is argued that caliphs in the 'Abbasid and Fatimid periods attempted to institute days of celebration during this period so as to draw people away from Twelver Shi'ism.)[26] A Bohra acquaintance of mine showed me in the Bohri prayer books which are read during 'Ashura the long list in Arabic of the blessings related to 'Ashura, which points out the sharp difference in attitude between the Isma'ili and Ithna'ashari positions on this point. The Twelvers hold that during the morning of 'Ashura one should abstain from food and water but after that one should break the fast with water after the afternoon prayers. The reason is that it was at this time that the Imam ceased his fighting and the order was given for "calamities to be visited upon the people of his household." The text states that we should cry over the calamities of the children of Husayn in much the same manner as we would cry for calamities visited upon our own dear ones, only to a greater extent as the sufferings of the children of the Imam are understood to be the worst ever experienced in human history. If one does this, then that person shall have recorded in his favor the spiritual benefit of "a thousand thousand *hajjs* and a thousand *umrahs* and a thousand thousand *jihāds* performed alongside of all of the prophets."[27]

Furthermore, it is considered to be the best of actions in the beginning of the afternoon on the day of 'Ashura for people to open their gowns and turn back their sleeves and, in the manner consistent with the occurrence of a calamity, stand upon the roof of their houses facing toward an uninhabited direction and with humility and tearful eyes perform the following actions. They should turn in the direction of the tomb of Imam Husayn, remember the battlefield of Karbala and the martyrdom of Imam Husayn, and making a sign with their finger, make an intention to read the *Ziyarat* of Imam Husayn. On the day of 'Ashura they should then read the *ziyarat*. The *ziyarat* is made up of three parts. The long *ziyarat* is followed by the curse of God upon those who killed the Imam and his companions. This is recited 100 times. After this a shorter *ziyarat* is recited 100 times. Then they should prostrate themselves and in this state of prostration ask God to curse the enemies of the *ahl al-bayt* and bless the Imam and his companions. At the end they should pray to God to keep the worshippers loyal to the Imam. After this they should perform another two *rak'ats* of prayer and then recite another supplication.[28]

An alternate method of action during 'Ashura is based on the teaching of Imam Ja'far as-Sadiq. The Imam has written that the best action on the day of 'Ashura is to begin by saying *namāz* (ritual prayers) with a pure heart. As in the other cases, a list of Qu-r'anic verses and *ziyarats* that can be recited following each *rak'at* of prayer is given. Once again those who perform these rites are promised that they will be held in a particularly close relation-ship with God as a result of their performance and will be granted spiritual and physical protection.[29]

The fourth section is considerably shorter than the others. It also relates Arabic supplications which, if read, will result in God protecting the worshippers from all kinds of disasters.[30]

We can deduce from the kinds of *a'mal* listed in *Tuhfat ul-'Awam* the importance of remembering the sufferings of the *ahl al-bayt* and being moved to tears and mourning by them. Engag-ing in grief for the sufferings of the *ahl al-bayt* is of great soterio-logical importance. To engage in these actions can lead to the forgiveness of sins and the blessings of God.

In the popular imagination the emphasis on this aspect of Mu-harram practice has led some Shi'i Muslims to complain that many Shi'a neglect their religious duties throughout the major-ity of the year and then attempt to make up for them during 'Ashura. As we shall discuss below, some Shi'a have argued that this attitude totally misses the point about what Imam Husayn was attempting to accomplish at Karbala. As one Shi'a told me, "If Imam Husayn did not die for prayer, then what did he die for?" Others have argued just as passionately that the troops of Ibn Ziyad also engaged in ritual prayers before the battle of Kar-bala, and thus what really was at stake was not the Shari'ah but the attitude of the Muslims toward the *ahl al-bayt*. Some have even argued that the entire concept of mourning *majlis* should be changed as the real intention of the *majlis* should be educa-tion of the masses about Islam.

Another dimension to arguments about the permissibility of 'azadari within the Shi'i community will be dealt with more thor-oughly in the final chapter which deals with physical *matam*. At this point it is sufficient to state that the influence of "fundamen-talist" and modernist ideas on the Shi'i community have caused many within the community to question the "Islamicness" of certain of these practices. This is evidenced by the existence of *fatwas* from contemporary *ayatullahs* on the question of the per-missibility of *matam*.[31] In general, these *fatwas* have argued that most forms of *matam* are indeed permissible, but the presence of the controversy within the community itself demonstrates the powerful forces at work upon it.

Majlis: The Educational Role of *'Azadari*

The soteriological dimension of acts of devotional mourning for Husayn are apparent from the above. But there is another important function of *'azadari*—education. This aspect of *'azadari* is most clearly found in *majalis* or "mourning assemblies." For example, the aforementioned arguments made by 'Ali Naqi regarding the permissibility of *'azadari* were made in the context of a *majlis*. Although the culmination of the *majlis* is the elaboration of the events of Karbala, the structure of the *majlis* renders it a powerful educational vehicle. This is because the longest portion of the *majlis* is a discourse on a religious topic. It generally begins with a Qur'anic verse, with the rest of the discourse acting as an interpretation of that verse, usually making a point about ethics or some social issue of concern to the community. Thus, because of the *majalis*, at least once a year—and in many cases once a week—Shi'a are exposed to what are quite often highly developed religious discourses.

A few important *zakirs* such as 'Ali Naqi have been trained in the Islamic universities of Iraq, and their *majalis* are important tools for the dissemination of traditional wisdom. One popular reader of *majlis*, the late Rashid Turabi, has read *majlis* on such diverse topics as "The *Bhagavad Gita* and *Najulbalagah*," "The *Qur'an* and Poetry," "Islam and Science," "Islam and Sufism," and "What Was Written of the Holy Prophet during his Lifetime."[32] The diversity of the titles in the repertoire of just one *zakir* gives some evidence of the range of topics which can be dealt with in these *majalis*. With the popularity of the cassette recorder, the *majalis* of important *zakirs* reach more people than ever before. Not only are *majalis* easily available for purchase at *imambargahs* for around 25 or 30 rupees, but there are lending libraries of cassettes as well. Thus, those Shi'a who wish access to religious education can obtain it easily. Indeed, during the month of Muharram it is difficult to avoid. Not only are nightly *majalis* broadcast over loudspeakers, but *marthiyah* and *majlis* can be heard in the streets and alleys over the speakers of cassette players for much of the day and night.

Because of the popularity of *majlis* and its central role in Shi'i piety, in some ways *zakirs* are more important to the religious education of the community in South Asia than the *'ulama*. Part of this is due to the simple fact that there are few real *mujtahids* in the region. Most of the important centers of Shi'i learning are in Iran and Iraq. Most of the important *mujtahids* and ayatullahs of the Shi'i world are from Iran. While there is a tendency particularly among those Shi'a who have been revitalized in their faith by the Iranian revolution to look more and more toward the Iranian *ulama* for the edification of their religious lives, many South Asian Shi'a see the role of the *ulama* in the limited sense as that of being expert in jurisprudence. The *ulama* do not enter into peoples' lives as intimately as they apparently do in Iran. As stated above, while there are few real *mujtahids* in Pakistan, there are many *zakirs*. This is not to say that the *ulama* are unimportant. Rather it reflects the logistical difficulty in becoming a *mujtahid* as there are no functioning *madrasahs* in the region able to administer the full corpus of instruction. Therefore, much of the responsibility for the religious instruction of the community falls on the *zakirs* (who may or may not be well-grounded scholars of Islam).

The Role of the *Zakir* in Shi'i Piety

Given the importance of the *majlis* in Shi'i piety, it is surprising that the role of the *zakir*—the reader of *majlis*—has received so little attention from scholars of Shi'i Islam. The importance of the *ulama* in Shi'i culture has become recognized, but the role of the *zakir*—who is usually *not* from among the *ulama*—has been all but ignored. An understanding of the role of the *zakir* and the function of *majlis* in Islamic society is particularly crucial in the study of Shi'i Islam in South Asia, where Shi'i Muslims have long constituted an influential minority. In this region—where *mujtahids* are few and *zakirs* are numerous—it can be argued that *zakirs* are in some ways the most important religious specialists in the Shi'i community.

As an expositor of religious and ethical doctrine, the *zakir* should be seen as speaking to two audiences—Shi'i and Sunni. Members of the Shi'i audience are already committed to ideas of 'Alid devotionalism. For these persons the *zakir* acts as a religious teacher expounding on the various levels of meaning in a Qur'anic text or an *hadith* or explicating the religious dimensions of this or that activity in the life of the Prophet or his *ahl al-bayt*. But once again there are two dimensions to this role. The first, like that of a Christian Protestant preacher, is to instill a deeper sense of commitment in the hearts and minds of his congregation or to persuade them of a particular point of view with regard to religious practice or attitude. The second is to put into the hands of his community, who occupy a minority position, the kind of information which will allow them to defend themselves against the arguments brought against them by Sunni Muslims.

A good example of this type of argument can be found in the above-mentioned *majlis* of Ayatullah 'Ali Naqi in which he attempts to prove the permissibility of Shi'i practices in Sunni terms. In making his argument—that *majlis* is not only a permissible but a fundamental part of Islamic practice—he attempts to show both Qur'anic evidence for the permissibility of *'azadari* and evidence from the Sunnah of the Prophet. Interestingly, the *hadiths* which he chooses to quote are *hadiths* from the standard Sunni sources rather than from the traditional Shi'i ones. His use of *hadiths* from *Sahīh Bukhārī*, which rely on the authority of Abu Hurayrah, are not meant to impress the Shi'a—who already accept the importance of *'azadari* and who would hold Abu Hurayrah in disrepute anyway—but rather to give to his Shi'i audience ammunition in their continuing debate with the Sunni concerning the permissibility of Shi'i practice.

But it should be remembered that it is not simply the content of the argument made in a *majlis* which gives it its power. To a large extent the effectiveness of a *zakir* in making his expository point lies in his skills as an orator and in the ritual context itself, which wraps the religious arguments in a cloak of emotion and sacred symbols, which in the hands of a particularly skilled *zakir* can drive home the point with remarkable intensity. *Zakirs* may begin learning their craft while quite young. Young *zakirs* begin by memorizing prewritten *majalis* which later serve as models for the *zakirs'* own creations. 'Ali Naqi has himself written a series of these *majalis*, published as inexpensive pamphlets.[33] From performing these *majalis* the young *zakirs* learn the performance aspect of the recitation and only later do they meld that with their own scholarship. Thus, it is not surprising that many *zakirs* are skilled showmen famed as much for their *persona* as their learning.

The Ritual Arena of *'Azadari*: The *Imambargah*

Given the importance of *'azadari* in Shi'i piety it is not surprising that special buildings exist whose primary purpose is to act as an arena for mourning performances. The large number of Shi'i Muslims in the city supports a substantial number of these buildings. *Imambargahs* are the primary arenas for the corporate activities of Shi'i Muslims, and they are the buildings used for the reading of *majlis*. They may also house *Husayniyya* or *ziyārat khānah*, in which ritual objects connected with devotion to the family of the Prophet are stored. *Imambargahs* are often part of a larger complex which may include a *masjid*, a *ghusl khānah*—for preparing corpses for burial—and perhaps a library or business offices. Sometimes small *imambargahs* are located in the homes of individual Muslims. In Karachi popular *imambargahs* are spread over many different areas of the city, each with its own distinctive personality. Certain *imambargahs* are associated with particular ethnic groups of Muslims. Some have reputations for attracting the best *zakirs*. Others may house important relics. Large *imambargahs*, such as Mehfil-i Shah Khurasan, located near the tomb of Muhammad Ali Jinnah, draw mixed crowds from different areas of the city. Mehfil-i Shah Khurasan boasts elaborate, full-size grave casings (*zarihs*), which I was told were originally designed for use at the tombs of the *ahl al-bayt* in Mecca and Medina. According to members of the Shiʻi community, as the Saudi Arabian government would not permit their importation, they have become sites of local pilgrimage—particularly on the occasions of the birth or death anniversaries of the Imams and Fatimah. Some of the *imambargahs* are highly politicized and are sites of agitation. Some have been targets of communal violence, such as Markazi Imambargah in Liaqatabad.

The ethnic and religious diversity of Karachi is mirrored in its *imambargahs*. The *imambargah* which was the focus of my research—Mehfil-i Murtaza—is a good example of the ways in which the *imambargahs* of Karachi may appeal primarily to one sector of the community while also attracting Muslims from other segments of the population. Mehfil-i Murtaza is a relatively young and very active *mehfil* established by Khoja Twelver Shiʻi Muslims who had migrated into Pakistan from East Africa. The Khoja Twelvers were originally converts to Nizari Ismaʻilism from Hinduism. In the late nineteenth century, following a falling out between certain members of the community and the Agha Khan (the Nizari Ismaʻili Imam), a portion of this community converted to Ithnaʾashari Shiʻism. Communities of Twelver Khojas are found throughout the Indian Ocean region. There are important Khoja communities in Bombay and East Africa (as well as a large community in Canada).

Currently, Karachi is the home not only of these Shiʻi Khojas from East Africa but also of *muhajirs* and indigenous Khojas. The East African Khojas are relatively affluent, and Mehfil-i Murtaza is located in the upper middle-class area of Karachi known as P.E.C.H.S. Mehfil-i Murtaza is a well-kept and modern complex. It contains a *masjid*, a *ghusl khanah*, and an *imambargah* with upper and lower sections for women and men, respectively. The *imambargah* opens up onto a large courtyard to allow for the larger congregations which come from all parts of the city to the *mehfil* on important occasions, such as Muharram. The ethnic origins of the *imambargah* can be seen in the fact that announcements of activities are written not only in English and Urdu, but also in Gujarati, mother tongue of most of the Khojas. Although established and administered by East African Khojas, it draws crowds from outside of its primary clientele, including Khojas from other parts of the city and non-Khoja Muslims. The popularity of Mehfil-i Murtaza is due in no small part to its reputation for consistently bringing in high quality *zakirs* to read *majlis*.

Not all *majalis* take place in large public *imambargahs*. Individuals may establish *imambargahs* in or near their residences as a pious action. For instance, during Muharram 1404 A.H./1983 A.D., ʿAli Naqi delivered *majlis* in Karachi at just such a small, private *imambargah* located near Mehfil-i Shah Khurasan. Because of his popularity he drew large crowds to the area. During the last few days of the Muharram cycle the streets around the residence were roped off, and closed-circuit television and loudspeakers broadcast his *majlis* to those unable to get inside. Besides the performance of *majlis* in *imambargahs*, local and visiting *zakirs* often read *majlis* in people's homes. All of this means that there is a great demand for *zakirs* in Karachi, particularly during Muharram, and subsequently that the most famous *zakirs* receive substantial remuneration for their services.[34]

The *Majlis* as Ritual and the *Zakir* as Performer

Majalis are the central rituals performed in *imambargahs* during the month of Muharram. They provide occasions both for the presentation of religious discourses and for the shared, public expression of a grief that is central to the nature of Shiʿi piety. The manifestation of grief in the context of Shiʿi ritual practice is understood as transformative and salvific. The intense nature of this grief indicates the strength of the love and devotion which underlies it—a love for the Prophet Muhammad and his family which constitutes the underlying fabric of Shiʿi Islam.

The *majlis* creates a ritual arena which facilitates the manifestation of this grief. During *majlis* Shiʿi Muslims gather in *imambargahs* to hear discourses on religious topics. These discourses culminate in the emotional rendering of some event indicative of the suffering of the Prophet's family. Although *majlis* is read throughout the year—particularly on Thursdays and on the birth and death anniversaries of the members of the *ahl al-bayt*—it is most closely associated with the yearly ten-day period of mourning for the martyred Imam Husayn, whose death on the field of Karbala is understood by Shi'i Muslims as a fulcrum in the history of the world and which remains to this day as a primary focus of spiritual reflection. The structure of the *majlis*—which consists of an expository discourse on religious and ethical matters, followed by an evocative, emotional rendering of the sufferings of the Prophet's family—allows not only for the evocation of grief but also for the continuing religious education of the Shi'i community. The *majlis* thus plays an important role in helping the community preserve its identity, as it is in *majlis* that Shi'i Muslims learn the arguments supporting their faith.

It is important to emphasize the fact that the *majlis* is a ritual and not merely a speech or recitation. *Majlis* allows for an emotional encounter with the characters of the sacred history of Islam—who have for the Shi'a a metaphysical as well as an historical significance. For Shi'a it is evidence of the verity of their faith that these symbols still evoke tears after 1,400 years. The fact that this story is so full of pathos that it can continue to generate powerful emotions—as if it had just happened—each and every Muharram in the hearts not only of Shi'a but many Sunnis and non-Muslims as well is taken as evidence of the special character of the events at Karbala. That the recitation of the events of Karbala should carry with it evidence of miraculous power is mysterious only until one realizes the station and position of the central characters. The miraculous is a central part of Shi'i piety, and the ritual arena of the *majlis* creates the possibility of miraculous encounter. By extension, the special and miraculous characteristics of the primary narrative of Shi'i Islam are evidence of the verity of the claims of Shi'ism as a whole.

The *majlis* allows for the creation of a liminal reality. At the height of the *majlis* the *imambargah* becomes transformed. It becomes simultaneously both Karbala and the "here and now." It is an intersection between the metahistorical reality of the Karbala drama and the ordinary reality of the participants in the *majlis*. The success of the *majlis* relies upon the ability of the participants to create and enter that liminal reality. This ability depends not only on the proclivity of the listeners and the eloquence of the *zakir* but on the structure of the *majlis* itself.

The Structure and Characteristics of *Majlis*

The structure of the *majlis* is processual. That is, its structure follows the tripartite scheme of separation, limen, and reincorporation first noted by Van Gennep and enlarged upon by Turner in his works on ritual. It remains the same throughout the year although it is most intense during the period of mourning associated with Muharram. The *majlis* generally follows immediately after the evening prayer at an *imambargah*. The most pious individuals usually arrive in time to perform ritual prayers before hearing the *majlis*, although this is not required.[35] No special preparations are required for hearing *majlis*.

Women and men are seated separately. At Mehfil-i Murtaza the lower section is reserved for men, with the women seated upstairs. At Mehfil-i Shah Khurasan a curtain is erected in the courtyard next to the *majlis* hall and women are seated there. In certain *imambargahs* loudspeakers or television monitors are placed in the women's section so that they can follow the *majlis*. This segregation of the sexes is to some extent ignored in relation to activities of *ziyarat*. Most *imambargahs* contain a *ziyarat khanah* which houses relics related to the *ahl al-bayt*. These may include representations of the standard of Husayn, coffins, the cradle of the infant 'Ali Asghar, or the tombs of the *ahl al-bayt*. Before the beginning of the *majlis* itself, persons attending the *majlis* may walk by and touch these objects as a way of receiving a blessing. Despite the segregation of the sexes at the reading of the *majlis*, I often observed mixed gatherings at these types of observances.

The most striking example of this is at the *ziyarat khanah* of Mehfil-i Shah Khurasan. The aforementioned *zarihs* or grave coverings, which were constructed during the 1950s to be sent to Saudi Arabia for the purpose of being placed on the graves of the family of the Prophet, have become a focus for devotion among the Shi'a of Karachi. Included are *zarihs* intended for use on the graves of Hazrat Fatimah and Hazrat 'Abbas. It is common for persons attending *majlis* to also come and read *du'a* at these grave markings. Such gatherings are generally mixed, with both men and women simultaneously performing these prayers. On the birthday of Fatimah the *zarihs* at Mehfil-i Shah Khurasan were a popular place of celebration. Merchants selling religious paraphernalia lined the street running alongside of the *imambargah*. *Zuljinahs* (horses symbolizing Husayn's mount) flanked each side of the iron gate leading into the room holding the *zarihs*. Inside the gate, *faqīrs* (Muslim ascetics) and dervishes wrapped in chains could be seen.[36]

What struck me immediately was the mixed gathering around the *zarihs*. The crowd was mainly women. And these women were not dressed in the dark, simple outer garment typically worn to such gatherings. Upon entering into the room where the *zarihs* are maintained, the women removed such garments and revealed extremely colorful *shalwar-kameez* (traditional long shirt and baggy trousers) and even *saṛis*. When I asked people in the community about this, the general response was that the intention of Islamic laws regarding the segregation of the sexes was to minimize inappropriate sexual thoughts and actions. In such an arena as this where one's thoughts are focused upon sacred personages, such thoughts are hardly possible, and thus such restrictions need not be so fully enforced. Similar mixed gatherings occur at many of the important Sufi shrines in the region, although there has been a move to restrict them at some of the shrines.

The central event is the recitation of the *majlis* itself. Following the prayers, the crowd begins to move gradually—a few at a time—into the *majlis* hall proper. The visual focus of the room is the *minbar*—a wooden staircase of about six or seven steps—which is located at the *qiblah* so that the audience faces toward Mecca. As people are getting settled, a series of recitations of poetry may take place. Generally the person or persons doing these recitations is seated or standing to the side of the *minbar*. There are several kinds of poetic recitations which take place before the *majlis*, of which *sozkhawani* and *marthiyah* are the most important types.

The *marthiyah* is followed by the delivery of the *majlis* by the *zakir*. Zakirs vary in style and in subject matter. Most wear a standard dress of *sherwānī* and *karakoli* hat. The *zakir* delivers his address from the *minbar*, seated on the step next to the top, as the top step is historically and traditionally reserved for the Imam. The *majlis* begins with the *zakir* entering into the room, usually to the shouts of "Salavat" for the family of the Prophet. The *zakir* then takes his seat on the *minbar*. Then there is a quiet communal recitation of *Surah Fatihah*, preceded by the same exhortation for the removal of the Shaitan (Satan) that is also a part of the daily prayers.

This is followed by the *khutba*, a formulaic recitation in Arabic consisting of praise of God, praise of the Prophet, and praise of the *ahl al-bayt*. Thus, the *majlis* begins with the demonstration of allegiance to the *ahl al-bayt*. This is followed by the discourse itself. The discourse generally begins with a verse of the Qur'an, with the rest of the discourse acting as a *tafsir* (exegesis) of that verse. During the mourning period of Muharram the *zakir* will deliver a series of discourses linked in theme and subject matter. Although the *majlis* is oriented around a Qur'anic verse, the subject matter can vary a great deal and the content of the presentations can contain references far afield from what one might normally consider the purview of Islamic discourse. For example, I have observed *zakirs* making reference to the Riddah wars as wars against "taxation without representation" and using quotations from Alvin Toffler's *The Third Wave.*

The last portion of the *majlis* is the *gham* or lamentation. The transition to the *gham* may be abrupt, but the most talented *zakirs* find ways to skillfully weld it into the context of the theme itself. The *gham* consists of an emotional narrative of the sufferings of the family of the Prophet. On each of the first ten days of Muharram the *gham* is traditionally linked to a specific event which is recounted by the *zakir*. For many people the *gham* is the central portion of the ritual. From the beginning of the *gham* people in the audience begin to sob and wail. As the incidents of Karbala are told, the crying becomes more and more intense. People strike their foreheads and chests. The *zakir* himself begins to cry. Generally the *gham* ends with the *zakir* overcome with emotion.

On certain occasions the *gham* is followed by *matam*, the physical act of mourning. The act of doing *matam* is profoundly emotional, as one might expect. From the seventh through the tenth day of Muharram the *matam* is extended. Rhythmic and musical variations of *nowhah* (lamentations) and *marthiyah* are sung by young men who stand near the *minbar*. The crowd joins in with a calling pattern of repetition. The rhythm of the *matam* is carried by the metrical striking of the hands against the chest (*hath ka matam*). Between the recitation of the different *nowhah*, simple chants of "Ya 'Abbas" or "Ya Husayn" are called out, and the sound of hands on chests becomes louder. *Matam* varies in length, depending on the evening. On the last three nights of the 'Ashura period *matam* may take the form of *zanjir ka matam*, in which young men flagellate themselves with chains and knives, although this activity is done out-of-doors to avoid the spilling of blood in the *imambargah* itself. Such activities are not required (in fact, some Shi'a are opposed to them), but they should be seen as manifestations of the same devotion to the Prophet which underlie the performance of the *majlis* itself.

On the last four days of these rituals small processions take place within the *imambargah* itself. Implements related to the stories of the martyrs of Karbala are carried throughout the crowd in the *majlis* hall. These may take the form of coffins wrapped in white and stained in red (perhaps bearing a black turban symbolizing the *ahl al-bayt*), a cradle symbolizing the young martyr 'Ali Asghar, or an *'alam* (standard) bearing a Fatimid hand and perhaps a silver waterflask symbolizing the standard of 'Abbas.

The *matam* concludes with the recitation of *ziyarat* in which the entire congregation turns in the direction of Mecca and Mashad while reciting salutations to the Imams, ending with the Imam Mahdi, the living Imam of the current age. This is normally followed by the sharing of food and tea and the dispersion of the crowd.

Analysis of the Ritual Process of *Majlis*

As stated earlier, Clifford Geertz has defined religion as "a system of symbols which acts to establish powerful, pervasive and long-lasting moods and motivations in men by formulating conceptions of a general order of existence and clothing these conceptions with such an aura of factuality that the moods and motivations seem uniquely realistic."[37] Clearly, *majlis* and its attendant rituals function in this way. The ritual of *majlis* allows people a chance to walk momentarily out of normal time into the realm of what Victor Turner has called the subjunctive mode— the realm of "what if" and "what could have been." In the ritual of the *majlis* people are able to enter into a sacred history but one with the possibility of certain alterations.

For example, Husayn is represented in the *julus* following the *majlis* by a coffin—the burial he deserved but was denied by Banu Umayyah. The hearers and mourners are allowed to experience Karbala and ask themselves the question: Had we been at Karbala would we have had the courage to stand with Husayn? This is part of the reasoning behind acts of physical *matam* such as flagellation and fire walking, a desire to demonstrate physically the willingness to suffer the kinds of wounds which they would have incurred had they fought at Karbala. The structure of the *majlis* allows for this entrance into a subjunctive realm removed from the normal day-to-day reality by creating a ritual space separated out from the ordinary realm, a liminal arena where one's attention can be focused on the symbolic paradigms which transcend any particular historical moment by penetrating all of history.

The central motif throughout the *majalis* is personal allegiance to the Imam. This is, after all, the focus of the narratives. In accordance with Geertz's definition, the *majlis* creates an atmosphere in which mourners not only encounter the "truth" of the necessity of personal allegiance through narrative and visual symbols but this atmosphere also induces a sense of heightened emotion which provides an internal assurance of the validity of their position. This is accomplished by gradually turning the attention of worshippers away from their own life experiences and on to the experiences of the *ahl al-bayt* so that those experiences become tools for reflection upon their own lives. Following the tripartite model of Van Gennep and Turner, the mourner is first pulled out of normal time through a series of acts of separation into the liminal realm of symbols and then, after the ritual has subsided, is allowed to enter back into the realm of normality.[38]

When the mourners come to the *imambargah* to hear *majlis* they generally proceed first to the *masjid* to begin by saying ritual prayers. (Most often the *majlis* is held immediately after evening *namaz*.) Having performed ablutions and thus having separated themselves from the realm of the profane, they further separate themselves from the realm of the ordinary by saying prayers, thus drawing nearer to the divine and re-creating the actions of Husayn on the eve of his martyrdom. There is a good deal of this type of paradigm-tracing in rituals of 'azadari in which people symbolically act out the kinds of actions which were performed at Karbala.

Upon leaving the *masjid* in the direction of the *majlis* hall to hear the *majlis*, they may enter the *ziyarat khanah*, where they are confronted with objects evocative of Karbala. These objects include symbols of the authority of the Imams and the Prophet. While there they may touch or kiss these objects connected to the *ahl al-bayt*. Entering into the *majlis* hall, they will hear *marthiyah* being read. These poems of mourning create an auditory environment evocative of Karbala. Participants in the *majlis* thus walk through a series of "doorways," all the time surrounding themselves more and more completely with visual and auditory phenomena that evoke the events of Karbala and serve to reinforce the sense of the presence of that place. It is as if the events of Karbala are always occurring just beneath the surface of everyday existence, and as if the act of going to hear *majlis* pulls back a veil revealing a reality that is in many ways more real than that in which people normally live.

It is into this already charged atmosphere that the *zakir* enters to recite the *majlis*. He enters amid shouts of allegiance to the Prophet and his family. He sits upon the *minbar*, which itself is symbolic of the authority of the Prophet and the Imams. The *minbar* may be flanked by *'alams* (standards) bearing the Fatimad hand—yet more symbols evocative of both the battle of Karbala and the authority of the *ahl al-bayt*. Many *imambargahs* have the names of the Imams written around the walls. Thus, everything in the room serves to focus the attention of the audience away from the mundane and toward events of the sacred narrative of Karbala.

The *zakir* begins by invoking the Qur'an. The Qur'an is no mere book. The speech of the Qur'an is the speech of God and therefore produces an automatic atmosphere of reverence. Many Muslims will not touch a Qur'an if they are not ritually clean. As Marshall Hodgson points out, the recitation of the Qur'an allows believers to taste to some small extent the experience of the Prophet as these were the very words he heard as revelation.[39] In the center of this charged arena the *zakir* expounds doctrines and religious arguments. Throughout the discourse he continues to evoke the name of the Prophet—calling on his audience to offer salutations to Muhammad and the *ahl al-bayt*. Members of the audience may spontaneously call out "*Nade Haidari*" to elicit shouts of "*Ya 'Ali!*"[40] As important points are made the audience is asked to reaffirm their allegiance to the *ahl al-bayt* as if the very logic of the arguments being presented is proof of the verity of the religion. Even during this portion of the *majlis* some may weep. The *zakir* uses his arms and the timbre of his voice to emphasize important points, while simultaneously heightening the emotional pitch of the crowd. By the time the discourse of the *majlis* has ended, the room is thoroughly charged with emotion.

This is followed by the *gham*, the dramatic climax of the performance. It is the heart of the liminal center of the *majlis*. Here the *zakir* must recreate the atmosphere of the events of the battle itself. Usually in tears himself, sometimes speaking in the present tense as if the events were happening before his very eyes, he attempts to evoke tears and wailing from his audience. Many in the audience may fall into a state of grief at the first mention of the events of Karbala. But it is not only the story which evokes grief. The quality of the narration and the narrator's ability to present the events in a way which touches the situation of his particular audience also brings about or enhances the desired emotional response. This emotional response is an important part of the piety of the participants in the *majlis* because it is evidence to them of the strength of their love for the people whom they mourn and thus of the strength of that personal allegiance which is so crucial in Shi'i Islam.

The *gham* may be followed by *matam* and the further chance for mourning. The mourning winds down into the recitation of the *ziyarat* in which the participants once more reaffirm their allegiance to the family of the Prophet through visitation of the Imams at their respective tombs. *Ziyarat* is, in fact, used for the close of many Shi'i rituals. It is significant that the final action which closes the ritual is one which affirms the allegiance of the believer to the chain of Imams, culminating in the twelfth Imam.

Following the *ziyarat*, the crowd breaks up only gradually. Food or tea is served, and each person has a chance to ask questions informally of the *zakir* or simply to visit with each other. There is time for each person to reflect upon his or her experience before entering back into the usual routine, each taking away a personally distinct and yet communally shared experience of the event.

The *majlis* thus moves from a series of steps of separation— slowly creating the atmosphere of Karbala—to a liminal stage in which participants are pulled into the Karbala drama itself. In the end people gradually reaggregate, taking with them the memories of their experience. Of course, the complexity and multivocality of the *majlis* allows for a good deal of difference of interpretation of the experience. One important point of disagreement concerns the function of the *majlis* within the community.

The Functions of the *Majlis*

From this analysis the two interrelated functions of the *majlis* can be clearly seen. As we have already discussed, the first of these is soteriological and devotional. We have already noted the spiritual benefit attached to mourning for the sufferings of the *ahl al-bayt*. Each *majlis*, unless it is a celebratory *majlis* for some blessed occasion, such as the birth of an Imam, ends in a section called the *gham* (lamentations). The *zakir*—the reader of *majlis*—through his skill as an orator is supposed to arouse in his audience tears of grief for the Prophet's family. As noted above, such tears are salvific and may make up for missed ritual prayers or other religious duties. The belief that Hazrat Fatimah and Hazrat Zainab will gather the tears of the devotees of Husayn and present them to God on the Day of Judgment as a sign of the sincerity of the believers' faith is a powerful symbolic incentive for people to come to *majlis* and publicly demonstrate their allegiance to the cause of the family of the Prophet.

The second function of the *majlis* is that of education. Because the chronological center and longest portion of the *majlis* is a discourse which is usually didactic and on a religious topic, at least once a year—and in many cases once a week—Shi'a are exposed to what are quite often highly developed religious discourses. Thus, the structure of the *majlis* allows not only for the evocation of grief, with all the aforementioned soteriological implications, but also through the discourse the *majlis* helps educate the community on religious matters, thus performing an important function in helping the Shi'i community preserve its identity as well as its intellectual superiority at the level of mass belief. The *zakir*'s function here is not simply to make his community better informed but also to supply it with the knowledge needed to defend itself from the intellectual assault of the Sunni community. The *zakir* attempts to use the *majlis* both directly—to any Sunnis who may be listening—and indirectly—through arming the Shi'a with arguments for use in debate—to convince the Sunni audience that the true interpretation of Islam is found in the Shi'i school.

Thus, the *majlis* is the ritual which plays the primary role in preserving the identity of the Shi'i community. For the most part, even my Sunni informants agreed that the average lay Shi'a is more highly educated than his Sunni counterpart in matters of religion. The single greatest reason for this may be the *majlis*. Even Shi'a who are not particularly pious in their daily practice will attend *majlis* for Husayn during the month of Muharram. Many will attend *majlis* on other days as well, and it is not unusual for many people to attend *majlis* at one or another of the *imambargahs* in Karachi every Thursday night.

Controversial Elements of the *Majlis*: The *Zakir* as Performer versus the *Zakir* as Scholar

The crucial importance of the *zakir* in Shi'i piety can be seen from the importance of the *majlis* itself. It is the *zakir* who sits at the center of this ritual. It is he who, seated upon the *minbar*, evocatively recreates the atmosphere of Karbala, which occupies such a central position in Shi'i piety. The *zakir* performs several interrelated functions. Some are primarily intellectual while others are more emotional. Some aspects of the *majlis*, particularly the soteriological ones, are addressed almost solely to the Shi'i members of the audience. These tend to be linked to the recitation of metahistorical narratives and thus to the evocation of the experience of the reality of Islam as a personal allegiance.

But certain dimensions of the expository portions of the *majlis* are meant both for the Shi'a and the larger Islamic audience. Because of the dual soteriological and educational nature of his performance, the *zakir* ideally must be both a learned religious scholar and a skilled showman able to create moods and evoke emotions. Although scholarship and a knowledge of the traditional sources upon which a *majlis* is based are important elements in the *majlis* performance, the presentation of a *majlis* is in no way a dry rendering of textual sources. The *zakir* is a performer. He presents his case emotionally and poetically in an atmosphere already highly charged with emotion.

The ability of the *zakir* to accomplish the expository end of his presentation is linked intimately to the soteriological dimension of the *majlis*. The tension between these two purposes of the *majlis* may not, in the final analysis, be as great as some members of the community understand it to be. In fact, the two purposes are intimately connected and help reinforce each other. At the most mundane level it can be noted that, if nothing else, the soteriological dimension of *majlis* helps to get people into the *imambargahs* so that they can hear the *majlis* in the first place. This is something that *zakirs* themselves know very well.[41]

A cogent discussion of this problem can be found in an article in the *Sarfaraz Weekly, Lucknow*, in which 'Ali Naqi answers criticisms from a reader concerning the state of *majlis* performance. The question from one Sayyid Sarfaraz Hussain had to do with the purpose of the *majlis*. Hussain argues that the real purpose of the *majlis* is education, particularly education about Islamic history. But, he writes, many *zakirs* ignore history and present a version of events at Karbala that is traditionally popular but historically inaccurate. He suggests that mourning *majlis* should be renamed "historical *majlis*" and treated primarily as lectures on history. In this way the real intention of the *majlis* will be preserved. 'Ali Naqi responded by arguing that, while it is important that *majalis* remain a source of historical information, they must continue to be *'azadari majlis* because it is *'azadari* which brings the people into the *imambargah* in the first place. Were it not for the *matam* and its promise of salvation, the educational

function of the *majlis* could not take place. People would not attend a *majlis* for history in the same numbers as they would a
mourning *majlis*.[42]

The quality of *zakirs* and the content of their *majalis* is a point
of intense discussion within the Shiʻi community of Karachi. Although there are highly educated and dedicated *zakirs*, there is
disagreement as to which *zakirs* are most fully qualified, and
some of the *majlis* readers are the object of scorn and derision by
segments of the community.

The controversy centers around the dual nature of the *majlis*,
discussed above. Is the primary function of the *majlis* educational or soteriological? Many Shiʻa feel that the accuracy of the
historical information in the *majlis* must be maintained at all
costs. Others feel that a little distortion of the facts is acceptable
as long as it facilitates a sense of passionate grief in the hearts
and minds of the listeners to the *majlis*.

A good example of this controversy relates to the commemoration on the eighth day of Muharram of the marriage of Qasim.
This is one of the most popular of all of the stories associated
with Muharram. It is particularly popular with women and is
the focus of the fire *matam* rituals that occur on this night,
known as Qasim's night. Qasim, Husayn's nephew and the son
of Imam Hasan, was to be wedded to one of Husayn's daughters
when they reached Kufa, but realizing that they would never
reach their destination, Husayn performed the wedding at the
battlefield of Karbala, and Qasim's bride was widowed on her
wedding night. This great tragedy is recited in most series of *majalis*. However, on the basis of the historical sources it is now believed by many knowledgeable Shiʻa that this event never took
place, or, if it did, it took place in a manner different from the
way it is usually presented in the *majlis*. Thus, the question
arises as to whether it is permissible for the *zakir* to include such
stories as this in the *majlis*, given their popularity and the fact
that they have been traditionally told in the region. Many Shiʻa,
particularly young, revitalized Muslims, feel that historical distortion is not to be allowed and refuse to patronize those *zakirs*
who play fast and loose with the historical facts in order to elicit
grief.

This dilemma is crucial to understanding the Shiʻi attitude toward the *zakirs*, which is ambiguous. At one *majlis* a young medical student from the Northwest Frontier Province told me that
in his opinion the primary function of the *majlis* was and is one
of political agitation. He noted, however, that for many people
the function of the *majlis* is solely to instill tears in the hearts of

the listeners, and thus many *zakirs* feel obligated to give the people what they want. He related to me an interesting anecdote. Noting the addiction of many Pathans to chewing tobacco, he told me of a poor *zakir* who had come to a village in the Frontier Province to read *majlis*. Try as he might, however, he could not induce his audience to cry during the *gham* portion of the *majlis*. At Karbala, he said, "Husayn and his companions were without food." But no one responded. Despite his description of the towering thirst of the Imam and his family, still not a tear was to be seen. The *zakir* was desperate. He had not reached his audience and could not figure out what to do. Then it dawned on him: People can only cry for things they can relate to. Thus, he said, "At Karbala, the Imam, may peace be upon him, had no chewing tobacco for three days." At this the crowd in the *imambargah* broke into uncontrollable sobbing.

This tells us something of the attitude toward *zakirs* held in certain circles: they will do anything to evoke the mourning response in their audience. Some are especially cynical about this, noting that *zakirs* are dependent upon the crowds at the *imambargahs* for their livelihoods and that this economic dependency causes them to pander to the desires of their audiences, even to the point of ignoring the educational function of the *majlis*.

Whatever the merit of these criticisms, it must be recognized that the *majlis*, by its very nature and structure, places the *zakir* in the center of a highly charged ritual arena in which the audience's attention is drawn toward a reflection on those tragic and sorrowful events which are central to Shi'i piety. The *majlis* is the most important of all of the activities performed during Muharram. It allows for an emotional encounter in a public arena with the most powerful symbols of 'Alid loyalism in the form of striking narratives and it allows the Shi'i community to reaffirm the fundamental principle of Shi'i Islam, which is personal allegiance to the family of the Prophet. As the central performer and narrator in these rituals the *zakir* plays an important and multifaceted role in Shi'i piety. His craft and his role in Shi'i society merit attention from scholars interested in coming to grips with Islam as it is practiced in South Asia.

The Sequence of the Muharram *Majalis*

The various activities of Muharram follow a traditional chronology.[43] They begin with the sighting of the first crescent of the first quarter of the moon. In case the moon is inadvertently mis-

PUBLIC PERFORMANCES

107

sighted an extra *majlis* may be delivered. (This was the case at Mehfil-i Murtaza during the Muharram in question.) The sequence of didactic portions of the *majalis* is dictated first by the topic at hand and the thesis which the *zakir* is attempting to make. But the content of the *gham* portions of the performance is governed by a traditional chronology, which may differ from region to region. These may particularly vary on the first through the sixth days. But, beginning with the seventh *majlis*, the order becomes more fixed. *Matam* begins on the fifth day of Muharram but it remains at first very short and not very intense physically.[44]

The sixth day is focused on the death of 'Ali Akbar, the eighteen-year-old son of the Imam who died in combat at Karbala. Among other reasons, he is significant in the story because he is said to have appeared to be an almost exact likeness of the Prophet and thus his death is held up as extremely evocative of the horror of the situation. The seventh day is related to the death of Qasim. As mentioned above, this narrative is a great favorite in South Asia. Small processions with replicas of coffins or other *shabi* (symbols) are held in the *imambargahs* following the *gham* on these occasions.

The eighth night is dedicated to the death of Hazrat 'Abbas. 'Abbas is a central character in the drama. In much the same way as 'Ali is the model disciple of the Prophet, 'Abbas is the model disciple of Husayn. He was the standard-bearer at the battle of Karbala. While on a mission to obtain water for the children of the camp he was brutally cut down. Although his hands were chopped off he did not allow the banner to fall. The *'alams* (standards) of 'Abbas are the most ubiquitous of all the *shabi* of Muharram.

The ninth evening is dedicated to the martyrdom of the infant 'Ali Asghar. This is perhaps the most emotional of all of the stories told during the month of Muharram. 'Ali Asghar is the paradigm of innocent ones killed for no reason. According to the narrative, the Imam carried the child forward to the battle lines to ask for water for the thirsty child. The army of Ibn Ziyad was almost moved by this action but the evil Hurmula fired an arrow which killed the child. In this story the innocence of the child is contrasted with the moral depravity of wanton infanticide. The purposelessness of the action demonstrates that the rejection of Husayn is, in fact, a rejection of the moral guidance without which humanity sinks to the level of the bestial.

There is generally a good deal of physical *matam* on this evening and it is also the evening called *Shab-i Bedar* during which persons stay awake all evening in acts of public and private devotion. The final day is *'Ashura*, the tenth day of Muharram itself. The *gham* on this day, performed in the afternoon, is dedicated to Husayn himself. During the day the *a'mal* is performed and *niyaz* (a food offering) is presented and shared. The evening following the tenth is *Shām-i Gharībān* (the Night of the Unfortunate Ones). On this evening the Shi'a remember the survivors of the battle of Karbala, in particular Hazrat Zainab. This is the last of the important *majalis*, although there is generally another *majlis* on the eleventh day. There is also a *ziyarat* recited on the next day and another *majlis* recited on the fortieth day of *Chhellum*, but the real culmination is the *majlis* on *Sham-i Ghariban*.

Julus in Muharram

Majlis is the most important part of the *'azadari* performances, but the procession of mourning or *julus* is significant as well. It is the most public of all of the activities associated with devotion to the family of the Prophet. *Juluses* can be of many kinds. In the city of Karachi daylong processions span the length of the city on the ninth and tenth days of Muharram. Small processions also are observed and participated in by the members of local communities. Throughout the city numerous mourning societies of young men come together to prepare for participation in the major *juluses*. *Juluses* are generally dedicated to the memory of an historic event. For example, in Rizvia Society a *julus* commemorates the murder of Muslim b. Aqil, Husayn's emissary to Kufa. A long *julus* in the month of Ramadan commemorates the martyrdom of 'Ali.

Processions allow people to reveal publicly their allegiance in powerful visual ways. People carry symbols, banners, and other articles through the streets. In some of the local *juluses* these symbols are carried by young boys into the houses of women in *purdah* so that the women can have the experience of connection with these symbols. An important element of *juluses* is the images carried in these processions which represent the Prophet's family and Karbala. The most important of these symbols are:

> *'Alams.* *'Alams* are poles or staffs reminiscent of the standard of Husayn carried by his half-brother 'Abbas at the battle of Karbala. The story of 'Abbas is central to the Karbala myth. 'Abbas was the standard-bearer for the camp of Husayn. Appealed to by the thirsty cries of the children—in particular,

Husayn's young daughter Sakina—'Abbas set out for the River Euphrates, from which the troops of Ibn Ziyad had cut them off for a period of three days. He arrived at the river carrying the staff and a water flask, but on the way back to camp with water for the children, he was engaged in battle. The water flask was punctured and in the ensuing combat his hands were severed. Miraculously, he did not drop the standard. The *'alams* which are carried are normally topped with a metal representation of the five-fingered Fatimid hand, which represents both the severed hand of 'Abbas and the five members of the holy *panjatan pak*—Muhammad, 'Ali, Fatimah, Hasan, and Husayn. The *'alams* are often draped in cloth, which is sometimes dyed to simulate bloodstains. The *'alam* is the symbol of the authority of the Prophet's family. Carrying these symbols allows the Shi'i Muslims to reaffirm their allegiance to the Prophet.

Zuljinah. These are the horses marched in the processions which represent the mount of Imam Husayn. In general they are white and of first-class quality. They are raised solely for this purpose and never ridden or used as work animals. Often the rearing of *Zuljinah* is undertaken by a mourning society (*anjuman*). During the large *juluses* which take place on and around the day of 'Ashura, the *Zuljinahs* are costumed elaborately in saddles painted as if stained in blood, with arrows protruding from the saddles in ways which are often quite realistic. The riderless horse is, of course, a symbol of martyrdom, as Husayn's death was realized by the women of the camp when his mount returned to the tents.

Ta'ziyahs. Ta'ziyahs are unique to South Asian Muharram performances. In Iran the term *ta'ziyah* refers to passion plays about the sufferings of the family of Prophet—in particular, Imam Husayn at Karbala. In Pakistan and India the term *ta-'ziyah* refers to large symbolic replicas of the tomb of Imam Husayn at Karbala. They are often made of paper and wood and are often transitory, being used for one Muharram and then buried.

The building and carrying of *ta'ziyahs* is an ancient tradition in South Asia, but the exact origins of the custom are shrouded in legend. It is commonly believed that Timur was the first to bring replicas of the tomb of Imam Husayn into India. Many stories current in the popular religious literature of Shi'i Muslims depict Timur as a pious Shi'a. In some of these stories miraculous elements are brought into play to demonstrate the power of devotion to the *ahl al-bayt* in granting the forgiveness of even the most heinous sins. In one such tale a minister of Emperor Timur is brought to heaven and castigated for his rancor against Timur because, although the Mongol conqueror had murdered many men, he was now a true devotee of the *ahl al-bayt* and as such should receive praise instead of criticism.[45]

The story of Timur's bringing of *ta'ziyahs* to South Asia is reported in *Tazk-e Taimuri*, but, as 'Ali Naqi Naqvi has pointed out, the credibility of this source is in question.[46] The basic thrust of the story is that while in Iraq Timur converted to Shi-'ism and became so deeply and emotionally attached to the area around Karbala that he would not move his troops from that spot. In order to deal with this situation, the *'ulama* of the region built a replica of the tomb which he could take with him out of the dust and clay of that place. It is reported that nightly sounds of mourning and lamentation could be heard arising from the model. It was this *ta'ziyah* which was brought to India by Timur during his invasion.[47] While the story is interesting as a pious narrative, its historical truthfulness is questionable as Timur invaded India before his stopover in Karbala.[48] The more likely reason for the development of this object of devotion may simply be the distance of India and Pakistan from the holy places of Southwest Asia. Pilgrimage to the tombs of the Imams in Iraq and Iran was simply beyond the means of most of the Muslim population of South Asia. *Ta'ziyahs* allowed people to pay homage symbolically to the tomb of the Imam while they remained in their own localities.[49]

The strength of this argument can be seen from the re-creations of local Karbala complexes and the types of activities which occur at them throughout Pakistan and India. Mircea Eliade has noted the importance of the re-creations of sacred places for the purposes of ritual. Just as Karbala is a kind of axis mundi in the sacred universe of Shi'ism, these "Karbalas" allow for yearly pilgrimages to that center, if only symbolically. I am here referring to certain areas which are designated as "Karbalas" in cities and towns throughout the region. During Muharram, processions will end at these "Karbalas" where the *ta'ziyahs* are then buried in emotional ceremonies.

Ta'ziyahs are an important part of Muharram processions. They become identified with the geographical nexus which they represent and ultimately they become foci of spiritual devotion. They allow participants in performances of *'azadari* to enter into the events of Karbala and, as is the case with *majlis*, to subtly change the outcome of those events, in this case by giving to the Imam the respectful burial he was denied at Karbala. Once again this practice resonates with Eliade's understanding of ritual as the re-creation and reenactment of a primordial cosmic event.

Historically, *ta'ziyahs* have been either buried or immersed in the ocean as a way of disposing of them. Part of this has to do with the universal religious problem of the disposal of sacred materials after rituals. Immersion in water is a common method, as water is often seen as a purifying agent. Immersion in water is the approved method for disposing of a worn out Qur'an, for example. In Multan, in the southern Punjab, large paper and wood *ta'ziyahs* are buried in the graveyard adjacent to the tomb of the great Shi'a-Sufi Saint Yusuf Gardezi. I observed these activities on a trip to Pakistan in 1989 and was able to talk with some of the participants in them. They were anxious to make it known that the reason for the burial of the *ta'ziyah* was that the Imam did not receive a proper burial at Karbala and that thus it was proper that his followers give him one now.

In Karachi it is generally the case that *ta'ziyahs* are taken to the sea. The most ornate and well-made *ta'ziyahs* however, are not destroyed. Rather the replica of the coffin of the Imam is removed and carried into the water, where a symbolic funeral is performed. If the *ta'ziyahs* are of particularly good quality they may be given to poorer *imambargahs* which do not have the resources to stock their *Husayniyya* with expensive relics.

Ta'ziyah are of differing sizes and quality. Some are permanent relics made of wood or metal which are only taken out once a year for processions or perhaps are kept only in the *Husayniyya* for purposes of *ziyarat*. Some are built specifically for processions and are used only once. These are often made of paper and wood, but there is still a great deal of time and labor put into them. An interesting element to this whole discussion is that historically some of the great *ta'ziyah* builders have been Sunnis.

Tabūts. Tabuts are models of coffins carried in processions. Generally they represent the coffins of Husayn, but they may also represent the coffins of 'Ali Akbar or one of the other martyrs of Karbala. Usually they are draped in a white cloth which has been painted with splotches of red paint to simulate the blood of the martyrs. Sometimes symbols of the battle of Karbala are added to the *tabut*. Cardboard arrows, or a black turban, a symbol of the head of Husayn and the authority of the Prophet's family, may be attached to the sides of the coffin.

Of the large models carried in processions *tabuts* are probably the most common. As stated above, in smaller, localized processions they may be carried into the homes of women in *purdah* so that they may take part in revering these sacred objects. As with *ta'ziyahs*, which are seen as a part of a subjunctive exercise in which history is reenacted and subtly changed, *tabuts* represent the burial which Husayn was denied and allow his followers to affirm the commitment to bring justice to an event in which justice was denied.

Palna. Of all of the stories which occurred at the battle of Karbala perhaps the most striking and emotional is that of the martyrdom of the infant 'Ali Asghar. The death of this innocent demonstrates that the battle of Karbala was no mere political struggle but rather was a struggle between good and evil. The wanton murder of an infant is seen as an act of the kind of depravity which occurs when one turns against God and loses moral guidance. The cradles (*palna*) representative of 'Ali Asghar are common in these processions and are particularly popular with women.

These objects are carried in the *julus* and sometimes are prepared at great expense by the donor. *Juluses* are also occasions for *matam* with the hands, and on the day of *'Ashura* and the martyrdom of 'Ali they are sometimes the occasion for *zanjir ka matam*. Many persons simply march along chanting. Children may recite *marthiyah*. An atmosphere of egalitarianism is maintained as all who participate have come together for a common end—a demonstration of their allegiance to the Prophet of Islam and his family.

Ziyarat

The third form of devotion has already been mentioned in the context of the other two. *Ziyarat* takes many forms over the course of the Muharram period. Many people pay their respects to the *ahl al-bayt* at the *Husayniyya* of important *imambargahs*, where the *rowzah* (replicas of the tomb) may be of gold or silver, and which may include crowns and arks as well as the articles already mentioned. Furthermore, many people set up household *Husayniyyas* with objects that are kept in storage the rest of the year. Some people erect elaborate displays in their yards, which are then visited by others. These visitations are metaphors of visitation to the graves of the *ahl al-bayt*. Such visitation is an important part of Shi'i piety because of the fact that the Imams are living entities and thus it is seen as an actual visitation. The *ziyarat* recited at the end of the *majlis* likewise is a substitution for physical visitation. The religious purpose behind these rituals is to present oneself before the holy family and to offer obedience to them.

Conclusion

The rituals of *'azadari* are central to Shi'i piety. They allow participants to experience the root paradigms of their faith through a direct encounter with the powerful spiritual presences who manifest those paradigms in their lives—Imam Husayn and his family and followers. These rituals create a liminal reality in which the metahistorical reality of Karbala intersects and interpenetrates into the world of ordinary space and time. This re-creation of Karbala fulfills several functions: it allows for the forgiveness of sins, it reinforces group identity and solidarity, and it facilitates the education of the community. Most importantly it allows for the revitalization of the personal allegiance and devotion which is the core of Shi'ism. In the subjunctive reality of these rituals participants can explore the question: What if I had been with the Imam at Karbala? The following chapter will examine an actual cycle of Muharram performances to gain a clearer sense of how that process takes place.

Figure 1. *Zakir* on the *minbar* at an *imambargah* in Karachi.

Figure 2. *Ziyarat khanah* at Mehfil-i Murtaza.

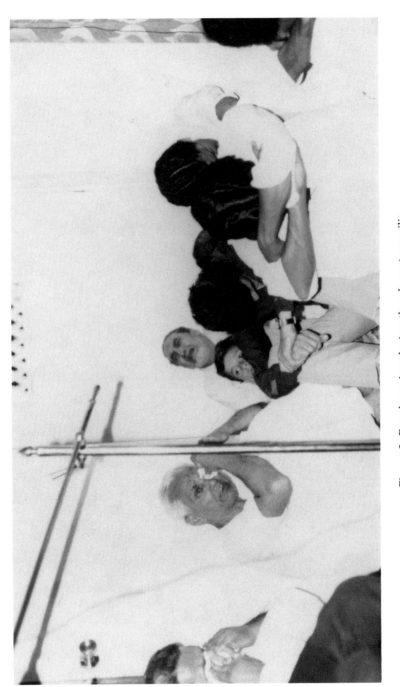

Figure 3. People crying during the *gham* at a majlis.

Figure 4. *Palna* of ʿAli Asghar being carried through an *imambargah* following a *majlis*.

Figure 5. *Taʿziyahs* made by the Husain Imami Tabut Committee Imambargah in downtown Karachi.

Figure 6. *Zuljinah*, the mount of Imam Husayn, prepared for Muharram procession.

Figure 7. *Matamdar* engaged in *zanjir ka matam*.

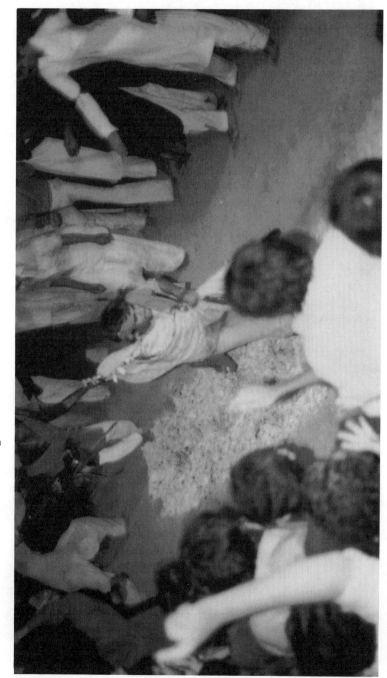

Figure 8. Fire *matam* in downtown Karachi.

CHAPTER FOUR

Muharram Performances
1404 A.H. (1983 C.E.)

The performances of Muharram are dramatic and follow in a processual sequence which builds towards a climax on the day of 'Ashura. The individual performances of *majlis*, *julus*, and *ziyarat* are parts of an overarching ritual which has its own momentum. This larger extended ritual mirrors the smaller rituals, and they in turn mirror it. Just as each of those internal rituals follows a pattern of process, building to an emotional climax and then falling off into a period of calm reflection, so does the entire ten-day period. It begins calmly and moves slowly but methodically toward the emotionally charged events of the ninth and tenth days. The processual nature of this period is best revealed by describing the activities in chronological order.

The following is a chronological description of some of the events as they unfolded during the ten days of 'Ashura in Karachi, 1404 A.H., which began on October 7, 1983 C.E. This description should help to place the individual performances of *majlis*, *ziyarat*, and *julus* in their proper contexts. While this type of description involves some repetition of arguments already raised, it is important for understanding the nature of Muharram performances to see how the symbols and rituals which underlie Shi'i piety are experienced by a Muslim community in a living context. The focus of the following exposition is the activities at Mehfil-i Murtaza, but occurrences in other parts of the city will also be included.

Over the course of the mourning period I interviewed a number of people whose understanding of the meaning of their participation in Muharram performances differed significantly. But one common thread running throughout all accounts was the way in which Muharram performances both intellectually and

emotionally reinforced the experience of Islam as a personal allegiance, which is the crucial element of Shiʻi piety. This unity of
experience facilitated the development of what is perhaps best
described by the term *communitas,* a term which Victor Turner
uses for the egalitarian relationships which predominate in the
state of liminality, for in this shared experience of the authority
of common symbols in the context of such emotional performances a sense of unity and equality was created, even in the
midst of the normal hierarchy of South Asian society.[1]

Muharram Begins: Evening of October 7, 1983

The sequence of Muharram performances at Mehfil-i Murtaza
began on the evening of October 7. (The Islamic calendar counts
its days from sunset rather than sunrise, in the manner of the
Jewish calendar.) Muharram begins with the sighting of the
moon, as do all of the months of the Islamic calendar. (This is
true for Sunni, Ismaʻili, and Twelver groups, but the Bohri Muslims have mathematically adjusted their calendar.) On the
twenty-ninth day of Zilhaj it was uncertain whether the moon
would be sighted. The *majlis* at Mehfil-i Murtaza was arranged
to take place whether or not it was. This is common practice.
The structure of this *majlis* was indicative of those that would
follow at this *imambargah,* although the crowds and the intensity
increased as the Muharram period continued. The *zakir* was a
young man from Sindh now living in Islamabad, who was gain-
ing quite a reputation. Although he was very bright and topical,
his training in Islamic matters was mainly self-taught. He read a
majlis on this evening, but it was not topically a part of the series
of *majalis* which were read during the rest of the week. The Mehfil-i Murtaza *majalis* were scheduled for 9:00 P.M., following *marthiyah* recitations, which began at 8:45 P.M. This allowed people
to come for evening prayers and proceed directly to the *imambargah* for the *majlis* immediately afterward. The reader of *majlis*
at Mehfil-i Murtaza, Hakim Syed Zaki Hyder Sahab, was reading *majalis* at several other locations throughout the city and was
often a bit late for the *majlis* over the course of the series of *majalis.* It was not uncommon for the timings of *majalis* throughout
the city to be staggered, so that one could attend several *majalis*
in one day. There were also daily women's *majalis* at Mehfil-i
Murtaza read by Dr. Shamim Rizvi Saheba. This began at 4:00
P.M. with *marthiyah* recitations, which were followed by the
hour-long *majalis* and thirty minutes of *matam* from 5:30 until

6:00 P.M. These *majalis* were held in the downstairs section, which was reserved for men during the evening *majlis*. Thus, the *imambargah* was a scene of constant activity during this period.

Before gathering for the *majlis*, many people would quietly converse with each other in the open area between the *masjid* and the *imambargah*, although there were signs discouraging people from loud conversations during prayers. The openness of the ritual was apparent from the willingness of people of many different perspectives to explain to me—as an outsider interested in Islam—the meanings of the rituals which I was observing. The dual purposes of education and soteriology were common topics in these conversations. One person told me during this first night that the major *maqsad* (intention) of *matam* was *tabligh* (the spreading and purification of religion). And yet he admitted that *thāwab* (the spiritual benefit) accumulated by engaging in *matam* was also important, although the greatest *thawab* is simply that which is gained by being a follower of Imam Husayn. This was a common theme over the period of the ten days.

When I arrived at 8:00 P.M., prayers were already in progress. People arrived sporadically to say their prayers. Some would go immediately from their prayers to the *imambargah*, others stopped to say a few words to friends or acquaintances. Families came as a group, but the women immediately went behind the curtains which led to the women's area upstairs directly over the men's section where they could watch the *majlis* on closed-circuit television. The *masjid* is located to one side of the *imambargah*. The *majlis* hall itself opens onto a large courtyard which is used to hold the overflow crowd on important holy days such as 'Id and 'Ashura. The *minbar* is located inside the *imambargah* against one wall, facing the *qiblah*. It consists of five or six wooden steps, covered in black cloth. Surrounding the *minbar* were four *'alams*, each draped in a different color—purple, green, blue, and white. Some told me that the different colors represented different members of the *ahl al-bayt*, but others said that the differences in color were merely aesthetic. In any event, over the course of the ten days the color and arrangement of the *'alams* varied. This change in decor was done by the women of the *mehfil* who, besides the nightly *majalis*, attended the daily ladies' *majalis* with women *zakirs*.

To the left of the *minbar* was a well-kept *Husayniyya* or *ziyarat khanah*. As Mehfil-i Murtaza is a reasonably affluent institution, the *Husayniyya* contains some stunning miniature *ta'ziyahs* called *rowzahs*, many crafted of precious metals. Many of these are models of existing tombs, while others are models of tombs for members of the *ahl al-bayt* for whom there are no tombs—such as Imam Ja'far as-Sadiq. There are also ornate crowns and *'alams*, both symbolic of the authority of the Prophet's family. Many of these *'alams* are topped with *panjatans* (Fatimid hands) of highly crafted metal and are draped in fine fabric. These objects are foci of reverential devotion which for some non-Shi'a appears as *shirk* or association of something that is other than God with God. The Shi'a counter that there is a difference between reverence and worship and showing respect to objects that are symbolic of the Prophet and his family is far from a sin, but rather is a sign of one's piety.

An important element of this process of *ziyarat* or visitation is the making of *mannat* or a spiritual vow. It was not uncommon to find small padlocks or pieces of red or green thread tied to the *ta'ziyahs* in the *ziyarat khanah*. These are tied to the relics as a part of a spiritual vow similar to those discussed in chapter two on *mu'jizat kahanis*. The declarer of the vow makes the *mannat* with the intention of returning after the request has been granted, at which time the lock or thread is removed. This activity is also performed at Sufi shrines and is further evidence of the connection between these two traditions.

The *ziyarat khanah* was simultaneously frequented by persons of both genders. I was told that although this did at times happen, men and women typically would visit the reliquary at different times.

The process of *majlis* actually got underway at 9:00 P.M. with the singing of *marthiyah*. The *marthiyah* was recited by a young boy seated on the floor to the side of the *minbar*. He recited into a microphone. In front of him was a small table bearing books and incense. As he recited *marthiyah* people began to flow in. At this time perhaps seventy-five persons were gathered. A group of traditionally dressed *madrasah* students sat near the front. On this date only a few were dressed in black, but the wearing of black became more common as the period of mourning progressed. While the *marthiyah* was being recited, people continued to pass through the *ziyarat khanah*, touching and kissing the objects in a pious manner before taking their seats. As in mosques, it is required to remove one's shoes, and shoes and sandals were stacked outside the entrance to the *majlis* hall.

There was a good mix of ages, but very few young children. Most of them were upstairs in the women's section, which I was told was slightly larger so as to contain the extra persons. Unlike many of the other *majalis*, only one *marthiyah* was recited. The *zakir* sat on the *minbar,* itself a symbol of prophetic authority, but not on the top step, which is traditionally reserved for the hidden Imam Mahdi. He recited *Surah Fatihah* and the formulaic *khutba* associated with *majlis.* By the time the *majlis* actually began there were about three hundred people in the hall. The *majlis* lasted about forty-five minutes and the *gham* was not followed by *matam.* The *majlis* was well received and people were informed at the end that a series of *majalis* on the topic of *Madarij-i Bandagī* (the stations of service to God) would begin the next evening.

The closing scenes of this *majlis* raise one of the most curious questions about mourning rituals. Although this was a time of mourning, there was an atmosphere of anticipation and almost excitement in the air. The *zakir* was a man of some reputation and people were clearly pleased with his preliminary *majlis* and showed a sense of aesthetic appreciation. Clearly there were elements of celebration even in these rituals of mourning. This apparent contradiction—that a ritual in some of its dimensions can be celebratory while remaining at its heart tragic—continued over the course of the days of Muharram.

The patterns for the rest of period of Muharram performances followed along the lines of these events. Things became more intense as the days progressed, but the structure of the rituals remained the same. From this day forward the visual environment of Shi'i neighborhoods began to change. Black banners bearing Shi'i slogans were stretched across intersections in the Shi'i neighborhoods. Special stalls called *sabīls* for the distribution of water, draped in black and staffed by young children, became commonplace. In Rizvia Society a shop opened up for the dyeing of cloth black. As the week progressed more and more people began to wear black. The auditory environment shifted as well. The sound of *marthiyah* and *majlis* filtered through the streets at different times of the day. All of this continued to increase in intensity as 'Ashura day approached.

1 Muharram/October 8

The next morning was the first day of Muharram. On this day I attended the first in a series of *majalis* of a somewhat different nature. This was a series of *majalis* by 'Ali Naqi Naqvi, known as Naqqan Sahab. He is quite famous throughout South Asia, and his *majalis* are very popular. His *majlis* was being held in a small *imambargah* in the courtyard of a private residence. This place—

called Masjid-i Shah-i Shahidan—was located in a pleasant garden about one block away from the important complex of
Mehfil-i Shah Khurasan. The tone of these *majalis* was highly
emotional right from the beginning. (The Khojas, who are the
dominant ethnic group at Mehfil-i Murtaza, are somewhat sub-
dued in their *matam*, but the *muhajir* groups who tend to frequent Naqqan Sahab's *majalis* are much more vociferous.) As is
the custom in Lucknow, Naqqan Sahab read only nine *majalis* at
this residence this year, the last being read on the morning before *'Ashura*—although he read *majalis* at different private
households throughout the city. Naqqan Sahab was an elderly
man and his health was apparently not good, but he was still an
energetic *zakir*, popular both for his skill as a performer and his
great learning. Following the *majlis*, tea was served and there
was conversation between Naqqan Sahab and his audience,
who were anxious to ask him questions.

The actual first day of Muharram at Mehfil-i Murtaza was not
visibly much different than that at the earlier day's proceedings.
There were more *marthiyahs* preceding the *majlis*. Some were
sung in groups and with harmony. The arrangement of the
'alams around the *minbar* remained the same as on the previous
evening and the crowd was larger. Of particular interest was the
visible presence of television cameras both to broadcast the
majlis into the women's section upstairs and to make videotapes
of the *majlis* for later viewing. The presence of video technology
is revolutionizing *majalis*. Great *zakirs* can now reach a large audience both visually as well as aurally. Not only can they be seen
once a year, but their performances can also be recorded and
used for educational purposes. The combined use of video and
audio cassette tape is bringing about a profound interest in religious activities among the youth of the Shi'i community.

2 Muharram/October 9

The next morning Naqqan Sahab delivered another *majlis* at
Masjid-i Shah-i Shahidan. As on the previous day, the scene
was more emotional than at Mehfil-i Murtaza. People were already crying during the recitation of *sozkhawani*, a special kind of
marthiyah. It is important to keep in mind the *thawab* or spiritual
benefit which accrues to a person from mourning for Husayn.
The evocation of grief and its manifestation in acts of *matam* are
central elements in these activities because of their soteriological
importance. When I arrived at 8:30 A.M. two young men were

singing *marthiyah*. At 8:45 the *sozkhawani* was still continuing. These continued until about 9:00 A.M., when Naqqan Sahab appeared amidst shouts of "*Salavat.*" Everyone rose as he passed by. A few touched his hands. Shouts of "*Nade Haidari*" and "*Salavat*" rose up in various parts of the crowd as he moved toward the *minbar*. Seated upon it, he recited the *khutba* and proceeded into his *majlis*.

The topic of his *majalis* was the concept of '*ismat*. '*Ismat* refers to the quality of the prophets and Imams by which they are protected from error or great sin. It is a crucial concept in Shi'i thought because the authority of the Prophet and the Imams derives from the fact that they possess '*ismat* and are thus *ma'sum*. Throughout the *majlis* Naqqan Sahab's skill as a performer was evident. In making his points 'Ali Naqi seemed to direct the crowd. He used poetry and repetition to reinforce his points. For example, he extracted a powerful response from his audience by the simple and powerful reiteration of the fact that the Prophet was not made pure so that he could become the Prophet, but rather he was the Prophet because he was *ma'sum*. This kind of discussion presents the crucial arguments which define the differences between the beliefs of the Shi'a and the beliefs of the Sunni majority. First, it emphasizes the element of personal allegiance. The primary allegiance is not merely to the message of the Prophet but to the Prophet himself, and that allegiance is due to his being *ma'sum*, a characteristic which he shares with the Imams. Furthermore, the station of the Prophet is inherent. The Prophet (*rasul*) is inherently and metaphysically the *rasul*. It is not something given to him from outside. The *majlis* ended with a *gham* which was quite emotional, but as of yet there was still no physical *matam*.

I arrived at 8:15 P.M. for the second in the series of Muharram *majalis* at Mehfil-i Murtaza. At that time very few people were about. On this evening I gave particular attention to the persons who were coming to pay their respects at the *ziyarat khanah*. I was once again struck by the similarities between Sufi shrines and Shi'i *ziyarat khanahs*. Each in their own way are places of visitation and pilgrimage although, whereas the Sufi shrine is actually a tomb of a sacred person, the *ziyarat khanah* is a place holding replicas of tombs. As stated above, there are in the *ziyarat khanah* locks and thread representing the making of spiritual vows, just as locks and thread are used at the important Sufi shrines in the subcontinent. The presence of sacred objects cloaks the place in an aura of sacrality and thus reinforces the possibility of the miraculous. The '*alams* and *rowzahs* are in some sense physical projections from a spiritual realm pointing to realities that exist in the metahistorical realm of symbols. *Ziyarat khanahs* are thus occasionally sites of apparent miracles.

I was told on this night—although I was unable to verify it—that in the Imamia Imambargah in Golimar mysterious voices can be heard arising out of the *imambargah* at night. This story mirrors the story of Timur hearing mourning voices arising out of his *ta'ziyah* made of the earth of Karbala. Belief in such occurrences is clearly within the bounds of the Shi'i worldview, which emphasizes the coexistence of beings possessed of spiritual power in the universe. Such miracles are often associated with the temporal appearance of Muharram. For example, I know of a family which has in its possession a *tasbih* (rosary) made from clay from Karbala which supposedly turns blood red every *'Ashura* at the time of the death of the Imam. I have seen a videotape of such a *tasbih* which is brought out in public in Multan every year as evidence of the power of the Imam. These types of occurrences are seen as proof of the authority of the Imams and of the necessity of allegiance to them.

The *majlis* began relatively on time at approximately 9:00 P.M. Once again I was aware of the fact that the persons in the Khoja *masjid* were much less vociferous in their reaction to the *majlis* than the audience at Mehfil-i Shah Khurasan or at Masjid-i Shad-i Shahidan—a fact which I do not see as any sign of lesser piety but more likely a fact of temperament, owing to class and historical background.

3 Muharram/October 10

This difference in temperament was clearly evident the next morning when I arrived slightly late at Masjid-i Shah-i Shahidan and found the crowds for Naqqan Sahab's *majalis* growing larger and larger. It was difficult to find a place to sit, and the crowd was vocal and emotional. As was also the case at Mehfil-i Murtaza, there were more and more people reading *marthiyah* and *sozkhawani* at the beginning of each *majlis* and the *gham* was becoming more and more intense.

That evening I attended two *majalis*. The first was in an urban courtyard in Kharadhar called Bāgh-i Zehra, which is best described as a vacant lot in the center of the old part of the city surrounded by old buildings. Kharadhar has a large population of indigenous and lower-class Khojas, as opposed to the African middle- and upper-class immigrant Khojas of Mehfil-i Murtaza.

The *zakir* who was reading *majlis* was very popular with that group of persons within the Khoja Shi'i community, who are usually classified as "fundamentalist." Muslim revivalist movements within Shi'i Islam place a great emphasis on *taqlīd* to *mujtahids*. The successful revolution in Iran has greatly enhanced the attitude toward the *'ulama* among certain groups within the South Asian Shi'i Muslim community. The Khoja community has been particularly attracted by this movement which understands Islam in terms of allegiance to the *'ulama*, who are seen as the best examples of religious practice in the absence of the Imam. The concept of *taqlid* is an almost universally accepted concept in the Shi'i world. But in South Asia, for a number of reasons, the role of the *'ulama* is for many people limited to questions of ritual behavior—for instance, how to pray, how to fast, and how to perform the pilgrimage to Mecca. For many persons the *'ulama* are only to be consulted on those matters and are generally ignored on other issues, such as politics or other aspects of Shari'ah law.

Revivalists of both the Sunni and Shi'i schools have shared a common belief that Islam is a perfect and complete way of life. By this they assume that the Shari'ah can and should inform *in a specific way* every action of a person's life—how to eat, what to wear, or how to conduct business. The element within the Shi'i community—I refer here to the majority school of *ūsūlī* Shi'i jurisprudence which accepts *ijtihād* (analytical reasoning) as a source of law—who emphasize *taqlid* have stressed that it is possible for the *'ulama* to enlarge the Shari'ah to include almost all possible activities of the modern world. They argue—quite reasonably—that most people do not have time nor skill to devote to the intensive study of the religious source literature necessary to decide for themselves what is or is not proper Islamic behavior. Thus, it is incumbent upon each Muslim to choose a learned Islamic scholar (*mujtahid*) to follow in all questions of Islamic law.

This argument is taken in its fullest sense by a sizable proportion of the Khoja community for two reasons. One is historical. The Khojas were originally Isma'ili until the turn of the century. They consciously chose to become Twelvers and depended upon the *'ulama* to help them to create a religious identity. These *'ulama* were from India and were Urdu speakers. This is unlike the case within many other groups of Twelvers in the South Asian milieu who have been comfortably defined as Shi'a in a cultural sense for generations and thus feel no need to make an intensive Shari'ah-mindedness a part of their very identity as

Muslims. This is not to argue that South Asian Muslims are impious with regard to the Shariʿah but that the role of the ʿulama among most South Asian Muslims is more limited than among Muslims in some other regions. Even within South Asia, this is not true for all ethnic groups. The Baltis in Gilgit are, for example, very conscious of taqlid. The second reason has to do with the Khoja community's vision of itself as a mercantile community. Members of the community told me that as business persons they did not have the time for intensive explorations into religion. Thus, strict taqlid allows them to discharge their religious duties with a minimum of inconvenience.

This type of Islam is quite popular with many young people. I interviewed a young woman who had taken on modest dress and a degree of purdah as a political action, even though her family had never before practiced purdah. For her, Islam was first of all a personal allegiance to the Prophet and his designated authorities. Islam was the only real spiritual path in the world today. The appearance of the Prophet, for example, rendered Christianity no longer viable. The way to demonstrate this allegiance was by the proper performance of Shariʿah, and the crucial element of this was giving taqlid to a mujtahid.

Likewise, the person who took me to this majlis shared this position and was quite explicit about his views. For him, Islam was essentially Shariʿah. It was the Shariʿah for which Husayn had given his life at Karbala, and thus it was the duty of all good Muslims to obey the Shariʿah in all of its particulars. In his opinion it was only in Iran, where the rule of the jurists had taken place, that real Islam was being practiced. This position is one which is a topic of intense discussion throughout the Shiʿi community, particularly since the Iranian Revolution, which for many young Shiʿi Muslims has offered a new sense of pride in Islamic culture and an alternative to embracing Western values.

The zakir reading the majlis was extremely popular. He was considered to be quite pious, and I was told that he would not shake my hand as I was not a Muslim and thus not pak (ritually pure) and therefore I would pollute him. This was the only time that I was told this during the entire period of my research, and apparently there is no agreement on whether this type of behavior is proper adab. The adherence to Shariʿah inherent in this zakir's majlis was evident from the fact that the majlis was interrupted for prayer after the evening azān (call to prayer) was broadcast during the majlis. The nature of the sermon part of the majlis concerned themes of justice in the Shariʿah. For example, the zakir told the story of a woman who had committed adultery and wished to be executed for her sin, but 'Ali would not punish her until she had first delivered and raised the child she was carrying as a result of her illegitimate union. Ultimately, according to the *zakir*, he carried out the execution. In this worldview there is absolute justice. If the woman had not been punished in this life, than she would be punished in the next.

Despite the severity of the message, this *majlis* was well received. I asked the person with whom I attended the *majlis* what the benefit was of crying at the end of the *majlis*. He replied that crying cleanses the brain and makes it easier to see the right path. I proceeded from Bagh-i Zehra to Mehfil-i Murtaza, where the pattern of the *majlis* was much the same as on the previous night. That evening there was a large commotion in the alley behind my house. Three very loud men had been hired by the Shi'i family which owned the house in which I was staying to make *halīm* (a kind of food especially made for Muharram) to distribute to the neighborhood. This distribution of food was customary with this family every year. The distribution of food and water is an essential part of Muharram observances. It allows the believers to alleviate the hunger and thirst of the oppressed as recompense for the fact that those who are seen as the ultimate expression of oppressed peoples were allowed to die while hungry and thirsty. Thus, they take part in actions which occur both in this realm and in the metahistorical realm of symbols. As stated earlier, *sabils* for the distribution of water spring up throughout Shi'i neighborhoods. They are generally staffed by children who dispense ladles of water to passersby in obvious symbolic reference to the thirst of the martyrs of Karbala. The Sunnis also build *sabils* but theirs tend to be gaily and colorfully decorated, in contrast to the simple, black draped ones of the Shi'a, a fact which often creates friction between the two communities.

4 Muharram/October 11

From the fourth day of Muharram things began to become much more intense throughout the city. The crowds at the various *imambargahs* and *majalis* became larger and more emotional. At Masjid-i Shah-i Shahidan, for example, the crowds began to flood out into the street, where the *majlis* was being broadcast on closed-circuit television to the people who could not get seats inside.

I spent the early part of the evening of the fourth day in the area surrounding Mehfil-i Shah Khurasan. Mehfil-i Shah Khurasan is a major place for the congregation of Shi'i Muslims during this period. Its importance as an *imambargah* and as a *ziyarat khanah* containing the *zarihs* of the *ahl al-bayt* has already been underscored. It is also located nearby to Nishtar Park (formerly Patel Park), the place from which the major *juluses* begin and the site itself of large and important outdoor *majalis*.

From the beginning of the mourning period the area around Mehfil-i Shah Khurasan became an arena for various kinds of religious activity. *Bazari* tables were set up for the sale of religious paraphernalia. Some tables had for sale *panjatans*, the five-fingered hands representing Muhammad, 'Ali, Fatimah, Hasan, and Husayn, and other objects for use in home devotional activities. Votive candles and incense for use in the *imambargah* could be purchased. Bumper stickers bearing such phrases in English and Urdu as "Live like Ali, die like Husayn" could also be purchased. There were also bookstalls selling various kinds of Islamic literature—Qur'ans and *tafsīrs*.

Although it was a time of mourning there was an almost carnival atmosphere to the place—a feeling perhaps best described by the aforementioned term made popular by Victor Turner, *communitas*. Turner used this term to refer to the kinds of relationships which exist between people during liminal periods, such as times of public rituals. During public rituals people in a sense exist both in and out of time. They exist partially in the realm of structured hierarchical relationships and partially in the transcendent realm of metahistorical events. Participants in these rituals experience a "generalized social bond that has ceased to be and has simultaneously yet to be fragmented into a multiplicity of structural ties." They have come together under a single higher ritual authority, and thus there is a weakening of the day-to-day system of hierarchy which separates people into "terms of more and less." Turner notes that during a liminal period society is either unstructured or rudimentarily structured and the community is relatively undifferentiated. It consists of equal individuals who submit together to the general authority of "the ritual elders."[2]

This aptly describes the nature of human bonds during Muharram. The experience of an intense human bonding as followers of the Imams—ritual elders whose existence is not so much spatial and temporal as symbolic—tends at times during this protracted period of ritual activity to eradicate differences of class and education and even of ritual piety. The soteriological dimension of the ritual implies the afterworld and the utopian social order associated with that realm. The rituals of Muharram share much in common with pilgrimage, and, in fact, some of the rituals are metaphoric pilgrimages. Pilgrims leave behind much of their structural identity and become simply pilgrims—a new and more rudimentary social role. During pilgrimage even those on the way to the tombs of martyrs share in the heady pleasure of *communitas*. Similarly, all of the participants in Muharram rituals are followers of the Imam, and all are comrades in arms, as it were, and all share in the ultimate victory of the martyrs. Thus, there is a sense of celebration underlying the sense of tragedy.

This sense of *communitas* was evidenced by the fact that people in the area around the *imambargah* were eager to discuss Islam with me and to accept me as a sincere person, even though I was not a Muslim in any technical sense of the word. For example, while there I encountered the gardener (*mali*) from the house of a Pakistani acquaintance. When I met with the *mali* near the *imambargah* he did not exhibit any behavior that showed that he felt the difference in social class between us or even the typical attitude toward foreigners that often affects conversations between them and Pakistanis. Some of his friends who had seen me earlier at Naqqan Sahab's *majlis* greeted me with "Ya 'Ali Madad" and bade me to offer the correct response, which is "Mawla 'Ali Madad."

One of these young men told me a fascinating account of his recent life history. He had been a Memon. According to some sources the Memon were originally Shi'a. Like the Khojas, they speak a dialect of Gujarati and share many culture traits with Bohris and Khojas. But, they at some point converted to Sunnism and are now strongly anti-Shi'a in their position.[3] Many are devotees of the Sufi saint Ghaus al-Azam Abdul Qadir Gilani, who is quite unpopular in the Shi'i community because of his attitude against Muharram performances. The young man told me that he had attempted to leave his religious community, and because of this his life had been threatened. He sought help from a number of sources, all to no avail, until he called upon Imam 'Ali for help and was granted it. Since that time he had been a Shi'a. The attitude of this person and his companions toward the Imams was interesting and striking. Although 'Ali and Muhammad are from the same light, it is 'Ali whom one should call upon in times of distress because 'Ali is Muhammad's lieutenant. Even if one calls upon the Prophet, he will delegate the task to the Imam rather than perform the miracle himself.

They also told me that many Sindhis believe that the real *Na'ib-i Imām* is the famous Sufi saint Lal Shahbaz Qalandar, whose tomb in Sehwan is an important site of pilgrimage for Shi'a and Sunni alike. This belief is further evidence of the connection between the Sufi and Shi'i traditions. When I asked about this connection they told me they were acquaintances with another young man from New Zealand who had come to Pakistan and had become a Shi'i *faqir*. I had met this man earlier that year at the *julus* of *Yaum-i Shahādat-i 'Ali*, the day of 'Ali's martyrdom, which occurs during the month of Ramadan. At that time he had told me that his *murshid* (Sufi master) was the *panjatan pak*. The importance of the authority of the *ahl al-bayt* in Sufism is a question which demands further research.

When I asked whether *qalandārs* (Muslim holy men) or *mujtahids* were higher in the Shi'i hierarchy, they told me that they were connected and that Lal Shahbaz Qalandar was helping Ayatullah Khomeini, who is a descendant of Husayn, to defeat Saddam Husayn, who is a descendant of Mu'awiyah and Yazid.[4] Before they left they told me that I should always say "'*Ali ke Dushman par La'nat*" ("Curses on the enemies of Ali") and that, although my name was Vernon, I should call myself "'Ali 'Ali."

I do not contend that these young men's beliefs are representative of Islam as understood by the *'ulama* or even a majority of Shi'i Muslims. But their beliefs do represent an important component of popular piety in the Shi'i community.

During our conversation I attempted to make it clear that I was not a Muslim. Their response was most telling. Since I obviously showed respect for the Prophet and for the Imams, this, they said, was sufficient. Besides, they said, it was Muslims (at least nominal Muslims) who killed Husayn. I encountered this attitude on more than one occasion. Once I was told that the fact that I wore black clothing during Muharram and showed respectful behavior at the *majalis* was evidence that I was in reality a Muslim, whether I knew it or not. This attitude stands in great contrast to the one I encountered at Bagh-i Zehra, and it indicates another pole of thought in the Shi'i community. For many who emphasize *taqlid*, the practice of Shari'ah is the essential part of one's Islam and is what defines a person as a Muslim. For other Shi'a, it is one's emotional attachment to the *ahl al-bayt* which is the crucial thing. Between these two poles lie an entire spectrum of attitudes.

I went from Mehfil-i Shah Khurasan to Mehfil-i Murtaza, where the *majlis* exhibited no difference in structure from the previous ones. However, from this day forward *matam* was performed at the end of the *gham*. *Matam* is the physical act of mourning. *Matam* can be seen as an extension of the *gham*, but it is more than simply that. During the next three days *matam* was solely done with the hands (*hath ka matam*)—the rhythmic beating of the hands on the chest. Although different ethnic groups have different ways of performing this *matam*, it is usually done with alternating hard striking of the hand against the chest. Often it is done to the refrain of special poetry about Husayn interspersed with fervent chants of "Ya Husain" or "Ya 'Abbas." *Matam* is in one sense a conscious manifestation of grief, but on another level it is a kind of *zikr*. One evening while I was conversing with a Shi'i friend in Mehfil-i Murtaza, we were asked to stop the conversation because it was possibly interrupting the concentration of those engaged in *matam*. In some places *matam* is done while moving in a circle, in others with the mourners standing in lines. On this first night the *matam* was kept short, and the end of the *matam* was signaled by the recitation of the *ziyarat* as usual.

5 Muharram/October 12

The next day at Masjid Shah-i Shahidan, 'Ali Naqi delivered the first *majlis* in which *julus* was held as a part of the *matam*. The *gham* concerned young 'Ali Akbar, and it had a devastating effect on the audience. Naqqan Sahab directed the audience into an emotional state. Suddenly, from behind the *minbar*, an *'alam* wrapped in a *chador*, which had been dyed to appear bloodstained was carried out into the crowd. Behind it was a small replica of a cradle. Everyone cried. The interjection of visual symbols into the already charged atmosphere of the *gham* is one of the most dramatically powerful elements of the *majalis*. It reaffirms all that has already been experienced in an auditory manner and in the imagination and is a penetration of the symbolic reality of Karbala into the present moment.

It is interesting to note that many of the same people attended different *majalis* throughout the city. The various *imambargahs* carried announcements for other mourning activities in other locales. The *imambargahs* were scenes of increased activity for the remainder of the ten days, as people attended as many *majalis* as possible and followed by word of mouth as to which *zakirs* were giving the best *majalis*.

In the early part of the evening I attended the *majlis* at Nishtar Park. In past years this had been one of the most important places for *majalis*, but with the death of the late Rashid Turabi attendance at this *majlis* had fallen off. Many people were wandering about and *bazari* tables had been set up. During the *majlis* I spoke with a young medical student from Peshawar whose views on 'azadari were quite different from those of the young men I had spoken with the night before. The person was a revitalized Muslim committed to accepting the authority of the 'ulama. He felt that the relationship of Sufism to Shi'ism was questionable. In particular, he balked at suggestions that perhaps Lal Shahbaz Qalandar Sahab was the *Na'ib-i Imam*. Perhaps, he said, such Sufis once served a purpose when they were all that there was to give guidance. As he put it, in the kingdom of the blind the one-eyed man is king. But now we have the 'ulama and they are better guides. He said that as a young man he didn't understand the *majlis*, but he recently lost his father, and now he understood something of suffering. He said that by comparing his sufferings to those of Husayn his were lightened. And yet for him the primary purpose of the *majalis* was political agitation—to raise the consciousness of the people so that they might challenge unjust authority.

Later in that evening of the fifth day I attended the *majlis* once more at Mehfil-i Murtaza. Things were much less intense here than at Mehfil-i Shah Khurasan. The *gham* on this night concerned 'Abdullah the son of Muslim b. Aqil, but no *nishan* (physical symbols) were carried through the crowd afterward.

6 Muharram/October 13

On the sixth day of Muharram there was an increase of emotional intensity throughout the city. Arriving late at Masjid-i Shah-i Shahidan, it was impossible for me to get anywhere near the *minbar*. A large crowd was out in the street watching the proceedings on closed-circuit television.

That afternoon in Rizvia Society there was a *julus* in memory of the martyrdom of 'Ali Akbar. It was a large parade of people. There were 'alams in the front, many of them carried by children who considered it to be a great honor. There was a *tabut* and a *zuljinah*, which were carried and led into the homes of women in *purdah* so that they too could take part.

Later that afternoon I had a conversation with the Shi'i woman who managed the boarding house in which I lived. She told me that the *julus*—which others had told me was for 'Ali Akbar— was for 'Ali Asghar. She said that in some areas it was customary to commemorate 'Ali Akbar on the sixth day and 'Ali Asghar on the ninth, although in this vicinity it was reversed. She showed me an ornate home *imambargah* which she had set up in her living room. The objects in this display were kept in storage every year until Muharram. This was the site of a daily women's *majlis*. Her family had certain traditions, such as the aforementioned distribution of *halim* on the fourth day, although she said that traditionally it could be done at any time. Her family also distributed *kabobs* on the morning of the seventh day as a *niyaz-i tabarruk* (blessed offering).

That night the *gham* at Mehfil-i Murtaza concerned the wedding of Hazrat Qasim. The *majlis* was a striking affair which clearly demonstrated the importance of this narrative in South Asian Shi'i piety. Flowers were draped on the *'alams*. Some interesting *marthiyah* was being sung. One of the *marthiyah* singers had others singing behind him making a tambura-like drone. The *zakir* was late for the *majlis*. At one point an official of the *imambargah* appeared and asked the *marthiyah* singers to continue until the *zakir* was ready. He was also reciting *majlis* at Markaz-i Imambargah in Liaqatabad and appeared quite tired, but, as in secular performances, the delay helped to build up tension in the crowd. People were already beginning to cry even before the *majlis* had begun.

It should be noted that this *zakir* was quite good at knowing how to play to his crowd. For example, he made considerable use of references to business dealings as metaphors as a way of reaching this largely mercantile audience. I witnessed him speaking to a different kind of audience at Markaz-i Imambargah and he spoke in a slightly altered manner.

Following the *gham* there was *matam*. The *matam*, while still limited to *hath ka matam*, was extended to a full thirty minutes and was more intense than usual. The *matam* was mainly performed by young men. Before the *matam* itself, a decorated coffin was carried clockwise through the crowd. There was a frenetic rush to touch it. After it had passed through the room, it was then passed on to the women's section. Ultimately, it was left to rest in the *ziyarat khanah*.

I arrived back at Rizvia Imambargah in time to observe *matam* following the *majlis* there. There was a procession of young boys. In the front of the procession was a young boy carrying incense on a tray, then another carrying candles and a cradle — probably representing 'Ali Asghar — and then *'alams*. The procession traveled clockwise through the *imambargah* and then outside, past a group of women who had gathered there. The young boys in the procession wore shrouds on their shoulders dyed as if bloodstained.

7 Muharram/October 14

The next morning 'Ali Naqi presented his *majlis* on the topic of Qasim. The crowd was very large. The *sozkhawanis* were punctuated by shouts of *"Salavat"* and *"Nade Haidari."* The *majlis* itself was very long, almost two hours. At the end there was a procession through the crowd. As at Rizvia Imambargah the night before, there was first incense followed by candles. The people would put their hands into the flames as the candles passed by. This was followed by *'alams* and finally by bowls of fruit wrapped in green cloth being carried on trays on the heads of young boys. The scene was strikingly emotional and quite moving.

Later that day I sat in a roadside restaurant in Rizvia Society talking with some of the local young men about the things I was seeing. They answered some questions which I had about what happened to the food after the commemoration of Qasim's *mehndhi* (a portion of the marriage celebration in which henna is painted on the hands of the guests in the wedding party). They said it was distributed to the poor as *niyaz* for those who came for *ziyarat*. The question was raised as to whether Qasim's *mehndhi* should be commemorated at all. One of the young men said that he was in fact boycotting a particular *zakir* because of certain references of his to Qasim which the young man considered inaccurate.

When I arrived at Mehfil-i Murtaza for the evening *majlis* on this night which was dedicated to the memory of Hazrat 'Abbas, I noticed that there had been a visual change in the *'alam* on the rear of the *minbar*. This *'alam* was recognizable as Hazrat 'Abbas's because it was draped with a metal model of a water flask. It was now draped with a *chador* dyed to appear bloodstained. Prior to the *marthiyah*, it was carried off into the back of the room. Following the *gham*, the *'alam* was brought forth and was carried around the chamber and there was extended *matam*.

This *majlis* of the seventh day was given over to 'Abbas. This is important in the narrative of Karbala because on the seventh day the water was stopped and on the eighth day 'Abbas went to obtain water. The next day at Mehfil-i Murtaza was devoted to 'Ali Akbar.

Later than evening there was the annual fire walking ceremony at Kharadhar. This was a major event in the city which I
will discuss at some length in chapter five.

8 Muharram/October 15

During the day there was a *julus* for Hazrat 'Abbas. It began at
Nishtar Park and was silent. There was no *matam* with knives
and only a few *'alams*. It ended with a camel and a *sabil*.

That evening there was a large crowd for the *majlis* at Mehfil-i
Murtaza. Before the *majlis* I had several discussions with people
on the subjects of *zanjir* and *āg ka mātam* (fire walking). Many
people were now coming to Mehfil-i Murtaza from different
parts of the city, particularly from Kharadhar. The hall was full.
The *minbar* was decorated differently on this evening. The
'Abbas *'alam* used on the previous evening was no longer on the
minbar but was kept in the *ziyarat khanah*. The *gham* this evening
concerned 'Ali Akbar, and the symbol carried through the
crowd was a coffin. There was no collection of money as this
nishan passed by, as I had previously witnessed in a predomi-
nantly Khoja *imambargah* in Toronto or in other *imambargahs* in
the city, such as Rizvia Society. The *gham* at Mehfil-i Murtaza focused on 'Ali Akbar, while the *gham* at Rizvia Society focused
upon Hazrat 'Abbas.

9 Muharram/October 16

On the morning of the ninth day I attended a small *majlis* at a
private home in a rather well-to-do suburb of Karachi. These
sorts of *majlis* are common during Muharram. The *zakir* was a
young man with a keen aesthetic sense. He was well aware of
and made good use of the appreciation of poetry, inherent in the
culture of Islamic South Asia. Few of the people in the room
were wearing black. There was no *minbar*, only a chair. There
was an extended period of *marthiyah* reading, after a rendition of
sozkhawani. At one point the atmosphere of the *majlis* almost became one of a *mushaira* (poetry recitation) with a young man
reading a series of poems to chants of "*vah-vah*." Elements of the
mushaira can be found in the *majlis* of many of the most popular
zakirs. People seemed to find no contradiction between the
sense of aesthetic enjoyment inherent in a good performance
and a series of well-turned phrases and the sense of tragedy in-

herent in the type of performance that was being given. Many of the poems were well known, and many of the older men would join in on the final lines of the poetry and offer excited hand motions. In the culture of South Asian Shi'ism there is apparently no contradiction between the emotions of aesthetic appreciation and those of religious mourning. A similar *mushaira* had been given earlier in the year in memory of the death of the daughter of a friend of mine in Karachi.

The next afternoon a large *julus* was brought out of Nishtar Park. Once again the general almost carnival-like atmosphere prevailed. There was very little *matam*, except for some done by some University of Karachi students. There were many *tabuts*. Some of these were carried into the women's sections of Mehfil-i Shah Khurasan so that women who were observing *purdah* would have the opportunity to pay their respects without violating their codes of moral decency. All of the standard elements of the larger 'Ashura julus were present, but they were not nearly as intense.

Around 5:00 P.M. of the same day there was another *julus* in Rizvia Society. Various *nishan* had been brought by cart from nearby Shah Wilayat Imambargah and were then openly marched back to that place. This was a large procession for such a local one, and many women dressed in black at one end of the courtyard of the *imambargah* watched the events as they took place. The procession ended about sunset.

Shab-i Bedar: 9 Muharram/October 16

Shab-i Bedar is the evening before *'Ashura* day. At Mehfil-i Murtaza there was a large crowd for the evening *majlis*. The *'alam* of 'Abbas was back on the *minbar*, still draped in its "bloodstained" *chador*. The *nishan* of 'Ali Asghar's cradle was in the *ziyarat khanah* covered with garlands. The *gham* was more intense and afterward there was *zanjir ka matam*.

On this night the end of the *majlis* was only the beginning of observances. It is customary to remain awake all evening because this is what the Imam did on the eve of the battle of Karbala, remaining awake all night in prayer and devotion. Remaining awake in prayer and devotion is a common manifestation of Islamic piety. Imam 'Ali was renowned for this practice as were many of the great Sufi saints. All of the features of the previous nights of mourning—*majlis, ziyarat, julus*—are present, but other customs are attached to this night's observances. It is customary for many people to remain in the *imambargahs* the whole night long, making up for ritual prayers missed during the regular year. It is particularly auspicious to visit seven different *imambargahs* during the course of the evening. Sometimes student groups will rent a bus to travel together from *imambargah* to *imambargah*. Again, one senses the paradox that even though this is a time of mourning and devotion it also is a time of camraderie and excitement and of anticipation of the coming events of the next day. On street corners there are men brewing huge urns of very strong and spicy tea so as to encourage people to stay awake throughout the evening. There is much conversation around these *chai* stands.

This is also the evening on which people stay up arranging their *ta'ziyahs* and other *nishan* for the *julus* on the following morning. This is the largest *julus* of the year. Over the course of the day it covers the entire length of the city from Nishtar Park to the sea, at Natty Pool where the *ta'ziyahs* are immersed in the water. Traveling from *imambargah* to *imambargah*, one sees many different *anjuman* (mourning societies) preparing for the events of the next morning. Passing through Sunni neighborhoods one can see the Sunni *ta'ziyahs* which are quite different in tone from their Shi'i counterparts. They tend to be more colorful and more jovial, made of bright paper and illuminated with the same type of lights used at weddings. The differences in the *ta'ziyahs* mirror the difference in attitude toward the events of Karbala as they are understood by the two schools of thought.

It is a mark of the importance of these events that they are considered by Sunni and Shi'a alike to be crucial in Islamic history. For the Sunni there is a sense that through his death Husayn had won an important victory for Islam and—of equal importance—Husayn was a martyr and as such did not die. Thus, for the Sunni there can be no need for mourning. Rather there should be an air of celebration.

Thus, the Sunni *juluses* carry about them this celebratory atmosphere. Whips are cracked. Drums are beaten. Brightly colored and ornate *ta'ziyahs* are marched cheerfully through the streets of the city.

When they reach the bay, they are dumped rather unceremoniously from a high bridge into the water below. This stands in sharp contrast to the Shi'i processions, which are in a very real sense funeral processions. The *ta'ziyahs*—although often well made—are far from aesthetically cheerful. The *Zuljinahs* and other symbols of the battle are covered with symbols of blood and violence. While the Sunnis see the battle of Karbala as in some sense ultimately a victory for Islam, and thus identify with Husayn and his comrades, they do not carry in their worldview the theological system which sees in the battle of Karbala a morality play that demonstrates eternal verities about the nature of humanity and God. As one Shi'i Muslim explained to me, while it is true that Husayn's death is a victory, the time for celebrating that victory is not while one is remembering his death. Just as the mother of a child must mourn the death of a loved one, so the world must mourn the death of the beloved of the Prophet. As one Shi'i told me, we can never forget that Husayn is more than simply an Islamic martyr. He is also the grandson of the Prophet—and that, he emphasized, we can never forget.

Throughout the city, people travel from *imambargah* to *imambargah* either to hear various *zakirs* or to simply pay their respects at different *ziyarat khanahs*. Each has its own atmosphere, but most of the important *imambargahs* are filled with activity. Young girls light candles in front of *ta'ziyahs*. Young men drink tea and discuss religious issues.

Shab-i Bedar is also the night of the most intense *zanjir ka matam*. This is the act of ritual flagellation, which is one of the most visibly provocative of all of the activities associated with Muharram. This phenomenon will be discussed in detail in chapter five. Suffice it to say here that it was performed at many different *imambargahs* throughout the city.

'Ashura Day: 10 Muharram/October 17

'Ashura day is the most active of all of the days of Muharram. It opens with the *azan* of 'Ali Akbar, in which a young man chosen for his handsomeness and beautiful voice gives the call to prayer. Events continue from early morning until late evening at which time the *Shām-i Gharībān majalis* are recited. Different *imambargahs* schedule the performance of various activities at different times of the day so that people can attend more than one event. For example, the Rizvia Imambargah held its *a'māl* (a series of prescribed Muharram observances) early in the morning. Traditionally, the *a'mal* at Rizvia Society is followed by a procession to an *imambargah* in nearby Golimar where the *ta'ziyah* are buried in the Karbala located there.

Through *Shab-i Bedar*, it was a topic of hot debate as to whether or not this procession would take place, as there had been a considerable amount of Sunni-Shi'i tension in that neighborhood, and the authorities were afraid that it might produce hostility and perhaps riots. Because the difference between the two schools of thought in the demeanor of their respective Muharram performances occasionally results in violent clashes, Sunni and Shi'i *juluses* are planned so that they may proceed without crossing each other's paths or even coming within hailing distance of each other. It had been a bad year for Sunni-Shi'i relations in Karachi. Violent clashes between Sunni and Shi'a had occurred earlier in the year, and leaders of the community agreed that nothing openly provocative should be said from the *minbar*.

Particularly inflammatory *zakirs* were kept from making speeches at central arenas like Nishtar Park. Possibly for this reason or possibly because of a general trend, there was little open *tabarra* in the *majalis* which I heard. *Tabarra*—the ritual cursing of the enemies of the *ahl al-bayt*—is a complex phenomenon, as has been discussed in chapter two. While there were *tabarra*-like elements in the *majalis* which I observed, they were subtle without direct curses upon Abu Bakr and 'Umar. In any event, the authorities did not permit the procession to take place.

I proceeded from Rizvia Society to the *majlis* at Nishtar Park so as to observe the beginning of the *julus* there. This is the largest of the Muharram processions and continues for most of the day. From dawn different *anjumans* gather together to carry banners, *'alams*, *tabuts*, and *ta'ziyahs*. There are *zuljinahs* and ornate replicas of the tomb of Husayn. First there is a *majlis*. The *zakir* sits at the end of a huge tent and speaks through loudspeakers. The *majlis* is followed by a period of *zanjir ka matam*. The *zanjir ka matam* is followed by the procession, there being *matam* within the *julus*. The various *anjumans* carry banners and *nishan* through the streets. The procession moves first past Shah Khurasan Imambargah and then on to Bunder Road (now Muhammad Ali Jinnah Road), reaching the sea by the early evening, just before the *Sham-i Ghariban majlis* at the Iraniyan Imambargah in downtown Karachi near Kharadhar.

The attitude and demeanor of this procession is a matter of controversy between different factions within the Shi'i community as well as between Sunnis and Shi'i Muslims. A major controversy this year was whether or not the *julus* should stop for prayers. In fact, the *julus* stopped and prayed as a whole over the course of the day. The proponents of prayer in the *julus* made the point that the Imam himself stopped for prayer during the battle of Karbala and thus to continue the *julus* during the *azan* would be tantamount to violating the same Shari'ah which

Husayn had died to protect. Proponents of this position included the *taqlid*-minded students of the Imamiyya Students Organization. They posted signs in *imambargahs* urging people to pray and drove around in cars with loudspeakers, announcing the same message. On the other side of this issue were many who felt that *jāzbat*, the emotional feeling of grief and mourning for the deceased members of the Prophet's family, must and does take precedence over any other dimension of the performances. Another important issue in this is undoubtedly the Shi'i students' response to criticism by the Sunnis of the fact that prayer, which is one of the "Pillars of Islam," should not be abandoned for the practice of *'azadari*.

I left the procession after it turned onto Bunder Road for its long march to the sea in time to attend the *a'mal* at Mehfil-i Murtaza at 11:00 A.M. The *a'mal* is one of the most important of the ritual actions of the entire cycle of Muharram activities. It consists of a long series of prayers, ritual movements, and prostrations performed behind a leader. At Mehfil-i Murtaza it preceded the actual *'Ashura majlis* and the *matam* which followed it. Some wander in throughout this process. Some go to the *masjid* and pray. The most compelling moment of the entire affair comes with a series of seven steps forward and seven steps backward undertaken by the entire congregation as a whole to commemorate the death of the infant 'Ali Asghar and the hesitation of the Imam to return to the child's mother with the terrible news of his demise.

The *a'mal* begins with four *rak'ats* of prayer followed by the recitation of the phrase "*Allahummal-'an qatalatal Ḥusayni wa awaladihī wa aṣḥabihi*" ("Oh God condemn and lay a curse upon the killers of Husayn, his family, and his friends") for 1,000 times. This is followed by the aforementioned seven steps of movement with the recitation of the phrase "*inna lillahi wa inna ilayhi raji 'una riẓan bi qaẓa'ihi wa tasliman li-amrihī*" ("Verily, we are Allah's and verily unto him we return. We are happy with his will and carry out his command"). Then they return to the place where they were standing and recite *Ziyārat-i 'Āshūrā*—a *ziyarat* especially related to this day which consists of curses upon the evil and blessings upon the good. Then, with hands raised and thinking of the enemies of Muhammad, another long Arabic passage condemning the murderers of the Imam is recited. Then curses upon the enemies of the Imam and a short *ziyarat* of blessings upon Husayn are each repeated 100 times. This is followed by two *rak'ats* of prayer and finally the recitation of *Du'a Al-Qa-*

mah. On the day of *'Ashura* at Mehfil-i Murtaza this was followed by the *azan* and the ritual *namaz.*

All of these activities help to set the mood for the *'Ashura majlis.* The long recitations in Arabic pull the minds of the mourners into congruence with an ancient paradigm. The words themselves are either from the Qur'an — as in the case of the *namaz* — or the Imams — who are the object of allegiance and *ma'sum* sources of guidance. The entire practice sets up the importance of the allegiance to the Imam and focuses the minds of the mourners on the symbols of Islamic authority. The *a'mal* ended with ritual prayer, the most ancient of all Islamic practices, which formed a fitting bridge to the *majlis* itself.

Before the *'Ashura majlis,* I noticed that all of the items in the *ziyarat khanah* had been covered with white cloths, and all of the *'alams* had been removed from the *minbar.* Since the *a'mal* was done late in the morning, few persons filtered out. More and more people came into the *imambargah.* After the prayer a *darud* was recited. Special carpets had been laid out for the large number of persons who had arrived to say their prayers.

An important element to be remembered in all of this is that there are different levels of knowledge in the community as to what different symbolic activities mean. When I asked people why the *rowzahs* in the *ziyarat khanah* were covered, one man told me that it was because of dust. Another told me that the *'alams* had been removed to make room for the *pesh imām* (prayer leader) to lead the *a'mal.* But another (apparently a more knowledgeable person) told me that it was simply a custom so that one could concentrate completely on Husayn to the exclusion of all other *nishan.*

Finally, the *zakir* took his position on the *minbar.* He was not wearing a *sherwani* but was dressed starkly in black. He wore no cap. The didactic portion of the *majlis* was very short. The *gham* was particularly moving. Following the *gham,* children appeared, bearing the *tabut* of Imam Husayn. Atop the *tabut* was a black turban, signifying the fact that Imam Husayn was of the blood of the Prophet. Everyone attempted to touch it as it passed by. Some men were so completely overcome with grief that they could hardly keep control. One man fainted, gasping from grief. The *matam* which followed was musical and terribly intense. While the *matam* was proceeding, the children carried the *palna* of 'Ali Asghar and the other *nishan,* including the *'alams* in the *ziyarat khanah,* to the center of the floor of the *majlis* hall, where they were wrapped in white cloths and decorated with green plant leaves of a type commonly found in graveyards.

Thus, it was both a sign of mourning and burial. The *matam* ended as usual with the recitation of *ziyarat*. Following the *matam* there was the breaking of the fast at the time of *'asr*, that is before sunset, with a meal of *halim*, *roti*, milk, and water. I was told that the congregation had increased by about 20 percent from the year before. The breaking of the fast on the day of *'Ashura* is an important element of Twelver Shi'i Muharram observances because it is believed that Ibn Ziyad's troops fasted on the day of *'Ashura* as a way of making it into an auspicious occasion.

The End of the *Julus*

Following the *niyaz* I went with some members of the *mehfil* to observe the end of the *'Ashura julus*. I met with the head of the Husaini Tabut Committee Imambargah, an *imambargah* in downtown Karachi which specializes in the construction of *ta'ziyahs* for the purpose of carrying them in *juluses*. He traveled with me to the bridge at Natty Pool where the *ta'ziyahs* are given burial. The *ta'ziyahs* from the Tabut Committee are large and ornate. They build one large one and one smaller one each year. Because of the amount of labor which goes into the building of these *ta'ziyahs*, the *ta'ziyah* itself is not buried. Rather, only the coffin is removed and given a burial in the shallow water of the bay. Mourners walk out into the sea and read *Fatihah* as if it were a real funeral. The *'alams* are held at the shore and are ultimately given as *rowzah* to small or impoverished *imambargahs* in the interior of the country.

Sunni *ta'ziyahs* were on the bridge as well. These were also disposed of in the water but the air of reverential respect which surrounded the burial of the Shi'i *ta'ziyahs* was lacking in the Sunni burials. As mentioned earlier, the Sunni *ta'ziyahs* were somewhat unceremoniously dumped over the side of the bridge from a relatively high point, from whence they crashed apart on contact with the water. This was in keeping with the whole demeanor of the Sunni procession, replete with cracking whips and beating drums. The tone of the Sunni *julus* is celebratory and thus is unacceptable to the Shi'a.

The authorities had taken great pains to ensure that the Shi'i *julus* would reach its destination at the Iraniyan Imambargah at Kharadhar well before the Sunni *julus* to avoid the type of confrontation which has occurred in the past. Loudspeakers within the *imambargah* chanted for people to stop their *matam* and enter into the *imambargah* so that the *Sham-i Ghariban majlis* could begin before the Sunni Muslims' *julus* passed by. In the past, incidents had occurred in the city when the Sunni *julus* would pass by, beating drums and singing at the very moment when the Shi'i Muslims were rapt in grief and mourning. Because of recent tensions in the area between the two communities, sober heads on each side prevailed and there was no conflict this year.

Sham-i Ghariban: 10 Muharram/October 17

The *Sham-i Ghariban majlis* is one of the most important events which takes place during the cycle of Muharram performances. "The Night of the Strangers" or "The Night of the Unfortunate Ones" commemorates the women and the children of the camp who remained as witnesses to the events of Karbala. The women had their veils pulled back and were paraded through the streets of Kufa and Damascus. The tents were burned. While the men had been martyrs, the women were witnesses. Thus, the women, and in particular Zainab, the sister of Imam Husayn, play an important role in the entire Karbala drama, for without their presence the world would have remained ignorant of the circumstances surrounding the death of the Prophet's grandson.

The emotional content of the *Sham-i Ghariban majlis* is much calmer but in some ways is more tragic than that surrounding the other *majalis*. The *majlis* at Mehfil-i Murtaza began right after *maghrib* prayers. The lights were dimmed and nearly everyone was clothed in black. The *minbar* was totally empty of ornament. To one side of the *minbar* a boy recited tragic poetry. The *ziyarat khanah* was also cast in dim light, and all of the holy objects within were covered with white cloths and sprinkled with sweet-smelling leaves of the kind which grow on tombs. Rather than sitting upon it, the *zakir* stood alongside the *minbar*. He recited calmly, standing in the darkness. The entire process took about one hour and then everything was over. Many of the people wished to get home early to see the official *majlis* by Allamah Ijtihadi on television that evening.

Other Activities

I returned for a *majlis* at Mehfil-i Murtaza the next evening. The visual demeanor of the *imambargah* had changed dramatically.

All of the *'alams* were back in their original positions in the *ziya-rat khanah*, but they were now cloaked in black and embroidered with silver lettering. This was also the case with the *ta'ziyahs*. I was told that it would remain this way until the eighth of *Rabbiul Awwal*, that is, for forty-eight days following *'Ashura*. During this period the *imambargah* would continue with less intensive mourning activities. There would be *majalis* on the tenth, twentieth, thirtieth, and fortieth days following *'Ashura*, as well as every Thursday. There would also be ten days of *majalis* between *'Ashura* and *Chhellum*—the large mourning celebration that falls on the fortieth day. This is called *'Ashra-i Zainabiyya* and can be held during any ten-day period. But generally the *majalis* are shorter and the *matam* is less intense or nonexistent.

The twelfth day is the ritual of *ziyarat*. Only ten or twenty people attended this ritual. This ritual follows the Islamic custom of reciting the entire Qur'an in the name of a deceased person and then distributing food in his or her name. As this was not done for Husayn at the time of his martyrdom, it is now done by his followers. People sat quietly and individually reciting *parahs* of the Qur'an. This was followed by a communal recitation in Arabic by a *pesh imam*, followed by the recitation of *ziyarat*. People entered through the *ziyarat khanah*. A boy carried a sweet dish through the crowd, and everyone took a bit. *Tabarruk* was distributed, and then everyone went home.

Conclusion

The rituals of Muharram are a central pivot in the religious lives of Shi'i Muslims. As the major public affirmations by Shi'i Muslims of the beliefs of their community, the impact of Muharram rituals on the lives of participants is difficult to overestimate. As independent rituals they create a series of liminoid arenas in which people are able to reflect in an emotional and immediate manner upon the root paradigms of Shi'ism. Taken as whole, the ten-day period is structured as an overarching ritual process which builds in intensity to the culminating rituals of the ninth and tenth days. Throughout this period people are confronted with the symbols of Shi'i authority and challenged to reaffirm their allegiance to the family of the Prophet in ways which are both public and personal. In the manner of Geertz's definition of religion, the participants are made aware of the "general order of existence" in ways which make it seem "uniquely realistic."

Although much of the information contained in the rituals is didactic and expository—as in the case of the *majlis*—the authoritative nature of that information is conveyed by an emotional interaction with a universe of symbols that in some ways seems to the participants to be more real than the mundane world in which they ordinarily live. The rituals are clear evidence of the dramatic nature of Shi'ism which is rooted in the metahistorical narratives of Shi'i sacred history. These rituals create a liminal arena separate from but still connected to historical reality which allows the mourners to take part in the events of Karbala in a symbolic manner and experience emotions which have a deep soteriological dimension. As each day succeeds the next, the individual stories of each of the major martyrs is not only retold but the characters are evoked. The *'alam* of 'Abbas, the cradle of 'Ali Asghar, the re-creations of the wedding of Qasim, all serve to pull the participants in Muharram rituals further and further into the Karbala paradigm. By the tenth day the atmosphere of Karbala is easily evoked; the death of Husayn and the remembrance of *Sham-i Ghariban* which follow it are able to induce a deep sense of grief at the suffering of the *ahl al-bayt* in the hearts of the participants. By suffering with the *ahl al-bayt* one stands with them at Karbala and, through that act of allegiance, shares in their reward. It is this aspect of the Muharram rituals which should be kept in mind as we examine physical *matam* in chapter five, as the wounds of Muharram are yet another sign of spiritual allegiance and devotion.

CHAPTER FIVE

The Wounds of Devotion:
Physical Risk as an Act
of Allegiance

Unfortunately, the profound theological and symbolic dimensions of the rituals of Muharram are often overwhelmed in the consciousness of non-Shi'a by the dramatic vision of physical *matam*. To some, the image of bloodstained men lashing their backs with knives or slicing their heads with swords is the definitive image of mourning in the context of Shi'i piety. This is unfortunate, not because such practices as self-flagellation and fire walking are not a legitimate part of Shi'i religious practice, but because they are seen only as bizarre and irrational aberrations rather than as coherent activities with an important place in the realm of Shi'i devotion.

Karbala was and—in the sense that it is a living reality—is the site of a military campaign. It was an event of physical suffering as well as one of moral courage. The visual images recalled through words in the *majlis* and through physical symbols in the *julus* are ones which give evidence of violence. Blood is a commonly portrayed symbol. It is splattered on the sheets which cover the *tabuts*. It is smeared on the blankets which cover the replicas of *Zuljinah*. Red, along with black, the color of mourning, is ubiquitous during Muharram. Red is the color of blood and, for some, the color of revolution.

Likewise, fire is an important symbol during Muharram because it represents the burning of the tents of the women following the martyrdom of Husayn. Yet fire is a multivocal symbol in Shi'i Islam. It represents, for example, the fire of hell. It is also a Qur'anic symbol for the oppression of the religious by those who reject God's guidance in the sense that it is a reminder of the attempt of Nimrod to kill Ibrahim by throwing him into the fiery furnace. Fire and blood are important constituents of the complex of symbols encountered by participants in the rituals of mourning during Muharram. For many participants in the rituals of Muharram, the immediate and direct experience of fire and blood in the form of *zanjir* and *ag ka matam* is an important proof of faith and devotion because it allows mourners to enter more directly into the paradigm of Karbala than is possible by simply listening to a *majlis* or marching in a *julus*.

Flagellation in Islam

Zanjir ka matam is the term used for cutting one's back with knives or chains as a ritual act of mourning for the death of Husayn. This activity is not limited to any particular class or ethnic grouping. Although at first glance it may appear to bear a good deal in common with Christian acts of self-mortification, it is in reality something quite different.[1] It is not an acceptance of pain as a way of scourging one's sins. There is almost unanimous agreement among participants in *zanjir ka matam* that it is a physically painless activity. Not only is it described as painless but it is also portrayed as ultimately noninjurious. Many different participants reported to me that in this type of *matam* there is almost never any serious, lasting injury. The mere application of rose water to the backs of the flagellants results in complete healing in a few days, sometimes without scarring. Furthermore, unlike Hindu *faqirs* who perform acts of self-abnegation to demonstrate that they have entered into another state of consciousness in which they are immune to the perception of pain, in Shi'i flagellation it appears that there is no obvious shift from one state of consciousness to another preceding an individual's participation in *zanjir ka matam*.[2] At one moment the participants may be engaged in conversation, and in the next they are engaged in the ritual of flagellation.

Several things should be noted about this practice. First, it is a public activity. It is not a solitary act of pious mortification but rather is the public performance of a deed of piety. Second, it is not only public but communal. To the best of my knowledge, it is never performed alone but always in the company of others who are also performing the same action. In this context it is almost like a ritual dance. It is done to the accompaniment of *marthiyah*, which lends a rhythmic dimension to it.

Thus, physical *matam* is a public, communal observance. However, it is not universally performed within the Shi'i community. Women, for example, do not take part.[3] In point of fact, the majority of men do not take part in it. A portion of the Shi'i community actively disapproves of these activities. But those who do engage in these activities do so publicly both in front of the larger Shi'i community and often before the even larger community of Sunni Muslims. *Zanjir ka matam* is based on religious ideas. Those who engage in these activities are demonstrating to others the efficacy of belief in the verities of 'Alid devotionalism — and thus the metaphysical status and power of the Imams. The power of God and the intercessory abilities of the *ahl al-bayt* are demonstrated through these actions. At the same time participants affirm to themselves the extent of their faith by risking personal bodily injury. By risking their physical safety they show themselves willing to follow in the footsteps of the martyrs of Karbala.[4]

Thus, the ritual of *zanjir ka matam* follows the pattern of the other public rituals of mourning associated with Muharram by facing in two directions simultaneously. It confers a benefit upon the flagellants in that they affirm the power of their own faith, and it challenges those who do not participate to evaluate the nature of what they are observing. What drives someone to do such a thing? And why is there no serious injury? *Zanjir ka matam* generally takes place within the context of another ritual, following after a *majlis* or during a *julus*. It is performed most often on the ninth and tenth of Muharram, when it generally follows the *majlis* of *Shab-i Bedar* or the *majlis* of 'Ashura. It is also performed in the context of *juluses* both on the ninth and tenth of Muharram and on other important days of mourning throughout the year, such as the *julus* commemorating the martyrdom of Hazrat 'Ali or the *juluses* of the fortieth day after 'Ashura (*Chhellum*). When it follows *majlis*, it is the culmination of the event — a physical expression of the experience of the event of Karbala which takes place during the *majlis* and the *gham*. Perhaps because of this fact there is no clear agreement as to the proper ritual preparations necessary for the performance of *zanjir ka matam*. When I interviewed young men about their participation in this activity, I wondered whether there was any act of ritual ablution necessary for *zanjir ka matam*. While many told me that it was recommended that one be *pak* (in the state of ritual purity required before prayer), it was not necessary. However, since the *matam* follows the *majlis*, which itself usually follows immediately upon the evening prayers, it is generally true that the participants are already *pak*.

When the *zanjir ka matam* is performed after a *majlis*, it takes place outside of the *majlis* hall since blood is ritually polluting. At Mehfil-i Murtaza the hall is protected by holding *zanjir ka matam* in an adjoining courtyard. The participants at Mehfil-i Murtaza are generally quite young. It was not uncommon to see boys between the ages of twelve and sixteen engaged in this activity on the ninth and tenth days of Muharram. Perhaps because of the young age of the flagellants the degree of intensity was not as great as I witnessed among older *matamdars* during the major *juluses*. This may be partially because of the renowned religious sobriety of the African Khoja community. The *zanjir ka matam* at Kharadhar and at Mehfil-i Shah Khurasan was much more intense.

The actual act of *zanjir ka matam* involves striking the back and shoulders with a series of sharp knives connected by six-inch chains connected to a wooden handle. They are available for purchase at the bazaars which spring up around the major *imambargahs* of the city during the first ten days of Muharram. The *matamdar* alternatingly swings the *zanjir* over his left and right shoulders, allowing the knives to fall across his back and draw blood. The *matamdar* is usually bare-chested and bare-backed during the entire process, which normally lasts ten or fifteen minutes.

There is no clearly visible transition into the act of *zanjir ka matam* following the *gham*. *Hath ka matam* begins as usual following the *gham*, and *sozkhawani* is sung over the microphone as mourners perform the rhythmic striking of the chest with the hands. While this is happening, those who are intent upon doing *zanjir ka matam* move out of the hall into the courtyard, where they remove their shirts and take up the *zanjir*. There is no obvious attempt by the *matamdars* to meditate themselves into an altered state of consciousness. It appears almost casual as the *matamdars* prepare. There is even a degree of conversation. As the *matam* continues there is apparently no experience of pain. It is important to note that in both *zanjir ka matam* and fire *matam* the *matamdars* claim to feel no pain. This is not an act of self-mortification, and its purpose is not to experience physical suffering.

There is good evidence that the basis of *zanjir ka matam* and the purposes for performing it are to be found in the very nature of the Karbala paradigm itself. First, it should be remembered that an important element of that paradigm is that it is a dramatic event whose major characters are people making a fundamental moral choice. This moral choice is linked to a fundamental religious choice. Does one follow the Imam? Is one willing to sacrifice one's life in the service of Islam? Clearly, a basic message of the Karbala narrative is that "talk is cheap." The Kufans had sworn that they would offer allegiance to the Imam when he arrived, but at the first hint of oppression from the caliphate they refused to come to his aid.

We have already examined the soteriological dimension of mourning for Husayn and the way in which showing solidarity with Husayn is understood to be a basic condition of true Islam. *Zanjir ka matam* is an extension of this same soteriological imperative. Thus, although Imam Ja'far as-Sadiq has given assurances that the spiritual blessing attached to passionate grief for the martyrs of Karbala is the same as if one had fought in Jihad with the prophets, for some this is not enough.[5] To engage in *zanjir ka matam* is to show a physical willingness to take upon oneself the same sorts of wounds that were inflicted upon the companions of the Imam at Karbala.

The *matamdar* thus enters *physically* into the Karbala paradigm. He becomes a warrior. By taking part in *zanjir ka matam*, the *matamdar* is hoping to demonstrate what he understands to be the truth of Karbala and through it to show to himself and others the validity of the authority of the Imams. The *matamdar* proves to himself the purity of his intentions through his act of risk taking, but more importantly he demonstrates to others the kind of devotion that Imam Husayn is able to engender after 1,400 years. Finally, the lack of pain and the lack of serious infection following this kind of *matam* are thought by many Shi'a to be proof of the miraculous intervention of the *ahl al-bayt* into this world, and this, they claim, constitutes proof of the entire Shi'i position.[6]

The question still remains as to the reason that there is no attempt to induce or endure pain in the process. I believe that there is a theological reason for this. Unlike the Christian penitent who wishes to endure pain, the focus of the *matamdar* is to show his willing allegiance to the Imam. Those who died with the Imam did not really die, as the Qur'an assures Muslims that martyrs do not die but enter into a special state of existence. Thus, the wounds of the *matamdar* like the deaths of the martyrs are only apparent and not real. The belief that there will be no pain is thus a part of the nature of the paradigm being encountered. Just as the martyrs of Karbala did not die but rather entered into a paradisiacal state, so also the wounds of the *matamdar* are in some sense as illusory as the deaths of the martyrs. For this reason it would be inconsistent theologically for the *matamdar* to feel pain or suffer disfigurement.

And yet there is controversy over this kind of *matam*. Not only in Pakistan but throughout the Muslim world, this type of activity has become a focus of criticism by Sunnis, Westerners, and some Shiʻa. Werner Ende in his article "The Flagellations of Muharram and the Shiʻite ʻUlama,"[7] has shown clearly the strong divisions within the Lebanese Muslim community over this issue and the effect Sunni fundamentalism has had upon this matter. The controversial nature of these activities can be seen by the very fact that modern *mujtahids* are still being asked to write *fatwas* on their permissibility. For example, a *fatwa* of Ayatullah Abu al-Qasim Khui of Najaf responds to the question of whether it is *jaʼiz* (permissible) to beat one's breast and back vigorously in *matam* by answering that it is permissible if there is not much over-injury or if it "does not ridicule Islam."[8] It is clear both from the question and the answer that there is a self-conscious concern among the Shiʻa about the permissibility of these activities in terms of how the rest of the world sees them. And yet the *ulama* are not willing to ban them. Shaikh Mirza Husain Naaʼini has argued that it is recommended (*mustaḥab*) to "make *matam* by beating with hands on chest and forehead even if it becomes red or black, also matam by chain (*zanjeer*) on shoulder and back even if it bleeds." He also has argued that it is permissible to "make *matam* with sword on head and forehead causing blood to come out provided it should not seriously hurt or cause injury to the bone which may result in bleeding profusely."[9]

And yet there is a sincere opposition to certain aspects of the practice of *zanjir ka matam*. For some it is distasteful and unacceptable. Some would replace this form of activity with another. An interesting example of this is the organizing of the Husayniyya Blood Bank at Mehfil-i Murtaza. In an interesting transformation the focus of *zanjir ka matam* has shifted from the act of flagellation itself to the blood which it produces. *Khūn* or blood is an important symbol, as already shown. The act of shedding blood symbolizes sacrifice (*qurbān*). At Mehfil-i Murtaza the Bilal Muslim Trust has arranged a less vociferous way for people to shed their blood for Islam. On the tenth of Muharram, a blood bank is set up in the *imambargah*. The blood is drawn and typed right at the *imambargah*. In fact, it is drawn in the *ghusl khanah* and then typed in the same field where the *zanjir ka matam* is performed. The typed blood is then distributed free to Shiʻi hospitals in Pakistan, although it is then given to Sunni and Shiʻa alike. By noon on ʻAshura of the year in which this research was

done, the blood bank had already processed 200 donors. Under-
standably, the people of Mehfil-i Murtaza are proud of their activities, particularly as there is a chronic blood shortage in
Pakistan.

But this kind of replacement for *zanjir ka matam* is not the
norm. *Zanjir ka matam* is actively engaged in throughout the city.
For example, on *Shab-i Bedar* as many as 600 or 700 people engaged in physical *matam* for almost an hour at Mehfil-i Shah
Khurasan, and the passion of that activity, although perhaps
not as socially useful, was a great deal more dramatic than lying
on a cot and giving a pint of blood.

Talvār ka Mātam

Another form of physical *matam*—but one which is much less
common—is *matam* with swords or *talvar ka matam*. In this practice the participant delivers a quick solid blow to the top of his
head with a sword which produces a great deal of blood. I was
unable to interview anyone who engaged in this form of *matam*.
Although I was unable to witness this *matam* on the day of
'*Ashura*, I did witness young men at the end of the *julus* with
their heads bandaged. This is a much more dangerous practice
than *zanjir ka matam* and under the auspices of the Khoja community one of the hospitals near the downtown area offers free
medical treatment to those injured while performing it.

Ag ka Matam (Fire Walking)

Another popular form of physical matam is *ag ka matam* or fire
walking. The origins of fire walking in South Asia as a means of
showing devotion to the *ahl al-bayt* are shrouded in mystery and
a great deal of folklore. An elderly poet from Bihar Province in
India told me that fire walking for the *ahl al-bayt* originated
among Buddhists who sought to find an original way to show
devotion. A more common explanation is that it signifies the
burning of the tents of the women at the camp of Karbala and
the women running in to rescue the children from the flames.[10]
A more interesting explanation is that in a petty kingdom in the
province of Sindh the British had entered into collusion with a
Sunni ruler to block all Muharram-related rituals. In order to
keep the faithful out of the *imambargahs*, the British and the
Sunni ruler set fires in front of the entrances of the *imambargahs*

but miraculously the people were able to walk right through without being harmed.

Whatever the historical origins of this custom, the image of fire, for the reasons mentioned above, is important and multi-vocal in the Islamic world. As mentioned earlier, fire symbolizes *jahannam* or hell, and the image of passing miraculously through flames is connected with the idea of deliverance from punishment. Another important image, taken directly from the Qur'an, is the aforementioned image of Ibrahim's deliverance from the fire where the flames became flowers and he was unharmed. This image is itself layered with meanings. It shows how God intervenes on behalf of his prophets and, in the case of Ibrahim, how he protects the *ahl al-bayt*, as the lineage of Muhammad can be traced back to Ibrahim. The connection with Ibrahim can be clearly seen in elements of this ritual.

The major performance of *ag ka matam* in Karachi takes place in Kharadhar in the large field adjacent to the Isma'ili Ja'amat Khanah on the evening of the seventh of Muharram. Although the fire walking itself was to begin at 2:00 A.M., I arrived at 11:00 A.M. and found a large crowd of people already milling about. It was a mixed gathering of men and women, although the number of women was much smaller. I discovered that many people wanted to talk to me about Islam and what I was about to see. The fire walking, I was told, was evidence of the *tufail* (intercession) of Imam 'Ali who was Mushkil Kusha. I was then told, however, that as all of the Imams share in the same light they are thus all Mushkil Kusha. Most of the people there were of the opinion that fire walking was permissible (*ja'iz*) in the opinions of the *'ulama*, but this was not unanimous.

At midnight there was a *majlis*. The street was filled with thousands of people. The *majlis* followed the usual format. A reading of the Qur'an was followed by *sozkhawani* and *marthiyah*. The *zakir* then appeared. He was a relatively young man. He sat on the *minbar* underneath a large photo of the Ayatullah Khomeini. Much was political in his *majlis*. It was critical of Israel and culminated in a call for Islamic unity. Throughout the *majlis* there was a great deal of reaction and interaction with the crowd. There were, for instance, frequent shouts of *"Husayniyat Zindābād! Yāzīdiyat Murdābād!"* ("Long live the path of Husayn, Death to the path of Yazid") as well as calls of *"Nade Haidari,"* with the answer of *"Ya 'Ali"* and *"'Ali ke Dushman par La'nat"* ("Curses upon the enemies of 'Ali"), answered with *"Be Shak"* ("Without doubt"). The *gham* was followed by a small procession with incense followed by a draped coffin.

During the *matam* I made my way to the fire walking arena. Several persons who had discovered that I was a researcher escorted me to the area where press photographers were standing upon trucks. The arrangement looked very much like a rodeo arena. In front of me was a trench approximately twenty feet long and six feet wide, filled with glowing coals. The trench was in the center of a square arena, surrounded by a wooden fence, and at the end opposite from where I was situated there was a chute with people lined up behind it. Along the outside of the left side of the fence surrounding the perimeter of the trench were women, mostly dressed in black, some of whom held hand cymbals. The men were on the right side of the fence.

The trench had been dug early in the morning, and wood had been piled up high within it. After the morning prayers the fire was lit, and all during the day the verse of the Qur'an referring to the miraculous saving of Ibrahim from death in the furnace was recited in shifts. Thus, the arena itself was miraculously charged in the minds of the Shi'a. Many of the people at this event told me that the intercession of the Imams had protected the area. Thus, anyone who walked upon the coals would be unharmed. The fact that *matamdars* would not be injured was not a proof of their own piety but rather of the power of the *ahl al-bayt*.[11]

As people began to congregate, the excitement and tension began to build. An attendant continuously raked the coals. Although the arena was illuminated by powerful lighting, at intervals those lights were dimmed, revealing the intensity of heat and light being radiated by the coals. In fact, I was able to take photographs without flash using the light of the coals alone. The heat from the coals even from where I was on the roof of a truck some thirty feet away was so intense that I had to continually move my camera to prevent the plastic parts of it from melting.

Within the arena were seven young men dressed in green overblouses and wearing sashes on their foreheads. They were carrying *'alams*. These young men represented Qasim, the unfortunate bridegroom (*dulha*) of Karbala. This is apparently a local and not universal custom. These young men were to be the first to cross the flames. There also was a child with *'alams*. He carried these around the flames several times and then the crowd began to chant to the clanging of cymbals: "Dulha! Dulha! Dulha!"[12] At one point a scuffle broke out. Apparently, a *matamdar* wished to cross the fire before these young men but he was prevented from doing so. The young men walked quickly across the flames with no injury as the crowd chanted louder and louder. Following these men, a stream of people headed across. They were all male but of many different ages. There were many children who walked across the fire as well. Of the people who crossed, I saw only one person—a young boy—who at the last minute ran around the side of the pit rather than go through the coals. To the best of my knowledge, no one was injured.

After about twenty minutes, the event ended quickly and with almost no warning. Attendants doused the flames with water and huge billows of smoke rose up filling the arena. As soon as it was over, people began to filter away. There was no *ziyarat* or similar activity that served as a clear ending point of the ritual.

Afterward I talked to one of the *matamdars*. Interestingly, he sought me out and not the other way around. He showed me his feet and the fact that there were no marks upon them. When I asked him if there had been any pain at all, he remarked that the only sensation was that of walking through cold water. Our conversation attracted a large crowd. When I turned to ask someone else a question, he became a bit irritated. I realized that I was being interviewed by him as much as he by me. He would not let me leave until I answered his *"Nade Haidari"* with *"Ya 'Ali,"* which I did on the second try. At this the crowd applauded and he was most impressed.

Here it was clear that the performance of *ag ka matam* is not merely an act of devotion but also is an act of witness to non-Shi'a. The *matamdar* saw his action as proof of the power of 'Ali and as proof of the truth of his religion. In the face of such evidence—that the natural order can be temporarily suspended—how could I deny the intercession of the holy family? By getting me to acknowledge Hazrat 'Ali, an important intention of the *ag ka matam* had been fulfilled. Not only had he reaffirmed his own faith but he had also demonstrated the verity of that faith to an outsider.

The next night at Mehfil-i Murtaza I spoke to a man forty-two years old who had been fire walking since he was a child of seven, and had walked on the fire the previous evening. He also remarked that there was no pain and no scarring. He confirmed that, as with other Islamic rituals, it is necessary to make a *niyyat* and then perform ablutions (*wuzu*); but again, because of lack of time, *namaz* is not necessary. This was in contrast to another informant who told me that one should pray two *rak'ats* of prayer before walking on fire. Others told me that even *wuzu* is not necessary. For some there is an almost matter-of-fact quality to the entrance into the performance. There is no rigid or even well-

defined distinction between the sacred and the profane or even
a clear-cut point of separation or reaggregation which one might
expect. This is possibly because the power in the event comes
from the Imams and is not dependent on the *matamdar*.

Throughout my investigations into this type of performance, I
sensed an uneasiness that I might misinterpret things. One
young boy at Mehfil-i Murtaza was greatly relieved to find that
Ayatullah Khui had given a *fatwa* that fire walking was *ja'iz* (permissible).[13] An Iranian journalist at Kharadhar assured me that
this kind of thing did not take place in Iran. There was, I sup-
pose, a logical feeling that this sort of activity might make Muslims appear irrational. And yet at the same time there was a
certain amount of pride involved in it. People pointed out to me
that *matamdars* include doctors and lawyers. In their day-to-day
lives they exhibit nothing that would set them apart as masoch-
istic or violent. And yet during Muharram these men may engage in acts of self-violence which to outsiders may appear
inexplicable.

Conclusion

The acts of physical *matam* may seem at first sight bizarre and
inexplicable, but seen in the larger context of Shi'i piety they are
another way in which people enter into the paradigm of Karbala
and demonstrate their piety and devotion. The miraculous element of these performances—the lack of injury in the case of
zanjir ka matam and the even more obvious lack of injury in *ag ka
matam*—are seen as demonstrations of the efficacy of faith in the
ahl al-bayt. This acts to convince non-Muslims and non-Shi'a of
the efficacy of Shi'i religious beliefs and thus is a form of proselytization as well as an act of devotion.

CONCLUSION

The subject of this study has been the practice of Shi'i Islam in the context of a contemporary South Asian community. This work is an attempt to link the ethnographic and textual study of religion in ways which enhance both of these approaches. It presents the religion of Shi'i Islam as it is lived in a particular context and demonstrates how the context and the religious worldview illumine each other.

Throughout I have attempted to define Shi'i Islam on its own terms rather than by comparing it to the larger Sunni tradition. Thus, Shi'ism is defined as the Islam of personal allegiance to the Prophet and those whom the Prophet loved. The centrality of devotion to Muhammad as a focus of Shi'i piety is difficult to overstate. While it is often argued that it is devotion to 'Ali that defines Shi'ism, it is clear that devotion to 'Ali emerges out of devotion to Muhammad, just as devotion to Muhammad arises as a corollary of devotion to God. Because this devotional allegiance is directed toward historical personages, the reflection upon history through narrative and ritual has become a crucial element of Shi'i piety. The characters of the sacred metahistory of Shi'ism are understood not as figures of a distant, unrecoverable past but rather as powerful entities who can be evoked—in fact, invoked—by the faithful, through the use of ritual, in ways which allow believers to demonstrate their allegiance to the Prophet and his family and reaffirm the verities of their religion.

This concept of personal allegiance to the Prophet and his family underlies all of Shi'i piety. The bulk of this work has examined various ways in which this allegiance is expressed in ritual performances in the particular environment of Karachi, Pakistan. Using Clifford Geertz's definition of religion as a system of symbols which acts to produce moods and motivations

157

concerning a general order of existence in such a way as to make that order of existence seem uniquely realistic in connection with Victor Turner's theory of ritual process, I have attempted to show how the Shi'i community uses ritual to convey the basic beliefs and root paradigms of the religion and inspire action on the basis of those beliefs.

Devotional allegiance is articulated in various rituals both public and private. On the level of household performances, the recitations of miracle stories used for the purpose of making spiritual vows are an important example of such rituals. These recitations create ritual arenas in which the participants evoke and encounter the important figures of Shi'i metahistory in an immediate way which allows them to experience the root paradigms of their religion. While these rituals are technically not enjoined as a part of the Shari'ah, they promote the same sort of values which undergird it. Furthermore, by evoking the spiritual power of the *ahl al-bayt*, they reaffirm the necessity of allegiance to the *ahl al-bayt* and — if the vows are fulfilled — the verity of their claim to authority.

On the public level the clearest examples of devotional allegiance are the large public rituals of Muharram. Again, the central theme of these rituals is allegiance to the Prophet's family — in particular, allegiance to Imam Husayn. The rituals of *majlis* and *julus* allow for emotional encounters with paradigmatic symbols. These rituals are understood to be efficacious both on the expository and soteriological levels (although both of these levels are connected to each other). These rituals allow for a spiritual encounter which simultaneously creates a sense of the reality of the spiritual existence of the *ahl al-bayt* and the efficacy of allegiance to them while engendering a sense of *communitas* among their participants.

Unlike household rituals, however, these performances face in two directions — one personal and the other public. The rituals are meant to reaffirm the faith of believers, while simultaneously drawing outsiders to the faith. These yearly public expressions of grief and mourning pull back a curtain which usually renders the Sunni and Shi'i communities culturally invisible to each other. The provocative nature of these rituals is in fact an essential element of them.

Even the most provocative of all Shi'i mourning activities in South Asia, such as flagellation and fire walking, must be seen against the backdrop of devotional allegiance. For many Shi'a these are proofs of one's allegiance to the cause of the Imam — that one is willing to take on the same sorts of wounds as one would have received at Karbala. The miraculous element of these performances once again acts as a proof of the efficacy of allegiance to the *ahl al-bayt*. This expression of emotion is shown to be one that is in accord with the basic attitudes of the Shi'i piety.

Thus, the rituals of Shi'ism arise out of the basic presuppositions of the religion and work to reinforce belief in the unique factuality of the power of the Prophet and his family. But they should not be seen as simply fulfilling the Durkheimian creation of a communal identity. While one aspect of these rituals is the creation of social solidarity and community identity, there is no single experience engendered by these rituals. All of the participants bring their own personal histories to these rituals, which cause them to focus on different symbols and to interpret them in individual ways. Thus, while there was a general tendency for the participants I interviewed in Karachi to become more Shari'ah conscious through their participation, there is a variety of interpretations of the meaning of the events of Karbala in people's lives. For almost all of the people I talked to during this research participation in these rituals played a large role in their creation of a Muslim identity.

Muslim Identity in the Modern World

To be a Muslim in the modern world is to participate in several interrelated identities. An individual is simultaneously a member of a nation state, a class, a gender, an ethnic group, and a linguistic community. Furthermore, each Muslim is also at least nominally identified as a particular kind of Muslim—Sunni, Shi'a, Isma'ili, or a member of a Sufi *tariqah*. The question of Muslim identity is a complex one that cannot be fully addressed or solved through a mere examination of Muslim "denominationalism." In fact, any attempt to reduce the question of Muslim identity to one single factor is flawed. Just as there are many kinds of Muslim there are many ways in which individuals define themselves as Muslims in the world.

For example, the Shi'a define themselves not only as Shi'a, but also as Muslims—members of the larger community of all the people who accept the authority of the Qur'anic event. From this standpoint the Shi'a themselves often downplay the controversial nature of Shi'i belief and practice, as they think of themselves as members of the *ummah*.

The complexity of Muslim identity in the world makes it crucial that researchers understand that analytical dyads like Shi'a and Sunni, Sufi and *ulama*, and "Great Tradition" and "Small Tradition," while useful for certain kinds of discourse, conceal as much as they reveal. The last of these provides a particularly useful example of this difficulty with a bipolar approach. It is tempting to organize the study of Muharram rituals around the bipolar opposition of folk tradition versus classical Islam. Many "rationalist" Muslims themselves deal with the material in this way, poking fun at their coreligionists' "superstitions" while arguing for the rationality of Islamic law. Flagellation and miracle stories are explained away as indigenous accretions onto the pure Islam of the Prophet and his family. But, in fact, such distinctions are misleading.

Throughout the period of mourning during Muharram there is a sense of the presence of the miraculous and the spiritual which one would normally think of in association with folk practice. To my surprise, as I asked deeper and deeper questions of the people I was writing about, I discovered that much of what I thought would be indigenous folk religion has its roots in the classical tradition. Furthermore, the miraculous aspects of the religion as experienced in the ritual context reinforced the observance of Islamic prescriptions in the day-to-day religious lives of participants in these events. That which was experienced in the liminal realm of ritual and performance was carried over into the world of structure.

Devotion to the *Ahl al-Bayt*: A Wall and a Bridge

While it is useful and accurate to describe Shi'i Islam as the Islam of personal allegiance, creating a bipolar opposition between Sunni Islam and Shi'i Islam in this way is problematic. Love and devotion for the Prophet and the *ahl al-bayt* is both a wall and a bridge between the Shi'a and other South Asian Muslim communities. Although devotional allegiance to the Prophet and his family is most fully worked out in the Shi'i worldview, except for the Wahabis and the *Ahl-i Hadith*, very few Muslims in South Asia deny the continuing spiritual existence of the Prophet and the efficacy of devotion to him. It is commonly believed throughout South Asia that the Prophet was created from light, that he hears the *darud* of pilgrims at his tomb in Medina, and that he can appear to devotees in dreams. Furthermore, through his designated spiritual descendants and *khalifahs*—the *awliyah* or Sufi saints—he continues to function as the spiritual governor of this world. Indeed, the popularity and strength of *tariqah* Sufism in South Asia has firmly maintained the belief that devotion to the Prophet is a crucial element of Islamic piety for both Sunni and Shi'a.

Similarly, 'Ali is almost universally seen as a living, spiritual presence among Sunni and Shi'a alike. *Qalandars* and *faqirs* often claim to have received their spiritual initiation in the "invisible realm" directly from Mawla 'Ali. The phrase "*Ya 'Ali Madad*" ("Oh, Help Me 'Ali") is uttered by Shi'a and Sunni alike.[1]

Although devotion to the *ahl al-bayt* is a determining factor for Shi'i Islam, pro-'Alid sentiments run through almost all of South Asian Muslim culture. Nowhere is this more clearly seen than in the rituals of pilgrimage to Sufi shrines. For example, the gates of the tomb of Shah Lal Baz Qalandar in Sehwan in Sindh are closed briefly every morning in a ritual that involves blessing the Prophet, Fatimah and the twelve Imams. Important shrines such as that of Shah Shams Tabriz in Multan are distinctly Shi'i in their orientation and iconography; however, they still attract Sunni pilgrims in droves. I recall once at the tomb of Shah Shams watching a crowd gathered around a black-clad *qalandar*. As the conversation continued it became clear that some of the people in the crowd identified themselves as Sunni and others as Shi'a. When I asked about this, one of the young men in the crowd spoke up and said that this was no problem as both the Shi'a and the Barelvi Muslims[2] accept the continuing existence of the Prophet and are devoted to the *ahl al-bayt* and are thus to be counted as real Muslims, unlike the Wahabis who deny the spiritual existence of Muhammad and have thus slipped outside of the bounds of true Islam.[3]

In fact, the normally clearly defined distinctions between Shi'a and Sunni are often quite blurred at the level of popular religion in South Asia. For instance, I have interviewed Muslims who have become Shi'a only recently as the result of vows made in the name of 'Ali or *Zuljinah*. I have also met Sunnis who flagellate themselves in the name of Husayn as the result of a *mannat*. While at one level the distinctions between Sunni and Shi'a are extremely important, at another level love for the Prophet and his family at times makes such rigid distinctions problematic. For the future there is much work yet to be done on the relationship between devotion to the *ahl al-bayt* and South Asian Muslim piety in general. It is, in fact, surprising that such questions have not been asked more frequently before.[4]

Islamic Studies as the Study of Muslim Experience

To my mind the discipline of Islamic studies should have at its center the experience of Muslim people. That experience certainly includes classical texts and scholarly, theological, and philosophical debate, but it also includes the experience of ordinary Muslims. Historically, the discipline of Orientalism understood its task as the creation of a canon for the study of Islam. Taking as their model the construction of the canon of Western civilization, the Orientalists sought to collect the most profound and valuable texts produced by Islam and to read them as one might read the "Great Books"—as artifacts contributing to the history of ideas. Such a reading of Ibn Al-Arabi or Ibn Rushd or Hafiz or Rumi is clearly possible. But it will tell us little about the experience of Muslim people. The study of Islam needs to take the context of Islamic practice seriously, because Islam is both a transcendent reality and an articulated series of responses to it. Particularly for the non-Muslim scholar of Islam, the question of Islam's transcendent truth—what God and Muhammad intended in the revelation—must remain to some degree or other shrouded from clear view. But the struggles of Muslims to engage the challenge of the Qur'anic event should draw the attention and respect of scholars both in and outside of the *ummah*.

The struggle of Shi'i Muslims is one common to all religions. Like all religious people they are engaged in a complex balancing act by which they exist in a multiplicity of roles simultaneously, all the while striving to remain true to what they see as essential to their religion. As they do this they in effect are continuously creating a new tradition. By examining the struggle of the Shi'a of South Asia we can learn much that is useful in examining the struggles of other people as they attempt to continuously adapt their religious life to the changing circumstance of the modern world.

This book has been an attempt at the exploration of the self-understandings of one particular group of Muslims but it raises issues that speak to the larger study of Islam (and religion). While this work has focused on the Shi'i Muslims of South Asia, I believe it raises important questions for the study of Islam in general. It is my hope that it provokes further interest not only in the study of Shi'ism and of South Asian Islam but in other contextual studies of Islam as well.

APPENDIX

A *Majlis*

The following is a description of the content of a *majlis* given by 'Ali Naqi Naqvi in Karachi on the morning of October 16, 1983. This *majlis* was delivered on 9 Muharram and was the last in his series of *majalis* at Masjid-i Shah-i Shahidan.[1] It is an excellent example of the ways in which moral and theological teaching and pious mourning come together in the single act of *majlis*. The *majlis* began with an announcer giving a list of other *imambargahs* where the *zakir* would also be reading *majalis* in the next few days. This was followed by an extended period of *sozkhawani* sung by one person.

The *maulana* began the recitation by asking the congregation to say a *du'a* for a man who had died. He then recited the *khutba* and after that called upon the crowd to offer salutations upon the Prophet and the *ahl al-bayt*. After this followed the actual beginning of the *majlis*.

Content of the *Majlis*

He began by saying that today was the last day of *'ashra* (the ten-day cycle) but that the things connected to the Qur'anic verse (which formed the basis of his *majalis*) were far from exhausted. However, he argued that as these things are of a permanent nature he did not feel it was necessary to give a complete list of them.

He then set up the basis of his discussion, which was that all of the *ma'sumin* are not of the same level. This tied in with the topic for his series of *majalis* which was *'ismat*—the protection of the *ma'sumin* from sin or great error. He argued that there are various *mansabs* or stations among the *ma'sumin* and that the basis of each of these *mansabs* is the degree of *'ismat* which they possess.

He used the analogy of light and the ways in which all light is the same in substance, while differing in its intensity. For example, there is a difference in the amount of light put out by a 25- and a 60-watt bulb but in each case it is still light. This is also true, he said, of 1,000-watt bulbs, and the sun also has light. But, he asked, are they all equal? (At this point in the argument the audience showed its appreciation of the

163

argument with shouts of "*Vah-Vah.*") He then argued that light is light no matter what its intensity, whereas there is only one type of darkness. Having set up this analogy he compared it with the possession of *'ismat* by the prophets whose names are found in the Qur'an and notes that they all possessed *'ismat* including Adam, Nuh (Noah), Ibrahim (Abraham), and Muhammad, but that it was not all of the same level. (At the mention of the names of the various prophets, people chanted "*Vah-Vah,*" responding most vigorously to the name of Muhammad.)

Having set this up as a foundation he went on to say that he knew of three levels (*mansabs*) of special relationship to God and that these are *nubbuwat*, *risalat*, and *imamat*. These three together, he said, would constitute the special topic of the day's *majlis*.

He began with *nubbuwat*. He stated that humanity was first introduced to *nubbuwat* by Hazrat Adam who was the first *nabi*. All of the prophets, *rasuls*, and Imams were *rahnumah* (spiritual leaders or guides) in that they showed us the proper path, but they were not all of equal standing. He said that there is one job to be done by all of them, but that the different *mansabs* involved in this work have different names. He used the courtroom as an analogy. Lawyers, judges, and justices are all involved in the work of bringing about justice but they have different standings. For example, if someone calls a judge a lawyer the judge could file a lawsuit claiming libel. Likewise, all of the three *darjah* (grades) of *rahnumah* do the same job—which is to show the right path to God—but they all have different standings. It is wrong to call a *nabi* a *rasul* or a *rasul* a *nabi* because there is a difference in their standings.

Having set up this argument he returned to his discussion of Adam. He argued that at the time when Adam was created there was nobody else. In the beginning there was only Abu'l Bashar (a title of Adam's meaning the Father of Humanity) but *Bashar*—meaning humanity—did not yet exist. This demonstrates the importance of prophetic guidance in God's plan as God did not want the people to be without a *nabi* for even a single moment. Although there was nobody yet in the world, God had still created Adam as a prophet because God desired that when people did come into the world there would be someone there to give guidance to them, as God does not want to leave his people for even one moment without someone to tell them right from wrong. (The audience responded to this with shouts of affirmation.) He continued with the fundamentally Shi'i point that there may be a guide without a people but there can never be a people without a guide. There was never a time when there were people and no *rahnumah*. First the guide came and then the people came. The existence of the people without a guide is not possible. So how, he asked, could it be that in the end there would be people but no guide? (At this point the crowd responds with vigorous shouts of affirmation. The *zakir* had made a major point that is crucial to Shi'i Islam—the necessity of Imamate. He called for *salavats* [blessings] on the Prophet and his family not once but twice, the second time calling for people to speak loudly.)

He continued arguing that the first type of person who came to give us guidance was the *nabi*. He stated that after Adam there were other *nabis* but that the historical data is not precise enough to give us exact dates. Thus, we do not know how long it was between Adam and Nuh. We do know, however, that from the time of Adam was the time of *nubbuwat*, but with Hazrat Nuh comes the beginning of *risalat*. The first *nabi* was Adam and the first *rasul* was Hazrat Nuh. We know, he said, from the Qur'an that Nuh's life was very long and that for 950 years he did *tabligh* (the preaching and purification of religion), although we do not know his entire age. Because he had a long life his title was *Shaikh al-Mursalin*, which means the aged and respected one. Having said all of this he reiterated that Adam and Nuh represent the first two stages of *rahnumah*—that of the *nabi* and the *rasul*.

He then turned his attention to Hazrat Ibrahim. He argued that just as we cannot be sure of the length of time between Adam and Nuh, we cannot be sure of the time which elapsed between Nuh and Ibrahim. But, when Ibrahim appeared he was both a *nabi* and a *rasul*. He then argued that with the coming of Ibrahim we have a new *mansab* which is called *imamat*. He bases his argument on the mention of Ibrahim in the last part of the first *parah* of the Qur'an (which he then quoted in Arabic).[2] In this verse it is mentioned that Ibrahim was tested by God. 'Ali Naqi told the crowd that although we don't know what questions God asked him, we do know what the results were—God made him an Imam. And we know that the station which he achieved after this is greater than that of a *nabi* and greater than that of a *rasul*. For if a *nabi* is an Imam or a *rasul* is an imam why would there have been a need for an exam? (At this point people are responding with chants of *"Vah-Vah."*) Ibrahim had been given a test so that he could be given a standing higher than that of a *rasul*. No one else before him had had the right to take this test for Imamate. Nobody attains this *mansab* without an exam and it is only given to those who are strong enough. 'Ali Naqi distinguished this kind of exam from a standard exam in the educational system. It is, he said, an exam of strength and faith. He compared this exam to the school exams by explaining the meaning of scores on these exams. When a student takes an exam and gets a 50 percent score, he has missed half of the questions and answered half of them correctly. This earns him a second division. The person who gets above 65 percent gets a first division. Then there is another person who gets 80 percent and that is also known as a first division. The person who gets an 80 percent still misses 20 points because he made mistakes. But Ibrahim achieved a 100 percent grade. He was a totally perfect person. If he had missed anything he would not have been called *mukammil* (perfect or completed) by God. Prior to Ibrahim there had been different grades but Ibrahim made no errors. And thus God said, "Oh Ibrahim, I make you an Imam of all of the people." Thus, Ibrahim became an Imam over all of humanity. (Here the *zakir* again called on the crowd to offer salutations to the Prophet.)

At this point in the *majlis* he distinguished between the three forms of *rahnumah*. *Nubbuwat* he argued may be for just one community or one region. *Risalat* is sometimes just for one family or for one tribe. Musa (Moses) is an example of this as he was only for one particular family. He was given the title of *Sahib-i Sharī'at* and is a *rasul*, but he was given *risalat* only for Bani Israel. Then he discussed Hazrat Isa's (Jesus) *risalat*. Isa's *risalat* was also only for Bani Israel. He referred to the Bible (probably Matthew 15:24) as evidence that Jesus saw his message as pertaining only to the people of Bani Israel. He argues that Jesus did not claim to have come for all mankind but only for one particular nation. If his preaching had come for the entire world, then the next prophet, Muhammad, would have appeared among the Romans. But the Prophet's forefathers were not Christians; they instead followed the religion of Ibrahim. If this had not been the case then God would have made the Prophet first a Christian. This proves that Christianity was only for the children of Jacob and Isaac; for the family of Isma'il, he argued, it was the message of Ibrahim which remained correct. There was no other *Rasul-i Alam* (World Prophet) between Ibrahim and Muhammad. Prophets were sent with specific messages for specific places.

Imamat, he said, is not used in reference to a particular people or a particular country. And when the Qur'an says of Muhammad that "I have sent you as a blessing for all humanity," this shows that it was meant for all humanity and not just one tribe. Ibrahim was made an Imam for the entire universe. Ibrahim asked God (according to this verse of the Qur'an) if his children would be Imams. God had made Ibrahim a *nabi* without asking and a *rasul* without asking, but Imamate could only come as the result of an examination. This is his reward for his exam. (Here he called for *salavats*.) He addressed the fact that *nubuwwat* will stop and *risalat* will stop but that Imamate will continue until the end of the world. (And here again he called for *salavats*.)

In accordance with this he again turned to the aforementioned verse of the Qur'an and translated it, noting that not all will agree with his interpretation. 'Ali Naqi noted that God responded to Ibrahim's request by saying that his covenant will not extend to the *zalimin*. He defined the *zalimin* as anyone who goes beyond the limits which God has set. In relation to Imamate, that post will not be given to anyone who is *zalim*. The *zalimin* in the Qur'an are those people who do not act according to the ways of God. There are limits set by God and to go beyond any of these is *zulm* and those people who do so are *zalimin*. He used as an example the act of disobedience of Adam and Eve in the garden of Eden when they approached the tree. This was not a thing against *'ismat*, he argued. It was not a sin; but they had been told not to go near the tree. Going near the tree was an action which was harmful to them but it was not against *'ismat*. He noted that he discusses this fully in a work of his that is published in India. Although it was not a sin in terms of *'ismat*, they went against what God had told them to do. He reiterated that those people are called *zalimin* because they go against the wishes of God and the *mansab* of Imam cannot be given to the *zalimin*. Adam had disobeyed God and thus he was only a *nabi*. (Here once again he called for shouts of *salavat*.) Ibrahim was a *nabi* without asking and a *rasul* without asking, but Imamate could only come as the result of an examination. This again is Ibrahim's reward for his exam. (Here the *zakir* called for *salavats*.) He addressed the fact that *nubuwwat* will stop and *risalat* will stop but that Imamate will continue until the end of the world. (And here again he called for *salavats*.)

Ibrahim he argued had all of the three posts—*nabi, rasul,* and Imam. Ibrahim was a descendant of Adam and was better than him. Likewise, Muhammad was a descendant of Ibrahim. But simple descent is not a reason for his position. Ibrahim was not an Imam simply because he was of the race of Adam. He was of Adam's lineage but he was greater than Adam. Then he asked the question, can a descendant of Ibrahim be greater than Ibrahim? (This was followed by a call for *salavats* and vocal affirmation.)

The Prophet is *afzal* (most excellent). He is greater than Ibrahim. Before Muhammad, Ibrahim was supreme, but now we follow the teachings and Shari'ah of the Prophet. If we were still following the Sunnah of Ibrahim we should have to sacrifice our children. But the Shari'ah of Muhammad has terminated the Sunnah of Ibrahim. If there is anything in the Sunnah of Ibrahim which is in conflict with the Shari'ah it is no longer valid. He made reference to recent cases in the newspapers where persons have received visions which led them to sacrifice their children,[3] but said that the only form of sacrifice of children which is acceptable in the present day is to send our sons off to fight in wars— but not by our hands.

He then argued that Muhammad is an Imam because if someone is greater than Ibrahim he must not only be a *nabi* and a *rasul*, but an Imam also. Muhammad was the end of *nubbuwat*, the end of *risalat*, and an Imam as well. At this point he quotes an *hadith* from the Sunni writer 'Abdul Haqq Dihlavi in which the Prophet said, "Oh 'Ali, son of Ibrahim. That which has reached me has now reached you." (He once more called for *salavats* to the Prophet and his family.)

He then quoted a line of poetry from the poet Khali linking Muhammad's and Ibrahim's message and work. The Qur'an is the final guide in written form and had to come through someone who is *ma'sum*. But guidance must also come through an Imam. Again referring back to the verse in the Qur'an, Ibrahim asks if Imams will be taken from among his children and God replies that they must not come from the *zalimin*. That title cannot be given to the *zalimin*. In his family there can be *zalimin* but the Prophet is not among those. He then quoted the Prophet himself as having said that this prayer of Ibrahim had reached him and thus he had become the Prophet. Ibrahim had never asked that all of his children should be Imams but that there should be one among them. Imamate shall only go to those offspring who are deserving. (Here once more the *zakir* called on the crowd to offer *salavats*.)

At this point he argued that *risalat* and *nubbuwat* have ended but that Imamate is not a thing which will be ended. He then went on to explain this through "dictionary meanings" of the terms. A *nabi* is someone who gives news (*khabardenevali*). As long as there was something to tell to the people there was a need for the institution of *nabi*. When all the news was told then there was no longer a need for a *nabi*. A *rasul* refers to the person who brings the message (*paygham*). As long as there was some message which had not come down there was a need for a *rasul*, but after it had all come down it was no longer necessary. An Imam is somebody who provides leadership. He is the person who travels ahead on the given road. As long as there is a path and there are followers there must be an Imam. (This statement evoked shouts of "*Nade Haidari*" from the crowd and other verbal affirmations. At this point the *zakir* called on the crowd twice to offer salutations to the Prophet and his family.)

Having established Imamate as one of the stations of the Prophet he proceeded to show how this authority is passed on to the Imams. He started by setting up the question of legality in successionship. If someone is a *jā nashīn* (someone who stands in the place of someone else), even if he holds the post for only one day, he will still be called by the title of that post. He gave several examples. If a *munsif* is taking the place of a judge who is on leave you will call him judge. If the vice president takes over for the president he uses the presidential seal. When a vice-chancellor takes a day off and somebody else fills in for him and something needs to be done he will stamp his signature. And when he leaves that position he also leaves behind that title. He continued that the Prophet has three positions. If a *nabi* has a *ja nashin* then he should also be called a *nabi*. But the work of *nubbuwat* is finished and so is the post of *nabi*. The same is true for a *rasul*. But a *ja nashin* is not necessary in *risalat*. There can be no question of a *ja nashin* for *nabis* or *rasuls* as the positions have been eliminated. But there is one more position and that is Imam. This post continues because the work is not yet finished. And the person who holds the highest *mansab* is the Imam. (Here there were two calls of "*Nade Haidari*" from the crowd, followed by two calls from the *zakir* for *salavats* on the Prophet and his family.)

After this he talked to the people almost casually. He apologized for the length of the *majlis* but said that there was one last thing that he wished to speak about. (He had spoken for almost an hour and a half at this point.) He said that he had differentiated between the three terms. Each station has special responsibilities and their followers have responsibilities as well. The *nabi* brings the news and it is the responsibility of others to do *tabligh*. The *rasul* brings the message and the job of the others is to respond to the message. The function of the Imam is to go forward and the job of his followers is to walk behind him.

What are the qualities of an Imam and what is the path of the Imam? He noted that this path is very dangerous. For example, when one goes to the mosque one follows the Imam and the term of his *imamat* is very short. But if you perform the prescribed actions ahead of the Imam during the congregational prayers when the Imam is praying then the prayer is lost. And this is only a minor *imamat*. The Prophet is the leader in the world. If prayer is nullified if we do not do it correctly, surely we must do more than simply talk about the Prophet. He criticized those people who remember the Imams and the Prophet but do not follow their example. He said that all of our lives we remember who the Imam was and then forget him in practice. We call him the Imam and then in practice we make others the Imam. For whom are you taking a stand, he asked, when you are making others the Imam? (At this point a few people started crying in remembrance of the abandoned path of the Imam.) We are siding with people who take the rights of other people, he said. Now, he said, tell me, are we a part of the good people or of the *zalimin*? We talk about supporting the oppressed and then in practice we follow the *zalimin*. We remember Karbala—but we do not remember the prayers they said there. Actually, he argued, if we did not remember, then we would not be mentioning it. We mention it; we listen to it; and we cry about it. But when it comes to practicing it we do not say our prayers. Husayn offered his life for *namaz* at Karbala, but we do not offer prayers. So will God consider us among his friends if we behave in this way? He then quoted a sentence that he had once heard at another *majlis*. He said, "We have remembered the dagger, but we have forgotten the prostration." But, he adds, "The dagger was Shimr's, while the prostration was Husayn's."

He continued by talking about how people allow the Qur'an to gather dust in their houses. Or if someone faints they revive them by fanning air on them with the Qur'an; but they do not read it. He continued, noting that there are mosques nearby but people never go to them to say their prayers. They invite *maulvis* to their homes for circumcisions, weddings, or to read prayers for the dead but never at other times. How, he asked, can the *'ulama* know the problems of the people if they never interact with the people? What can you learn from the *'ulama* or from the *pesh imams* if you never let them know your problems? It is desirable for people to learn from the *'ulama*.

He then moved from this point of learning about Islam from the *'ulama* to the *gham*, noting that the discussion about Karbala is for the welfare of Muslims and the world and that it is done for the very survival of Islam. He said that the sacrifices made by the grandchildren of the Prophet are an example for us to follow. If we follow their tradition then they will consider us their followers. Was not the condition of those who accompanied Husayn like that of Husayn?

He based his *gham* on the portion of the *a'mal* where the congregation takes seven steps forward and seven steps back, and then recites the Qur'anic words which are recited when a person dies in order to remind those who are hearing them about their final return to the Lord. Husayn's hesitation should not be seen as indecision, as the *mawla* always knew what he had to do. But he was in sorrow (*gham*). He would have to go to the tents and tell the women. What, he thought, will I tell the mother of the dead child—that he has joined the Prophet? At this point he equated the condition of Husayn with that of Ibrahim and *ahl-i Ibrahim*. In a similar fashion, seven times Hagar went back and forth between the mountains seeking water for her child Isma'il. Husayn moved back seven times before he finally entered the tents, where he gave the corpse of the child to its mother.

He then quoted a *marthiyah* which was related by 'Ali Asghar's mother which, although not historical, is according to the *zakir* indicative of the feelings of Husayn. "Mawla, you should not be sad because the sacrifice is great. You never thought that such a thing could happen."

(During this time the crowd continued to cry more and more intensely.) Now Husayn was left alone. There was no one else. It is not part of the teaching of Islam to appear weak before one's enemies. As long as one can one must stand and fight. (As he continued the crying in the audience grew louder and louder.) He recited how the Imam said his farewells to his sisters, his wives, and then the women in the camp whose husbands and other relatives had already given their lives in combat. And he asked them to offer greetings to all of the followers of Muhammad and the friends of 'Ali back in Medina and to tell them to remember the thirst of the Imam while drinking cold water as the Imam was thirsty for three days.

(As he continued the crying became more and more intense.) He said that after saying all of this the Imam went to the battleground. The *zakir* noted that before this day it was the name of 'Ali that was renowned for bravery but after Karbala it was that of Husayn. He described how Husayn rode alone into battle having had no food and no water and upon the back of the same horse where he had earlier carried 'Ali Asghar. But now, he said, the back of the horse is empty. The grandson of the Prophet has fallen to the ground. And there was no one else there. If 'Abbas had been there or if 'Ali Akbar had been there *Zuljinah* would have gone to them. But he went to the tents of the women as there was no one on the battlefield. And it was Sakina who saw him first and cried, "Oh my father."

(At that point the audience expressed a great sigh of grief and the *matam* began.)

NOTES

Introduction

1. Clifford Geertz, *The Interpretation of Cultures*, pp. 90–91.

2. I am here using the term "multivocal" in the manner of Victor Turner. See Victor Turner, *From Ritual to Theatre: The Human Seriousness of Play*, pp. 62–84.

3. Emile Durkheim, *The Elementary Forms of the Religious Life*.

4. Rudolph Otto, *The Idea of the Holy*.

5. Victor Turner, *The Ritual Process: Structure and Anti-Structure*, p. 96.

6. For my use of this term see Turner, *From Ritual to Theatre*, pp. 82–84.

7. Turner, *The Ritual Process*, pp. 106–7.

8. Victor Turner, *The Forest of Symbols*, pp. 100–101.

9. Ibid., pp. 102–3. It should be noted that Turner understands these *sacra* to be secret. This is clearly not the case with Muharram rituals which are purposively public.

10. Victor Turner, *Dramas, Fields, and Metaphors: Symbolic Action in Human Society*, p. 64.

11. Ibid., p. 64.

12. Zamir Akhtar Naqvi, *Urdu Marthiyah Pakistan Mei*, pp. 191–94. This is an interesting work by a young *zakir* living in Pakistan. He has based much of the historical portion of his book on Sibtul Hasan Hansawi's *'Azadari ki Tarikh*. I am not an historian of South Asia and cannot claim to speak to the historical verity of these sources. What is important from the perspective of this work is not whether this represents actual history but history as it is understood by the Shi'i community.

13. This will be more fully discussed in chapter 3.

Chapter 1: The Nature of Shi'ism in Its South Asian Context

1. Edward W. Said, *Covering Islam: How the Media and the Experts Determine how We See the Rest of the World*, p. 82.

2. H. A. R. Gibb, *Mohammedanism: An Historical Survey*, pp. 82–85.

3. Ignaz Goldziher, *Muslim Studies*, vol. 1. A good example of this can be found on p. 23 where Shi'ism is contrasted with orthodox Islam.

4. Fazlur Rahman, *Islam*, pp. 203–21.

5. Once again, an excellent example of this can be found in Goldziher's discussion of saint veneration. Goldziher, *Muslim Studies*, 1:209–39.

6. I am deeply indebted to Professor Karrar Hussain of the Khurasan Islamic Research Center for his insights. Karrar Hussain is a highly learned man (although not a member of the *'ulama*) as well as a respected reader of *majlis*.

7. Marshall Hodgson, *The Venture of Islam*, 1:79–82.

8. Karrar Hussain, personal conversation.

9. Yousuf N. Lalljee, ed., *Ali the Magnificent*, pp. 89–95; and Shaykh al-Mufid, *Kitab al-Irshad: The Book of Guidance into the Lives of the Twelve Imams*, pp. 127–38.

10. This is probably best expressed in the *Hadith al-Thaqalyn* which reads, "Verily I am leaving among you two objects of high estimation and care: the book of God and my dear kindred my family. They are my Vice-Regents after me and *will not part from each other until the return at the Pool*." See Abdulaziz Abdulhussein Sachedina, *Islamic Messianism: The Idea of the Mahdi in Twelver Shi'ism*, pp. 102–3.

11. Karrar Hussain, personal conversation.

12. See the analysis of the Qur'an in Sunni piety, in Hodgson, *The Venture of Islam*, 1:366–72.

13. I interviewed many different Muslims—Sunni and Shi'a—whom I met in Pakistan from Ramadan through Muharram about their feelings on this definition and encountered literally no one who disagreed with it.

14. This argument can be found in almost any Shi'i history. See, for example, Allamah Sayyid Muhammad Husayn Tabataba'i, *Shi'ite Islam*, pp. 42–50.

15. Ha'im Chisti, *Mushkil Kusha*, pp. 37–38.

16. *Hadith Kissa'*.

17. Hodgson, *The Venture of Islam*, 1:372.

18. Ibid., 1:238.

19. This argument is taken from *Tuhfat ul-'Awām Maqbul*. It will be further discussed in chapter 3.

20. Sachedina, *Islamic Messianism*, p. 122.

21. Tabatabai, *Shi'ite Islam*, p. 48.

22. Abu Bakr al-Kalabadhi, *The Doctrine of the Sufis (Kitab al-Ta'arruf li-madhhab ahl al-tasawwuf)*, p. 57.

23. Muhammad Baqir al-Majlisi, *Hayat ul-Qulub*, 2:122–278.

24. Mufid, *Kitab al-Irshad*, pp. 229–65.

25. Ibid., p. 229.

26. Ibid., pp. 229–67.

27. Michael Gilsenan, *Recognizing Islam: Religion and Society in the Modern Arab World*, pp. 116–42.

28. Turner, *From Ritual to Theatre*, pp. 82–84.

29. An important concept underlying these events is that of the maintenance of proper *adab* or courtesy. Relationships with powerful personages like rulers or Sufis require that one observe prescribed patterns of respect. *Adab* is an important concept in Islam in South Asia. The reader is referred to Barbara Daly Metcalf, ed., *Moral Conduct and Authority: The Place of Adab in South Asian Islam.*

30. Mufid, *Kitab al-Irshad*, p. 125.

31. Ibid.

32. Maulana Sayyid Husayn Riza, *I'jaz-i Khitabat*, p. 25.

33. Ibid.

34. Ibid.

35. See S. V. Mir Ahmed Ali, *The Holy Qur'an.*

36. Lalljee, *Ali the Magnificent*, p. 7; and Mufid, *Kitab al-Irshad*, p. 229.

37. See, for example, Lalljee, *Ali the Magnificent*, pp. 49–55; and Mufid, *Kitab al-Irshad*, p. 40.

38. Hodgson, *The Venture of Islam*, 1:146–89.

39. Ibid., 1:216–17.

Chapter 2: Household Rituals: The Uses of Miraculous Narrative

1. Hodgson, *The Venture of Islam*, 1:394.

2. Susan S. Wadley, "Vrats: Transformers of Destiny."

3. As stated in chapter 1, the concept of *adab* is extremely critical in Islamic piety. Readers are once again referred to Metcalf, ed., *Moral Conduct and Authority.*

4. *Mu'jizat wa Munajat*, p. 3.

5. This version is based upon the version in *Mu'jizat wa Munajat* and two pamphlet versions.

6. Maulana Jalalu-d-din Muhammad I Rumi, *The Teachings of Rumi: The Masnavi*, p. 4.

7. I am indebted for this interpretation to Abbas Hussain who teaches English at the University of Karachi and has considerable insight into *tariqah* Sufism in Pakistan.

8. Surah 21:69.

9. I learned this through discussions of *majalis* literature with Professor T. H. Naqvi with whom I studied Urdu in Karachi.

10. Hodgson, *The Venture of Islam*, 1:238.

11. I am grateful to Margi Robinson who first made me aware of this (and the miracle stories themselves) during the 1982 Berkeley Urdu Language Program.

12. *Das Bibiyan ki Kahani*, pp. 2–5.

13. Ibid., p. 5. Surprisingly, Khadijah, the Prophet's wife, does not make this list.

14. Ibid., pp. 5–6.

15. Ibid., pp. 6–7.

16. Ibid., p. 7.

17. Ibid., p. 8.

18. Idries Shah, *Caravan of Dreams*, pp. 114–22. This version of the story is considerably different than the one which is current in Pakistan.

19. Ibid., p. 114.

20. This version is based on the version in *Mu'jizat wa Munajat* and a pamphlet version.

21. *Fatihah* here refers to a ritual in which certain *surahs* of the Qur'an are recited in the name of 'Ali and then food is distributed.

22. This is an older version that was published together with the *kahani* connected to the *niyaz* of Imam Ja'far as-Sadiq.

23. A. J. Arberry, *Sufism: An Account of the Mystics of Islam*, p. 28.

24. For example, there is a water-giver in the Gilgamesh epic who serves this function.

25. I raise this only as a possibility, not to imply that these stories are primarily Isma'ili in content. However, Shi'ism did spread in the subcontinent early on as a result of Isma'ili proselytization and this has left its mark on the region.

26. I discovered that it was difficult to find out information about this ritual. At one point at Mehfil-i Murtaza a number of people were insulted that I asked if this ritual was related to the death of Mu'awiya until an older gentleman assured me that the 22d of Rajab was in fact the day of Mu'awiya's death, although it was not the reason for the *niyaz*.

27. "Mu'jizat Imam Ja'far as-Sadiq," *Mu'jizat wa Munajat*, pp. 34–38.

28. Interestingly, *kir* (rice pudding) is not mentioned, although it was usually present when I observed this ritual.

29. This is the version printed with the pamphlet version of *Mushkil Kusha Kahani* mentioned above.

30. *Mu'jizat wa Munajat*, pp. 3–4.

Chapter 3: Public Performances:
The Ritual Encounter with Karbala

1. This can be readily seen from examining any Shi'i calendar such as the one published by the Mostazafan Foundation of New York.

2. 'Ali Naqi Naqvi, "Qatil-i 'Abarat," in *'Azimat-ul Husayn*, p. 104.

3. 'Ali Naqi Naqvi, *Azadari: A Historical Review of the Institution of Azadari for Imam Husayn*, p. 1.

4. I am here using the term in the manner of Victor Turner. See Turner, *From Ritual to Theatre*, pp. 62–84.

5. See chapter 1.

6. Sibtul Hasan Fazil Hansawi, *'Azadari ki Tarikh*.

7. Fida Hussain, *Ainah-yi Muharram Sharif*, pp. 12–19.

8. 'Ali Naqi Naqvi, *'Azimat-ul Husayn*, p. 105.

9. Ibid.

10. I am indebted to Abdulaziz Sachedina for pointing out this aspect of the *majlis* to me.

11. 'Ali Naqi Naqvi, *'Azimat-ul Husayn*, p. 105.

12. Ibid., p. 107.

13. Ibid., p. 108.

14. Ibid., p. 109.

15. Ibid., p. 108.

16. Ibid., p. 116.

17. Hansawi, *'Azadari ki Tarikh*, p. 81.

18. Mahmoud Ayoub, *Redemptive Suffering in Islam*, pp. 77–78.

19. *Tuhfat ul-'Awam Maqbul*, pp. 242–43.

20. Ibid., p. 243.

21. Ibid.

22. Possibly as a way of staving off criticism of *shirk* or *ghulluw* the Imams enjoined the recitation of *surah-i tauhid* on all believers at least once in each *salat*.

23. *Tuhfat ul-'Awam Maqbul*, p. 243.

24. John T. Platts, *A Dictionary of Urdu, Classical Hindi, and English*, p. 3.

25. *Tuhfat ul-'Awam Maqbul*, pp. 243–44.

26. Hansawi, *'Azadari ki Tarikh*, pp. 38–39.

27. *Tuhfat ul-'Awam Maqbul*, pp. 243–44.

28. Ibid., p. 245.

29. Ibid., p. 246.

30. Ibid., p. 249.

31. Unpublished material obtained from A. A. Sachedina.

32. Zamir Akhtar Naqvi, *Urdu Marthiyah Pakistan Mei*, p. 204.

33. See the series of books by 'Ali Naqi Naqvi, *Zakiri ki Pehli Kitab*. These small books contain a series of prewritten *majalis*. Beginning *zakirs* use such books when they are starting out until they develop the skill to write their own.

34. They may receive as much as 5,000 to 10,000 rupees a *majlis*. Naqqan Sahab contributes his fee to a Shi'i institute in Lucknow.

35. My experience at most *imambargahs* was that there was a distinction of purity between the place of *sajdah* (prostration) and the *Husayniyya*. As a non-Muslim it was sometimes the case that I was denied access to the *masjid*, although this was not always the case and there was a disagreement even among learned Muslims as to whether or not a non-Muslim could in fact enter the *masjid*. All visitors, however, were encouraged to attend the *majlis*.

36. I interviewed some of these chained dervishes and learned that they wore these chains in memory of the survivors of Karbala.

37. Geertz, *The Interpretation of Cultures*, pp. 90–91.

38. Turner, *The Ritual Process*, p. 96.

39. Hodgson, *The Venture of Islam*, 1:394.

40. This is sometimes spontaneous but sometimes it is done by people in the audience called the "spoons" of the *zakir*. Sometimes they are paid and their job is to heighten the intensity of the *majlis*.

41. Hazrat Maulavi Sayyid Shakir Husayn Sahib Naqvi, *Mujahid-i 'Azam*.

42. "Sawal-o Jawab Besilsileh Yad-o Yadgar az 'Ali Naqi al-Naqvi," pp. 5–13.

43. I took this list from the study of Muharram in Lucknow and Delhi done for the 1961 Census of India. In actual practice I found that there was a great deal more fluidity in this list than I originally thought that there would be.

44. I am not sure of the reason for this; perhaps it is because it is the halfway point of the ten days.

45. Hansawi, *'Azadari ki Tarikh*, p. 27.

46. 'Ali Naqi Naqvi, *Azadari*, p. 128.

47. Shakir Husayn Naqvi, *Mujahid-i 'Azam*, p. 335.

48. Ibid., p. 336.

49. 'Ali Naqi Naqvi, *Azadari*, p. 129.

Chapter 4: Muharram Performances 1404 A.H. (1983 C.E.)

1. For my use of this term see Turner, *The Ritual Process*, p. 96.

2. Ibid.

3. For a good discussion of this see Wladimir Ivanow, "The Sect of Imam Shah in Gujarat," *Journal of the Bombay Branch of the Royal Asiatic Society* 12:19–70.

4. It should be remembered that this discussion took place during the height of the Iran-Iraq war.

Chapter 5: The Wounds of Devotion: Physical Risk as an Act of Allegiance

1. This was also observed by Keith Guy Hjortshoj, *Kerbala in Context: A Study of Muharram in Lucknow, India*, p. 145. His explanation, however, does not fully explain the relationship between *zanjir ka matam* and Shi'i theology.

2. This was also observed by Hjortshoj.

3. This may be only because of the ideal of feminine modesty in Islam. I did, however, observe *hath ka matam* among women and talked to people who had seen fire *matam* practiced by women. I think it more likely that the reason for this is that Shi'i law disallows female participation in combat (a fact mirrored in the role of the women at Karbala and a contrast drawn by some Shi'i writers between Fatimah and Aisha). It is the act of *zanjir ka matam* as surrogate warfare which, I believe, makes it solely a male phenomenon.

4. This argument is verified in the popular Urdu work by Muhammad Wasi Khan, *Husain Husain*, 1:35.

5. See chapter 3.

6. Again, this was also observed by Hjortshoj, p. 162, in relation to fire *matam*.

7. Werner Ende, "The Flagellations of Muharram and the Shi'ite '*Ulama*."

8. Unpublished material obtained from A. A. Sachedina.

9. Ibid.

10. This is the explanation in Khan, *Husain, Husain*, 1:36.

11. This was also observed by Hjortshoj, *Kerbala in Context*, p. 162.

12. This aspect of the ritual is also described in Ja'far Sharif, *Islam in India or the Qanun-i Islam*, pp. 158–59.

13. Unpublished material obtained from A. A. Sachedina.

Conclusion

1. In an attempt to counter this practice, which they consider to be *shirk*, one "reformist" Muslim organization devised bumper stickers which read *Sirf Allah Madagar He* (Only God is the Helper).

2. The Barelvi are the largest Sunni "sect" in Pakistan. They define themselves as the school of tradition and they accept the authenticity of the Sufi tradition.

3. At the level of popular Islam the connections between Sunni and Shi'a are close but reform movements like the *Jammat-i Islami*, the *Deobandis*, and the *Ahl-i Hadith*, suspicious of popular religion in general, have exacerbated tension between the two schools.

4. I returned from a year of fieldwork in Multan in 1989 under the auspices of a Fulbright Grant where I was engaged in research on Sufi pilgrimage. These sorts of questions continually moved to the forefront of that research. I have presented two conference papers based on this research at the 1989 and 1990 national meetings of the American Academy of Religion. I am currently compiling this research for a book on popular Sufism in Pakistan.

Appendix: A *Majlis*

1. According to A. A. Sachedina it is the custom in Lucknow to give the final *majlis* on the ninth day.

2. Surah 2:124: "And when his Lord tried Ibrahim with certain words, he fulfilled them. He said: Surely I will make you an Imam of men. Ibrahim said: And of my offspring? My covenant does not include the unjust, said He." Similar arguments are to be found in the English *tafsir* of S. V. Mir Ahmed Ali and the Urdu *tafsir* of Maulana Sayyid Zafar Hasan Sahab.

3. Earlier that year a man and his family had walked into the sea at Hawkes Bay on the authority of just such a dream in an attempt to walk to Karbala. The women and the children were carried into the water in metal boxes and almost all of them drowned. The survivors of the

Hawkes Bay incident were at the center of a great deal of controversy and discussion. Salman Rushdie used this incident as the basis for an episode in *The Satanic Verses*.

GLOSSARY

The following is a glossary of some of the technical terms which occur most frequently in the text. The meanings of the terms are confined to the contexts in which they are used in the book.

āg ka mātam: fire walking performed as an act of devotional mourning for Imam Husayn.

ahl al-bayt: "the People of the House"; it includes the Prophet, 'Ali, Fatimah, Hasan, Husayn, and the other Imams from among the descendants of Husayn.

'alam: a representation of the standard of Husayn often topped with a five-fingered hand representing the *panjatan pāk*.

'Alid loyalism: concept developed by the late Marshall Hodgson referring to loyalty to the 'Alid family and the complex of attitudes associated with that loyalty.

'ālim: a scholar-jurist; one of the *'ulama*.

a'māl: a series of prescribed ritual actions performed on the day of *'Āshūrā*.

anjuman: a society of persons who come together for the purposes of mourning Husayn.

'Āshūrā: the tenth day of the month in Muharram; the day on which Husayn was martyred and the center of the ritual mourning period of Muharram.

āyatullah: the highest level of *mujtahid*.

'azādārī: the complex of rituals and performances used in mourning for Husayn.

azān: the call to ritual prayer.

bid'a: innovation; an action that is inappropriate because it was not a part of the practice of the Prophet or his companions.

179

Bohris: name given to a division of the Isma'ili Muslims of South Asia. They are neither Twelver Shi'a nor followers of the Agha Khan.

Chhellum: the fortieth day after '*Ashura*. This is a day of ritual mourning and the end of the major mourning cycle which begins on the first day of Muharram.

darūd: a recitation of blessing or praise for the Prophet.

da'wa: the agents of the Imam who spread the doctrines of Isma'ilism.

du'ā: personal petitionary prayer to God. Often it is performed at the end of *namāz*.

fiqh: Islamic law.

gham: the final portion of a *majlis* in which the *zākir* evokes the incidents of Karbala and induces tears of grief in the congregation.

ghūllūw: "extremism"; believing extreme things about 'Ali such as ascribing divinity to him.

ghusl khānah: area in an *Imambargah* where corpses are prepared for burial.

ḥadīth: a report about the actions or speech of the Prophet or one of the Imams.

Ḥadīth Kissa':   important *hadith* which tells of the Prophet gathering Fatimah, 'Ali, Hasan, and Husayn under his cloak, producing a concentration of light which attracted the Angel Jibra'il from the heavens. For this reason they are called the "People of the Cloak."

halīm: special kind of food served during Muharram.

hāth ka mātam: the act of mourning Husayn through the rhythmic striking of the chest with the hands.

Ḥusayniyya: an area of an *imāmbārgāh* where devotional objects are kept. Also called a *ziyārat khānah*.

ijtihād: the use of independent reasoning in the formulation of Islamic law.

imāmbārgāh: building used for the performance of Shi'i religious activities.

'iṣmat: "infallibility"; the state of being protected from error.

ja'iz: refers to that which is permissible under Islamic law.

jāzbat: emotional attraction.

julūs: mourning procession.

Khojas: a group of Gujarati-speaking Shi'i Muslims. They are divided into Nizari Isma'ili and Twelver groupings.

khuṭba: a formulaic Arabic recitation performed near the beginning of the *majlis* which greets the *ahl al-bayt*.

kundah niyāz: ritual performed in the memory of Imam Ja'far as-Sadiq in which rice pudding is served in clay pots.

majlis (pl. *majālis*): mourning assembly; a recitation by a *zākir* consisting of an expository discourse followed by an evocation of Karbala called the *gham*.

mannat: a spiritual vow.

marthiyah: lamentation poetry written about Imam Husayn.

ma'sūm: the state of being protected from sin or error.

Ma'sūmah: Fatimah; so called because she is *ma'sūm*.

ma'sūmīn: the fourteen *ma'sūm* ones; Muhammad, Fatimah, and the twelve Imams.

mātam: physical acts of mourning.

mātamdār: one who does *mātam*.

mehndhi: "henna"; the term refers here to the remembrance of the wedding of Qasim who is believed to have been killed at Karbala on the eve of his wedding.

minbār: the staired platform from which the *zākir* delivers his *majlis*.

muhājirs: those persons and their descendants who migrated to Pakistan after the partition of India.

mu'jizāt kahānīs: miracle stories; tales concerning the miraculous intervention of the *ahl al-bayt* used for the making of spiritual vows.

mujtahid: a scholar-jurist; one capable of exercising *ijtihād*.

Mushkil Kusha: "remover of difficulties"; a title of 'Ali.

Na'ib-i Imām: deputy of the Imam.

namāz: the Urdu and Persian word for ritual prayers; equivalent to the Arabic *salāt*.

Nade Haidarī: a call given at *majlis* meaning "cry out Haydar ('Ali)!" The proper response is "Yā 'Ali!"

nass: designation; the process by which each consecutive Imam is designated by his predecessor.

nazr: a religious offering.

nishān: a symbolic artifact respresentative of the *ahl al-bayt*.

niyāz: an offering made in the name of a holy person.

niyyat: intention; in Islam any religious act, such as *namāz* or fasting must be preceded by a formal intention.

pāk: the state of ritual purity.

palna: a replica of the cradle of the slain infant 'Ali Asghar.

panjatan: the five-fingered hand representing the Five Holy Ones.

panjatan pāk: the Five Holy Ones; Muhammad, Fatimah, 'Ali, Hasan, and Husayn.

purdah: the practice of the segregation of women.

qalandār: Muslim holy man; they are often Shi'a and wear chains and other unusual garb.

rowzah: replicas of the tombs of the *ahl al-bayt* displayed in *ziyārat khānahs*.

sabīl: stands set up for the distribution of water as a pious action during Muharram.

ṣalāvāt: a call for blessings upon the Prophet and his family.

Shab-i Bedār: the evening before the day of *'Ashura* on which it is customary for people to stay awake all night in acts of devotion.

Shām-i Gharībān: The Night of the Unfortunate Ones; the night following the day of *'Ashura* on which the final evening *majlis* is given.

sherwānī: a long coat worn on formal occasions.

sormah: a mascara-like eye decoration worn by men.

sozkhāwāni: a type of sung lamentation poetry.

tabarra: the ritual condemnation of the enemies of the *ahl al-bayt*.

tabarruk: blessed food.

tabūt: coffin; the replicas of coffins carried in *julus*.

takrīr: the unspoken approval of the Prophet.

talvār ka mātam: physical *mātam* in which the *mātamdar* strikes his head with a sword.

taqlīd: the act of giving obedience to a *mujtahid* in questions of Islamic law.

tasbih: a rosary.

ta'ziyah: model of the tomb of Imam Husayn carried in processions.

thāwab: the spiritual benefit gained by performing an action.

ṭufail: intercession; the intercession of the Imams.

wuzū: spiritual ablutions before prayer.

"*Yā 'Ali Madad*":   "Oh Help, Imam 'Ali."

zākir: the person who delivers *majlis*.

zanjīr ka mātam: *mātam* that consists of flagellation with chains and knives.

zarih: a decorative grave covering.

zikr: "remembrance"; refers to Sufi meditative techniques for focusing concentration on God.

ziyārat: pilgrimage to the tomb of an Imam or a replica of it. It also refers to a type of formulaic recitation which is a symbolic pilgrimage.

ziyārat khānah: place for displaying religious artifacts evocative of the *ahl al-bayt*.

Zūlfiqār: the sword of ʿAli.

Zūljinah: a horse which serves as a representation of the mount of Husayn in processions.

BIBLIOGRAPHY

Urdu and Persian Sources

Chisti, Ha'im. *Mushkil Kusha.* Faisalabad: Khalid Mahmud Khan, 1983.
Das Bibiyan ki Kahani. Karachi: Mahfuz Book Agency, n.d.
Hansawi, Sibtul Hasan Fazil. *'Azadari ki Tarikh.* Karachi: Muslim Sulman Mission, n.d.
Hussain, Fida. *Ainah-yi Muharram Sharif.* Itava, U.P., 1966.
Khan, Muhammad Wasi. *Husain Husain.* Vol. 1. Karachi: Mashur Offset Press, n.d.
al-Majlisi, Muhammad Baqir. *Hayat ul-Qulub.* Vol. 2. Tehran: Kitab Befarsi Islamiya, 1977.
Mu'jizat wa Munajat. Karachi: Ahmad Book Depot, n.d.
Naqvi, 'Ali Naqi. *'Azimat-ul Husayn.* Karachi, n.d.
_____. *Shahid-i Insaniyat.* Lucknow: Thani Barqi Press, 1966.
_____. *Zakiri ki Pehli Kitab.* Lahore: Imamia Kutub Khanah, n.d.
Naqvi, Hazrat Maulavi Sayyid Shakir Husayn Sahib. *Mujahid-i 'Azam.* Jaipur, n.d.
Naqvi, Zamir Akhtar. *Urdu Marthiyah Pakistan Mei.* Karachi: Sayyid and Sayyid, 1983.
Riza, Maulana Sayyid Husayn. *I'jaz-i Khitabat.* Karachi: Sindh Offset Press, 1983.
"Sawal-o Jawab Besilsileh Yad-o Yadgar az 'Ali Naqi al-Naqvi." *Sarfaraz Weekly Lucknow.* 1976.
Tuhfat ul-'Awam Maqbul. Lahore: Ansaf Press, n.d.

Sources in English and English Translation

Ahmad, Imtiaz, editor. *Ritual and Religion among Muslims in India.* New Delhi: Ramesh Jain for Manohar, 1981.
'Ali b. Abu Talib. *Nahjul Balagha.* Translated by Syed Mohammed Askari Jafery. Elmhurst, N.Y.: Tahrike Tarsile Qur'an, 1977.
_____. *Supplications (Du'a).* Translated by William C. Chittick. London: Muhammadi Trust of Great Britain and Northern Ireland, 1980.

185

al-Amini, Hassan. *Islamic Shi'ite Encyclopedia*. Vol. 1. Beirut, 1968.

Ali, S. V. Mir Ahmed, translator. *The Holy Qur'an*. Pakistan: Peerma-homed Ebrahim Trust, n.d.

Arberry, A. J. *Sufism: An Account of the Mystics of Islam*. London: Allen and Unwin, 1950.

Arberry, A. J., translator. *The Doctrine of the Sufis*. Cambridge: Cambridge University Press, 1977.

Attar, Farid al-Din. *Muslim Saints and Mystics*. Translated by A. J. Arberry. London: Routledge and Kegan Paul, 1966.

Ayoub, Mahmoud. *Redemptive Suffering in Islam*. The Hague: Mouton, 1978.

Behishti, Muhammad Husayni, and Javad Bahonar. *Philosophy of Islam*. Translated by M. A. Ansari. London: Islamic Seminary Publications, 1982.

Census of India 1961. Monograph Series, volume 1 part 7-B. Monograph no. 3. *Muharram in Two Cities (Lucknow and Delhi)*.

Chelkowski, Peter J., editor. *Ta'ziyeh—Ritual and Drama in Iran*. New York: New York University Press, 1979.

Chittick, William C., translator. *A Shi'ite Anthology*. Selected by Allamah Sayyid Muhammad Husayn Tabataba'i. London: Muhammadi Trust of Great Britain and Northern Ireland, 1980.

Douglas, Mary. *Purity and Danger: An Analysis of Concepts of Pollution and Taboo*. New York: Praeger, 1970.

Durkheim, Emile. *The Elementary Forms of the Religious Life*. Translated by Joseph Ward Swain. New York: Free Press, 1965.

Eliade, Mircea. *The Myth of the Eternal Return*. Princeton: Princeton University Press, 1954.

Enayat, Hamid. *Modern Islamic Political Thought*. Austin: University of Texas Press, 1982.

Ende, Werner. "The Flagellations of Muharram and the Shi'ite 'Ulama,'" *Der Islam* 55. Berlin, 1978.

Faridi, Shahidullah. *Inner Aspects of Faith*. Karachi: Mehfil-e-Zauqia, 1979.

Faruki, Kemal A. *Islam Today and Tomorrow*. Karachi: Pakistan Publishing House, 1974.

Fischer, Michael. *Iran: From Religious Dispute to Revolution*. Cambridge, Mass.: Harvard University Press, 1980.

Geertz, Clifford. *The Interpretation of Cultures*. New York: Basic Books, 1973.

———. *Islam Observed*. Chicago: University of Chicago Press, 1968.

al-Ghita, Ayatullah Kashif. *The Shia—Origin and Faith*. Translated by M. Fazal Haq. London: Islamic Seminary Publications, 1982.

Gibb, H. A. R. *Mohammedanism: An Historical Survey*. Home University Library, 1949; 2d ed. revised reprint, New York: Oxford University Press, 1973.

Gilsenan, Michael. *Recognizing Islam: Religion and Society in the Modern Arab World*. New York: Pantheon, 1982.

Goldziher, Ignaz. *Muslim Studies*. Edited by S. M. Stern. Vol. 1. Albany: State University of New York Press, 1967; second printing 1977. Vol. 2. Albany: State University of New York Press, 1971.

Guillaume, A. *The Life of Muhammad: A Translation of Ishaq's Sirat Rasul Allah*. Oxford: Oxford University Press, 1978.

al-Hilli, Ibn al-Mutahhar Hasan b. Yusuf. *Al-Babu 'l-Hadi 'ashari. A Treatise on the Principles of Shi'ite Theology*. Translated by William Miller. London: Royal Asiatic Society, 1928.

Hjortshoj, Keith Guy. "Kerbala in Context: A Study of Muhurram in Lucknow, India." Ph.D. dissertation, Cornell University, Ithaca, N.Y. Ann Arbor, Mich.: University Microfilms International, 1977.

Hodgson, Marshall. *The Venture of Islam*. Vol. 1, *The Classical Age of Islam*. Vol. 2, *The Expansion of Islam in the Middle Periods*. Vol. 3, *The Gunpowder Empires and Modern Times*. Chicago: University of Chicago Press, 1974.

Hollister, John. *The Shi'a of India*. London: Huzac, 1953.

Hughes, Thomas Patrick. *A Dictionary of Islam*. Lahore: Book House, n.d.

Al-Hujwiri, 'Ali B. 'Uthman Al-Jullabi. *The Kashf Al-Mahjub*. Translated by Reynold A. Nicholson. London: Luzac, 1976.

Hussain, Jassim M. *The Occultation of the Twelfth Imam*. London: Muhammadi Trust of Great Britain and Northern Ireland, 1982.

Ibn Babuya, Muhammad b. 'Ali. *A Shi'ite Creed*. Translated by A. A. A. Fyzee. London: Oxford University Press, 1942.

Ivanow, Wladimir. "The Sect of Imam Shah in Gujarat." *Journal of the Bombay Branch of the Royal Asiatic Society*, 1936.

Jafri, Syed H. *Origins and Early Development of Shi'a Islam*. London: Longman, 1979.

al-Kulayni, Muhammad b. Ya'qub b. Is'haq. *Al-Kafi*. Vol. 1, part 1, "Al-Usul—The Book of Reason and Ignorance," translated by As-Sayyid Muhammad Hasan ar-Rizavi. Tehran: A Group of Muslim Brothers, 1978. Vol. 2, part 2, "Al-Usul—The Book of Excellence of Knowledge," translated by As-Sayyid Muhammad Hasan ar-Rizavi. Karachi: Khurasan Islamic Research Centre, n.d.

Lalljee, Yousuf N., editor. *Ali the Magnificent*. Bombay, n.d.

_____. *Know Your Islam*. Elmhurst, N.Y.: Tahrike Tarsile Qu'an, n.d.

Lewis, Bernard. *The Origins of Isma'ilism*. "A Study of the Historical Background of the Fatimid Caliphate." Cambridge: W. Heffer and Sons, 1940; reprint ed., New York: A. M. S. Press, 1975.

al-Majlisi, Muhammad Baqir. *The Life and Religion of Muhammad (Hayat al-Qulub)*. Vol. 2. Translated by James L. Merrick. Boston: Phillips, Sampson, 1850; reprint ed., Texas: Zahra Trust, 1982.

Metcalf, Barbara Daly, editor. *Moral Conduct and Authority: The Place of Adab in South Asian Islam*. Berkeley: University of California Press, 1984.

Mohy-Ud-Din, Ata. *Ali the Superman*. Lahore: Sh. Muhammad Ashraf, 1980.

al-Mufid, Shaykh. *Kitab al-Irshad: The Book of Guidance into the Lives of the Twelve Imams*. Translated by I. K. A. Howard. Qum, Iran: Ansariyan, n.d.

Muhurram A' Amal: A Chapter from The Prayer's Almanac (Mafaati ul Jinaan). Karachi: Peermahomed Ebrahim Trust, n.d.

Naqvi, 'Ali Naqi. *Azadari: A Historical Review of the Institution of Azadari for Imam Husayn*. Translation of "Aza-i Husaini par Tarikhi Tabsera." Karachi: Peermahomed Ebrahim Trust, n.d.

_____. *The Martyr of Karbala*. Translated by S. Ali Akhtar. Karachi: Islamic Culture and Research Trust, 1984.

Nasr, Seyyed Hussein. *Ideals and Realities of Islam*. Boston: Beacon, 1966.

Otto, Rudolph. *The Idea of the Holy*. Translated by John W. Harvey. London: Oxford University Press, 1923; 2d ed. reprint, 1977.

Platts, John T. *A Dictionary of Urdu, Classical Hindi, and English*. Oxford: Oxford University Press, 1974.

Rahman, Fazlur. *Islam*. Garden City, N.Y.: Anchor, 1968.

_____. *Major Themes of the Qur'an*. Minneapolis: Bibliotheca Islamica, 1980.

Rizvi, Sayid Athar Abbas. *A Socio-Intellectual History of the Isna'Asharis in India*. Vols. 1, 2. New Delhi: Munshiram Manoharlal, 1986.

Rumi, Maulana Jalalu-d-Din Muhammad I. *The Teachings of Rumi: The Masnavi*. Translated by E. H. Whinfield. New York: E. P. Dutton, 1975.

Sachedina, Abdulaziz Abdulhussein. *Islamic Messianism: The Idea of the Mahdi in Twelver Shi'ism*. Albany: State University of New York Press, 1981.

Said, Edward. *Covering Islam: How the Media and the Experts Determine How We See the Rest of the World*. New York: Pantheon, 1981.

_____. *Orientalism*. New York: Vintage, 1979.

Schimmel, Annemarie. *Mystical Dimensions of Islam*. Chapel Hill: University of North Carolina Press, 1975.

Shah, Idries. *Caravan of Dreams*. Baltimore: Penguin, 1972.

Shari'ati, Ali. *On the Sociology of Islam*. Translated by Hamid Algar. Berkeley, Calif.: Mizan, 1979.

Sharif, Ja'far. *Islam in India or the Qanun-i Islam*. Translated by G. A. Herklots. Oxford University Press 1921; reprint ed., London: Curzon, 1975.

Subhan, John A. *Sufism: Its Saints and Shrines*. New York: Samuel Weiser, 1970.

Tabatabai, Allamah Sayyid Muhammad Husayn. *Shi'ite Islam*. Translated and edited by Seyyed Hossein Nasr. Albany: State University of New York Press, 1975.

Turner, Victor. *Dramas, Fields, and Metaphors: Symbolic Action in Human Society*. Ithaca, N.Y.: Cornell University Press, 1974.

_____. *The Forest of Symbols: Aspects of Ndembu Ritual*. Ithaca, N.Y.: Cornell University Press, 1967.

_____. *From Ritual to Theatre: The Human Seriousness of Play*. New York: Performing Arts Journal, 1982.

_____. *The Ritual Process: Structure and Anti-Structure*. Ithaca, N.Y.: Cornell University Press, 1977.

Wadley, Susan S. "Vrats: Transformers of Destiny," in *Karma: An Anthropological Inquiry*, editors Charles F. Keyes and E. Valentine Daniel. Berkeley: University of California Press, 1983.

Watt, W. Montgomery. *The Faith and Practice of Al-Ghazali*. London: George Allen and Unwin, 1953; 4th ed., 1970.

Watt, W. Montgomery. *The Formative Period of Islamic Thought*. Edinburgh: Edinburgh University Press, 1973.

_____. *Muhammad at Mecca*. London: Oxford University Press, 1953; reprint ed., Pakistan: Oxford University Press, 1979.

_____. *Muhammad at Medina*. London: Oxford University Press, 1956; reprint ed., Pakistan: Oxford University Press, 1981.

Weber, Max. *The Sociology of Religion*. Boston: Beacon, 1922.

Zaker. *Tears and Tributes*. 3d and revised ed. Vancouver, Canada: Hydery, 1978.

INDEX

of, 1, 6-10, 11-33, 36-39, 74-75,
77-80, 91, 109-11, 123-24, 131,
133-34, 151, 157-58, 160-62;
Twelver, 7, 88, 93, 116, 123,
140; worldview of, 9, 122, 125,
157, 160
Sindh Province, 6, 7, 20, 116,
128, 151, 161
Sozkhawani (mourning poetry),
97, 120-22, 132-34, 148, 152,
163
Spiritual vow. *See Mannat*
Stories: *Das Bibiyan ki Kahani*
(Story of the Ten Women), 38,
54-58, 66; importance of, 21-25,
29, 31-32, 37; *Janab-i Sayyidah ki
Kahani (Bibi Fatima ki Kahani)*,
38, 39-54; *Mu'jizat kahanis*
(miracle stories), 2, 8, 9, 24-25,
28-29, 36-70, 118, 158, 160;
weddings in, 41-42, 44-45, 48,
51-52, 53, 65, 105, 131-32, 143,
153
Student participation, 118, 130,
134, 135, 138
Subjunctive mode, 3, 4, 24, 99,
112-13
Succession. *See Imamat*
Sufis, 7, 8, 14, 20, 22-23, 27, 36,
47, 49, 52, 58, 65, 76, 77, 90,
97, 111, 118, 121, 127-28, 130,
134, 159-61
Sughra (bint al-Husayn), 55
Sunni Muslims, 7, 8, 9, 14-20,
29, 30, 35, 37, 39, 58, 66, 71,
74-75, 78, 81, 83, 84, 91-92, 95,
103, 111, 116, 121, 123, 128,
135-38, 140-41, 147, 150, 151,
157, 159-61, 167
Symbols: *'alam* (standard), 99,
101, 108-09, 117-18, 120-22,
129-34, 137, 139, 140, 143, 153;
fire, 49-50, 145-46, 152; gold,
49; *palna* (cradle), 112, 129,
131, 134, 139, 143; *panjatan*
(Fatimid hand), 19, 99, 101,
109, 118, 126; *tabut* (coffin),
111-12, 130, 131, 133, 134, 137,

139, 145, 152; turban, 99, 112,
139; *ta'ziyah* (replica of
Husayn's tomb), 109-12, 117-
18, 122, 135, 136, 137, 140;
water, 63, 65, 111, 135, 140;
use of, 1-5, 6, 8, 25, 49, 74, 92,
99-100, 106, 108, 115-16, 122,
125, 142-43, 157; *zarih* (grave
casing), 93, 96-97, 126; *Zuljinah*
(horse), 96, 109, 130, 135, 137,
145, 161, 170. *See also* Colors;
Husayniyya

Talha, 23
Taqlid (obedience), 123-24, 128
Ten women of Islam. See Stories
Timur, Emperor, 109-10, 122
Toffler, Alvin, 98
Toronto, 133
Transformation, of individual, 2,
3, 6, 27, 94. *See also* Identity;
Liminal realm
Troeltsch, Ernst, 15
Tufail (intercession), 19, 22, 25,
35, 40, 46, 49, 51, 52, 57, 69,
147, 149, 152-54
Turabi, Rashid, 90, 130
Turkish Muslims, 77
Turner, Victor, 2-5, 25, 47, 96,
99-100, 116, 126, 158
Twelver Shi'a. *See* Shi'i Muslims

Uhud battle, 82-83
'Ulama (religious scholars), 20,
90-91, 110, 123, 128, 130, 152,
160
'Umar (b. Sa'd), 16, 17, 28, 86,
137
Ummah (Muslim community), 14,
30, 74, 159, 162. *See also*
Identity, Shi'i Muslims
Umm Habibah, 43, 52
Umm Kulthum, 55, 57
Unconscious state, 40-42, 44-46,
49, 50, 51-53, 59, 68
Uthman, Caliph, 37, 66
Uttar Pradesh, 78
Uways al-Qarani, 36